TRAINING TO TEACH IN THE LEARNING AND SKILLS SECTOR

Visit the *Training to Teach in the Learning and Skills Sector* Companion Website at **www.pearsoned.co.uk/keeley-browne** to find valuable **student** learning material including:

- Electronic versions of tables and templates that appear in the book allowing you to easily customise, print and use them in your teaching or training
- Additional practical tools such as examples of proformas, record sheets, checklists and an ILP (Individual Learning Plan)
- Weblinks including a direct link to QTLS standards

PEARSON
Education

We work with leading authors to develop the
strongest educational materials in education studies,
bringing cutting-edge thinking and best
learning practice to a global market.

Under a range of well-known imprints, including
Longman, we craft high-quality print and electronic
publications which help readers to
understand and apply their content, whether studying
or at work.

To find out more about the complete range of our
publishing, please visit us on the World Wide Web at:
www.pearsoned.co.uk

TRAINING TO TEACH IN THE LEARNING AND SKILLS SECTOR
From Threshold Award to QTLS

Liz Keeley-Browne

PEARSON
Longman

Harlow, England • London • New York • Boston • San Francisco • Toronto • Sydney • Singapore • Hong Kong
Tokyo • Seoul • Taipei • New Delhi • Cape Town • Madrid • Mexico City • Amsterdam • Munich • Paris • Milan

Pearson Education Limited

Edinburgh Gate
Harlow
Essex CM20 2JE
England
and Associated Companies throughout the world

Visit us on the World Wide Web at:
www.pearsoned.co.uk

First published in 2007

© Pearson Education Limited 2007

ISBN: 978-1-4058-1238-2

British Library Cataloguing-in-Publication Data
A catalogue record for this book is available from the British Library

Library of Congress Cataloging-in-Publication Data
Training to teach in the learning and skills sector/Liz Keeley-Browne. -- 2nd ed.
    p. cm.
  Includes bibliographical references and index.
  ISBN 978-1-4058-1238-2
    1. Teachers--Training of--Great Britain. 2. Effective teaching--Great Britain. 3.
  Occupational training--Great Britain. 4. Individualized instruction--Great Britain. I.
  Keeley-Browne, Liz

LB1725.G6T73 2007
370.71'1--dc 22   2006052712

10 9 8 7 6 5 4 3 2 1
11 10 09 08 07

Typeset in 9.5 pt Palatino by 30
Printed by Ashford Colour Press, Ltd, Gosport

The publisher's policy is to use paper manufactured from sustainable forests.

Dedicated to happy times when the house rings with laughter from family and friends, and to colleagues and friends who commit to provide opportunities to those denied (for whatever reason) the right to an inspirational and motivating experience of education.

Teachers in the lifelong learning sector value all learners individually and equally. They are committed to lifelong learning and professional development, and strive for continuous improvement through reflective practice.

The key purpose of the teacher is to create effective and stimulating opportunities for learning through high quality teaching that enables the development and progression of all learners.

Introduction to the new professional standards: teacher/tutor/trainer education for the learning and skills sector

Contents

11 Enhancing learner behaviour: establishing and maintaining an effective learning environment — **182**

12 Continuing professional development: developing by participating in formal and informal professional activities — **193**

Supporting resources

Visit **www.pearsoned.co.uk/keeley-browne** to find valuable online resources

Companion Website for students
- Electronic versions of tables and templates that appear in the book allowing you to easily customise, print and use them in your teaching or training
- Additional practical tools such as examples of proformas, record sheets, checklists and an ILP (Individual Learning Plan)
- Weblinks including a direct link to QTLS standards

For more information please contact your local Pearson Education sales representative or visit **www.pearsoned.co.uk/keeley-browne**

List of figures and tables

Figures

Tables

List of examples

Web resources

Listed below are the document templates, useful information and weblinks that accompany this book, which are available to download at **www.pearsoned.co.uk/keeley-browne**. Boxes in the margins throughout the text guide you to the relevant documents on the website.

Portfolio front page	Web 1
IT skills assessment	Web 2
Observation log	Web 3
Assessment record proforma	Web 4
Individual learning plan	Web 5
QTLS standards	Web 6
Health and safety assessment	Web 7
Learning log	Web 8
Lesson plan	Web 9
Scheme of work	Web 10
Shared observation sheet	Web 11
Reflective practice criteria	Web 12
Lesson plan (ii)	Web 13
ICT standards	Web 14
Logic Model	Web 15
Lesson plan (iii)	Web 16
Extended scheme of work	Web 17
ILPs for your learners	Web 18
Information on disabilities	Web 19
Behavioural strategy analysis	Web 20
PCP framework	Web 21
CV template	Web 22

Preface

The aim

The aim of this book is to introduce new and already trained teachers, tutors or trainers working in the learning and skills sector to the routes towards becoming licensed to practise. Each chapter is designed as a journey from 'survival' to 'success', helping all practitioners to become reflective professionals in a challenging and changing sector of education and training. This sector is not unaccustomed to change, and one of the challenges in writing this text has been keeping abreast of and reporting on the reforms currently under way.

The title

The title of this book reflects new approaches to training, resulting from a number of government reports and initiatives that place greater focus on the role of the teacher/trainer in this sector. There is, more than ever before, a government focus on the need for such staff to be competent, flexible, well trained, able to adjust to change and informed about the key issues involved in teaching and training in the twenty-first century. This is not to say that all practitioners need training. In fact this sector has a strong record of supporting the diverse needs of learners and has been the 'second chance, best chance' for many individuals failed by the school system. Recent Ofsted reports (for example, Ofsted, 2003), however, have identified the need for greater dissemination of the good practice that exists and the need to formalise the position of those working in the sector by ensuring they are qualified to a suitable level.

This book has been written to support existing lecturers and those intending to join a newly framed learning and skills environment which is beginning to examine teaching, learning and assessment with a clear focus on helping individual learners to reach their full potential. Reference is made throughout the book to the personalisation agenda, a key element of government reform. Key focus is given to the concept of safe learners. Those working in the sector need support in addressing the agenda for reform. This book has been written to provide that support.

The historical context

In February 2004 the Department for Education and Skills (DfES) published a report on the quality of teacher training in the post-16 sector. The report followed a thorough review of the training delivered in universities and colleges as carried out by Ofsted. This review described the landscape to the government's agenda for change, aptly called *Success for All* (DfES, 2002a). *Success for All* marked the launch of the creation of the Learning and Skills Council with a brief which places this sector of education as the major player in the strategy to widen participation, remodel the workforce and offer degree-level opportunities to a much wider section of the population.

This sector, traditionally known as the post-16 sector, now opens its doors to those aged between 14 and 16 who might benefit from accessing a different curriculum from that which is traditionally offered in our schools. Curriculum reform will focus on the personalisation of learner experience, with learner journeys (attendance at schools, colleges or workplaces) likely to vary according to the individual and their needs. These initiatives make the term post-16 somewhat inaccurate as it becomes apparent that learners from aged 14 and beyond will access courses in a variety of environments, including school, colleges and the workplace (DfES, 2005b).

In addition, a shift is occurring away from post-16 education and training focused solely in a further education college. Larger numbers of students are now trained in the workplace, in community centres, in hospitals, military installations and in prisons, thus rendering the terms 'further education college' and 'further education lecturer' of limited use. For this reason the title of this text has identified the increasing use, in government documents, of the terminology 'learning and skills sector'.

A further element of change constitutes justification for this text. Workforce regeneration, the introduction of foundation degrees (many of which are and will be delivered in institutions other than universities), place additional pressures on those working in the sector. There are expectations, as set out in policy initiatives, that staff in the sector will play a lead role in making the UK more socially inclusive, specifically by widening participation, adopting more inclusive practices and supporting a diverse student group. In addition, the government target for experiencing higher education is as high as 50 per cent of the population by 2010. At the end of the 1990s, only 20 per cent of the school-leaving population went on to further study. Clearly, our universities, as we know them today, cannot accommodate such an increase in student numbers. This planned expansion of higher education will result in a number of changes to how university education is delivered. We are already witnessing an increase in degree-level opportunities being offered in further education colleges and greater reliance on dif-ferent delivery methods such as distance learning and the use of computer technologies to facilitate course delivery. The learning and skills sector is already responding to these changes. Many further education colleges are working in partnership with their local higher education institutions (HEIs) to provide greater degree-level opportunities for the student body. The relationship between an HEI and a further education college needs to be one of mutual support. Each institution has much to learn from the other.

All these changes are placing fresh demands on teachers and trainers in the workforce. As outlined above, the target audience for the book is those new to teaching and the experienced facing new challenges. The aim is to provide technical advice on the skills associated with managing teaching, training and learning. The strategy has been to provide a set of toolkits for early survival with activities that then extend and increase the lecturer's repertoire of available skills. The set tasks have been designed to encourage and support the practitioner. As well as encouraging the development of skills, advice is offered on how to use information and communication technology (ICT) to work 'smarter rather than harder'. In addition, through set tasks and discussion, the book is intended to promote wider debate.

Each chapter contains activities associated with the very personal act of teaching/ tutoring/training, providing the participant with opportunities to produce evidence of their developing skills. Tasks have been designed to guide the teacher/tutor/trainer through the experiences they will meet in their role. The aim is to provide advice and support, as well as a toolkit of short activities, to give lessons a focus and provide pathways to engage the reluctant or less confident learner. Throughout the text you will find activities in the form of tasks to focus your thinking. In addition, a number of portfolio tasks are set to support those wishing to prepare for accreditation as qualified practitioners and working towards either the level 3 award (PTLLS) or the licence to practise in the learning and skills sector. It is intended that the tasks, once completed, should form part of your evidence towards your chosen accreditation route leading eventually to qualified teacher status (QTS) in this sector (QTLS). The tasks are intended and designed to do more than demonstrate evidence. They are intended to create a document to record activity and encourage reflection, thought and philosophical debate, to ground the act of teaching and training as a rational and principled activity. The portfolio tasks have been designed to act in an additional role, namely as suggestive of evidence that might be provided by those wishing to use the Accreditation of Prior Learning (APL) route into QTLS status. The tasks and portfolio tasks involve practical activity rather than extensive research and essay writing. This is deliberate and has been done to address the criticism made by Ofsted (Ofsted, 2005) that training courses focus too much on formal assessment methodologies resulting in a high degree of overassessment.

The set tasks provide opportunity for a gradual development in skills, using a step-by-step approach from observation to small periods of practice on to planning and delivering whole class sessions. Guidance is provided on how to work with subject learning coaches and mentors to gain the most from them. Core teaching skills are introduced progressively throughout the text in a guided and supportive way, emphasising the role of collaboration and reflection in development as an effective teacher. In addition, more advanced teaching approaches are encouraged as the reader is guided towards opportunities for post-qualification training and development.

I hope you will find this book a useful guide. Reading it does not guarantee you will become an excellent teacher/tutor/trainer. I hope it will help.

Liz Keeley-Browne

Acknowledgements

We are grateful to the following for permission to reproduce copyright material:

Figure 5.2 after *How the Brain Learns* (Sousa, D.A. 2001) Sage Publications (Corwin Press), Thousand Oaks, CA, USA; Table 5.2 from Hung, D. (2001) Theories of learning and computer-mediated instructional technologies. Education Media International 38(4): pp281–287, Taylor & Francis Ltd. http://www.tandf.co.uk/journals; Figure 6.1 from *E-Learning Standards LLUK Skills for Learning Professionals* (2005) Lifelong Learning UK, p. 2 and Figure 12.1 from Institute for Learning website: http://ifl.ac.uk/cpd_portal/cpdcd/guidance/planning_cycle.html. These figures are reproduced with the permission of the Institute for Learning. At the time of publication initial teacher training is in a period of significant change with the implementation of *Equipping our Teachers for the Future*. Within its remit for advancing the teacher professionalisation agenda the Institute for Learning is developing a new model of professionalism which supersedes these figures. For the latest information on the professional development agenda please visit www.ifl.ac.uk; Chapter 7, extract on pp. 110–11 from Huddersfield University website: http://associate.hud.ac.uk, ASSOCiate Online, 251 Health and public services ... 15.5 Law and legal services, Huddersfield; Example 9.4 from Curtis, S.A., Zajicek, M. (2005) 'Structuring an on-line assessment of students' learning', Proceedings IADIS International Conference e-Society, Malta, June 2005; Figure 11.1 adapted from *Entry to Employment Resources* (2003), Wheel of change diagram. Crown copyright. Reproduced under the terms of the Click-Use Licence.

In some instances we have been unable to trace the owners of copyright material, and we would appreciate any information that would enable us to do so.

The new qualifications

The rationale for the reform of the standards for teacher training in the learning and skills sector is one based on a clear argument for closer alignment between the expectations placed on those working in the sector and their counterparts in schools and higher education. The proposals are for a basic minimum standard (PTLLS, also known as the initial award or passport to teach) to be attained by those teaching, tutoring or training for a minimum period weekly with a framework and structures in place beyond this leading to a benchmark qualification (Qualified Teacher Learning and Skills) resulting eventually in a licence to practise.

Level 3 Award in Preparing to Teach in the Lifelong Learning Sector (PTLLS)

PTLLS is a generic award offered to anyone likely to be delivering education or training apart from visiting speakers. It is designed to include approximately thirty guided learning hours excluding teaching practice and observation of teaching/tutoring/training.

A **portfolio front page** template can be downloaded from the companion website (Web 1)

Qualified Teacher Learning and Skills (QTLS)

For those for whom teaching is their chosen profession, full licence to practise to achieve QTLS status will be an expectation. The initial training consists of 120 guided learning hours plus at least eight teaching practice observations. Individual licensing will be monitored with clear expectations of engagement in continuing professional development activities on an annual basis. Former experience of working with learners may be counted towards qualification status.

The e-learning standards

New standards for the application of information technologies have also been produced replacing the ILT (information and learning technology) standards written by the Further Education National Training Organisation in 2002. The new standards represent the continued importance of embedding ILT into the curriculum. Opportunities for the practice and implementation of the new standards, prepared by Lifelong Learning UK, are presented throughout this text.

How to use this book

This text has been designed for four types of practitioner broadly identified as follows:

- *Those new to teaching and/or teaching for a limited number of hours per week and needing to achieve Preparing to Teach in the Lifelong Learning Sector (PTLLS).* The book aims to develop your skills and provides tasks and portfolio activities that you can present towards accreditation for your passport to teach.

- *Those working towards full Qualified Teacher Learning and Skills (QTLS).* Again, identified tasks and portfolio activities are suggested, but of a more developed nature and closely linked to the extended standards for qualification beyond those required for the passport.

- *Those already qualified (PGCE, Cert. Ed.,)* who may wish to use the Accreditation of Prior Learning (APL) route to gain QTLS qualification. The portfolio tasks, designed around your existing practice, are suggested here to support your preparation towards full QTLS accreditation.

- *Remaining in good standing.* Practitioners who are fully qualified may wish to refresh their skills and knowledge as part of the requirement for continuing professional development (CPD). In addition, they may wish to begin to work towards full degree-level qualification or master's qualifications. Chapter 12 provides a brief overview of available opportunities for modules of learning, seen as CPD, for those working in the sector. It is anticipated that the CPD framework will offer varied delivery options including the accreditation of prior learning, (DfES, 2005a).

The chapters in the book have been designed to support achievement of the standards for teachers working in the sector. Explanation and advice are provided, interspersed with set tasks culminating in a portfolio referencing guide at the end of each chapter which maps the set activities against the production of evidence for a number of awards. The three awards identified are:

- PTLLS (initial award)
- training awards leading to full QTLS
- the e-learning CPD award (a newly framed award which will provide the educational workforce with the opportunity to develop their e-learning skills).

The tasks have been designed to provide opportunities for the reader to practise their skills and begin to prepare a portfolio of evidence to demonstrate their competence in the defined area. Completing the tasks does not guarantee you the award but it gives practitioners confidence to progress, evidence to present to an awarding body and the benefits of prepared resources for use in your teaching.

Using the standards

The standards are described in terms of scope (identified using a number system plus the letter S) knowledge (identified as K) and practice (described as P). They are further separated in domains, so, for example, within the domain Professional Values, issues of equality and diversity are in scope AS3 'Equality, diversity and the need for inclusion in relation to learners, the workforce, and the community'. To support this focus the knowledge expectations for AK 3 are 'The issues of equality and diversity and inclusion.' In terms of practice AP 3, the expectation is for the application of principles to evaluate and develop own practice in promoting equality and inclusive learning and engaging with diversity.

Areas in scope S are identified at the beginning of each chapter. At the end of the chapter, tasks are delineated with a knowledge reference (K) or a practice reference (P) dependent upon the nature of the expectations involved.

List of abbreviations

ACE	adult and community education
AD/HD	attention deficit/hyperactivity disorder
AEA	Advanced Extension Award
AEB	Associated Examining Board
AoC	Association of Colleges
APL	Accreditation of Prior Learning
AQA	Assessment and Qualifications Alliance (merger of AEB and NEAB)
AVC	Advanced Vocational Qualifications
BECTA	British Educational Communications and Technology Agency
BSA	Basic Skills Agency
CAA	computer-assisted assessment
CEL	Centre for Excellence in Leadership
CETT	Centre for Excellence in Teacher Training
CKSA	common knowledge, skills and attributes
CPD	continuing professional development
CUREE	Centre for the Use of Research and Evidence in Education
DfES	Department for Education and Skills
ESOL	English for Speakers of Other Languages
FE	Further Education
FENTO	Further Educational National Training Orgainisation
FERL	Further Education Resources for Learning
GCE	General Certificate of Education
GCSE	General Certificate of Secondary Education
GNVQ	General National Vocational Qualification
HEFCE	Higher Education Funding Council for England
HEI	higher education institution
IAG	information, advice and guidance
ICLT	information, communication and learning technologies
ICT	information and communication technology (term used mainly in schools)
IfL	Institute for Learning (further education professional body)
ILP	individual learning plan
ILT	Institute for Learning and Teaching (higher education professional body); information and learning technology (term used mainly post-school)
ISP	internet service provider
ITALS	Initial Teaching Award Learning and Skills
JISC	Joint Information Systems Committee
LEACAN	Local Education Authority Curriculum Advisers Network

LLUK	Lifelong Learning UK
LSC	Learning and Skills Council
LSDA	Learning and Skills Development Agency
LSN	Learning and Skills Network
LSS	learning and skills sector
NATFHE	National Association of Teachers in Further and Higher Education
NEAB	Northern Examining and Assessment Board
NEET	not in education, employment or training
NETP	National Employer Training Programme
NIACE	National Institute for Adult and Continuing Education
NLN	National Learning Network
NQF	nationally recognised qualification framework
NQT	Newly Qualified Teacher
NVQ	National Vocational Qualification
Ofsted	Office for Standards in Education
OMR	optical mark reader
PAL	peer-assisted learning
PCP	professional and career profile
PELTS	personal employment, learning and thinking skills
PGCE	Postgraduate Certificate in Education
PTLLS	Preparing to Teach in the Lifelong Learning Sector
QCA	Qualifications and Curriculum Authority
QTLS	Qualified Teacher Learning and Skills
QTS	qualified teacher status
RARPA	recognising and recording progress and achievement
RDN	Resources Discovery Network
RLO	reusable learning object
RLR	reusable learning resource
SAT	Standard Attainment Test
SSC	sector skills council (an employer body)
TTA	Teacher Training Agency
VAK	visual, auditory and kinaesthetic
VCE	Vocational Certificate in Education
VLE	Virtual Learning Enviroment
WBL	work-based learning
WBLP	work-based learning provider

1

The context for change
New professional standards for teachers in the learning and skills sector

Learning outcomes

By the end of this chapter you will:

- be aware of the place of the learning and skills sector within the wider context of policy change
- begin to think about what it means to be a licensed teacher in the sector having an awareness of national developments and how they might impact on that role
- begin to identify your own professional development needs
- begin to prepare evidence, through the set tasks, and by producing a portfolio of evidence which might be used towards your preparation award and the licensed to practise qualification.

Areas in scope in this chapter in relation to the standards for teachers, tutors and trainers working in the sector are AS 2, AS 3, AS 6, BS 2 (in part only).

This introductory chapter describes the range of provision covered by the learning and skills sector (LSS) and provides a brief history of the current context for change. Previously referred to as further education, adult education and/or post-compulsory education, this area of education and training is currently the focus of much government attention.

The context for change

Prior to the full publication of *Success for All* (DfES, 2002b) in which the government set out the current agenda for reform, a discussion document, *Success for All: Reforming Further Education and Training* (DfES, 2002a), identified a number of weaknesses in the sector. These related specifically to the lack of attention paid to teaching and learning in a sector staffed by an underdeveloped workforce suffering from 'significant recruitment and retention problems' (p. 20). The document also records 'good practice in learning delivery, often involving inspirational creativity by front-line staff'(p. 6). There is a clear acknowledgement, however, that this is not consistent across the sector. The *Success for All* strategy is very explicit in setting out four goals for the reform agenda:

Goal 1   Meeting needs, improving choice

Goal 2   Putting teaching and learning at the heart of what we do

Goal 3   Developing the teachers and leaders of the future

Goal 4   Developing a framework for quality and success.

The third goal, 'Developing the teachers and leaders of the future', and the reforms to teacher training that are becoming associated with it, are the impetus for this text.

New professional standards

Statutory requirements

A Statutory Instrument (DfES, 2001) made a qualification in teaching achieved within a specified period a requirement for all new teachers appointed to further education colleges. New legislation and government targets are driving the reform agenda requiring training and qualification leading to a preparation award (for those teaching only a few hours per week) and a full 'licence to practise' for new and experienced lecturers. Achievement of the full licence qualification will lead to the award of Qualified Teacher Learning and Skills (QTLS) award. There is an expectation that 90 per cent of those teaching in the sector will hold a qualification by 2010 (DfES, 2002a). In addition, there are a number of other legislative requirements associated with race, equality and disability that will impact on your role. These are discussed later in this text. You will also need to be mindful of health and safely legislation and the requirement to address the concept of the 'safe learner'.

The minimum core

In 2003, the endorsement body for post-16 teacher training, FENTO, stipulated that courses of teacher training should include a core of training in language, literacy and numeracy. The established requirement included two different approaches:

● A requirement that those teaching in the sector would themselves possess a certain level of proficiency in the core subjects (literacy, numeracy and ICT).

● A requirement that lecturers should be aware of cultural and social factors that restrict the ability of their learners to be functional in these core skills and in demonstrating their understanding of these factors, and be in a better position to understand the individual needs of those they teach.

This book approaches the minimum core requirements in a three-pronged way: first by providing advice for the skill development of lecturers approaching certification of their competence (see Chapter 2); second, through the discussion of learners' needs, differentiation and inclusion (see Chapters 7, 8 and 10); and third, in the discussion of e-learning and proficiency in ICT skills, as threaded throughout this text and addressed in detail in Chapter 6. Tasks set in Chapters 7 and 8 focus on subject-specific approaches to meeting the needs of different types of learners. In Chapter 10 focus is given to disability needs and awareness of possible barriers to learner achievement.

Professional recognition

Lifelong Learning UK (LLUK) is the sector skills council responsible for the professional development of those working in the UK lifelong learning sector. In designing the new qualification framework, LLUK has established that the following amounts of time will be involved:

- 30 guided learning hours excluding teaching practice and observation for the preparation award.
- 120 guided learning hours plus at least 8 teaching practice observations for QTLS.

Former work experience with learners may be used to count towards these totals. It is also LLUK's responsibility to ensure that those in training are assigned an appropriately qualified and experienced mentor in their subject or occupational area. The role of coach/mentors is discussed at the end of this chapter.

As part of LLUK, a new professional body, the Institute for Learning (IfL), has been formed to raise the standards of professional practice in the LSS sector, to provide formal routes for accrediting continuing professional development (CPD) for its members and raise the status of the post-compulsory education and training (PCET) profession (www.ifl.ac). The IfL has been charged with delivering the following services:

- Registering all who enrol on the preparation award and those who complete it as holding a threshold licence to practise.
- Registering all those who complete the full award and awarding QTLS to those who complete the full qualification.
- Continuing to register those who complete appropriate CPD (see Chapter 12).

LLUK will be the statutory body required to approve the quality of courses leading to the awards here discussed.

Star awards

One early recommendation recorded at the launch of the IfL is the award of Star status to those nominated as inspirational teachers. Awards are made on an annual basis in an attempt to reward excellence in the sector and acknowledge areas of good practice.

Many of the ideas in this book should help the aspiring Star member of the teaching staff. The text provides appropriate help and support whether you are already fully qualified (to PGCE/Cert. Ed.) level, studying for these qualifications or working towards the foundation and certificate courses such as the City and Guilds Certificate in Further Education Teaching. Such qualifications will be phased out and replaced by the preparation award and the licence to practise, a qualification offered at the initial minimum academic level of level 4, with progression to level 5 for full accreditation, in the nationally recognised qualification framework (NQF).

Continuing professional development

The chapters in this book have been designed not only to give coverage to all aspects of training required by those working in the sector but also to act as a quick reference for the experienced, to refresh their skills and enable them to return to the classroom enthused and reinvigorated with new ideas to implement. The set tasks have been designed to develop your thinking and in some cases to provide opportunities for you to gather evidence which might be presented for assessment at a later date. Those already qualified may wish to compile a portfolio using the set tasks as evidence of CPD.

The learning and skills sector

Created by an Act of Parliament in 2000, the learning and skills sector is a very complex and diverse sector providing education for a variety of different interest groups. Operating in the sector to provide skills and training are staff in:

- further education colleges (there are over 400 such institutions)
- those working in sixth forms in schools and colleges, adult and community education (ACE) tutors funded by local education authorities
- those working on lifelong learning projects
- work-based learning providers (WBLP)
- lecturers offering basic skills provision for adults in prisons, colleges, community venues
- staff working in the voluntary sector.

Recognising the skills of lecturers in the sector

Data collected in 2001 based on full-time staff employed in further education colleges suggested that the sector employs 227,837 teaching and support staff, 58 per cent of whom are women. Of the quarter of a million staff employed, just over half were on permanent contracts. These data fail to include the army of staff, again mainly female, who teach in work-based environments, prisons, hospitals and in service organisations. This workforce too, is known for 'unhealthy levels of casualisation' (DfES, 2002a: 20).

More recent research carried out by LLUK reveal that in 2005 the college workforce is still predominantly female. Just 37 per cent of all staff and 30 per cent of part-time staff employed by colleges are men. It also revealed that the bulk of college staff are in their forties and fifties with 19 per cent aged under 35, while 44 per cent are aged 45 and over. Seven per cent of male employees were found to hold management posts compared with 5 per cent of women. Eighty-eight per cent of further education staff class themselves as 'white British', with 3.4 per cent Asian and 2.9 per cent black (www.lluk.org.uk).

Task 1.1

Consider the qualities you might expect to find in a member of staff working in the learning and skills sector. You may wish to choose a specific type of lecturer such as an engineering lecturer, a social care lecturer or a business lecturer. An example of how you might approach this task is provided in the example answers section at the end of the book. This particular answer was produced by a group of in-service lecturers enrolled on a university course leading to a teaching qualification, who chose to tackle the task pictorially.

1

Task 1.2

Taking what you have produced for Task 1.1, list the components of the effective teacher, tutor or trainer under the headings given below. Consider, specifically, diversity and difference among learners, the needs of employers, the local community, and health and safety issues.

Professional knowledge and expertise
Examples:

_____
_____
_____

Skills and attributes
Examples:

_____
_____
_____

Commitment to teaching and the needs of learners
Examples:

_____
_____
_____

Task 1.3

Consider the importance of each of the three categories in Task 1.2. You may wish to consider whether the focus of the categories changes when used to describe a lecturer working on foundation degrees, an A level mathematics teacher, a teacher of a vocational course such as health and beauty or a teacher of basic skills.

Portfolio task 1.1

It is now time to set up your portfolio. This will be the record of your ideas, thoughts and achievements during the training period and beyond. Start by designing your front page to give information on who you are, your role in your institution, the skills and the qualifications that you bring to the role of teacher/tutor/trainer.

The new technologies for teaching

It will be a requirement of those gaining a licence to practise that they are competent users of technology. A whole chapter is dedicated to the use of technology in learning and teaching to demonstrate how technology may be used in a variety of ways in the learning and teaching process (Chapter 6).

All lecturers in the sector will be required to complete modules of continuing professional development on an annual basis and it is likely that modules of learning associated with the use of information and communication technology (ICT) will be given high priority. A recent report from the National Association for Teachers in Further Education identified ICT as an area where professional development for lecturers is most required, stating that

> considerable unplanned development of on-line learning is leading to work isolation, reinventing the wheel, undertaking tasks that could be shared and potentially not using IT to best effect.
> (www.ifl.ac.uk/news-index).

The use of ICT in the support of the lecturer is a key focus in this text in acknowledgement of the government publication of its e-strategy (DfES, 2005b) entitled *Harnessing Technology: Transforming Learning and Children's Services*. This strategy, which applies to schools, 14–19 and lifelong learning (and other service sectors) describes the increased deployment of digital and interactive technologies in the service of education and training.

Training to use the new technologies

If you are new to the world of computers then it is recommended that you register for a course of training as soon as possible. The role played by ICT and ILT (information learning technology) in the arenas of learning and teaching is expansive and likely to increase. Large amounts of government funding have been made available to ensure better access to free training programmes. You need to contact Learndirect, the national learning advice centre that will have a base near you. The best way to contact your local Learndirect centre is through the local library or, if you apply some basic computer skills, to search the internet at www.learndirect.gov. Learndirect is likely to be defined as an online service in 2008 and will probably be renamed at this stage. You may wish to register for the European Computer Driving Licence course that will offer training in basic computer skills. You can complete the course at a registered centre or online via the internet.

Example 1.1 Evaluating your training needs

To help you evaluate your training needs in the use of the technologies that support learning you may wish to complete the table below.

Application of ICT/ILT	Statement of your experience	Needs analysis
Word processing Assignments Letters Worksheets Importing clip art		
Using PowerPoint (or similar) To present basic content Importing clip art Additional facilities: Moving images Music		
Evaluating websites To use in teaching or for research		
To support learners Email Creating handouts Creating acetates Using digital camera Scanners Specialist software Electronic whiteboard Website design		

1

Impact of technology

At the start of the academic year 2006/07 all participants completing an initial teaching qualification will be required to enter and pass nationally designed external tests in numeracy, literacy and ICT. In 2007 it is intended that the same national tests will be a formal component of the new arrangements for all those participating in any training award. These tests will measure the functional skill level of all those in training. You will need to be able to demonstrate an acceptable level of operational ability in all three areas.

Technology tip

If you are concerned about your level of competence in numeracy and literacy (in respect of the minimum core requirements) or just want to refresh old skills, then contact Learndirect (www.learndirect.co.uk) or phone 08080 200 800. An advisor will be able to provided you with the opportunity to complete task to assess your skills, will give you a Preparing For Testing course on which to practise and enable you to take a short test, free of charge, which, when you pass, leads to a Certificate in Adult Numeracy or Literacy recognised as an equivalent-level qualification to GCSE.

E-learning standards

In addition to the standards expected of lecturers in relation to their abilities to teach, the LSS has also developed standards for the use of e-learning. These are discussed in full in Chapter 6. At the moment you need to be aware that tasks set in this text have been mapped against these standards as well as the standards for LSS teacher training. Evidence of this mapping against the standards is, where feasible, presented at the end of each chapter.

Portfolio task 1.2

Having reviewed your skills in the use of ICT return to your portfolio front page. Here you need to identify any training needs you may have in relation to the use of the technologies for teaching.

Observation log and assessment record sheet

An observation log can be downloaded from the companion website (Web 3)

For those new to teaching, following what is known as the 'pre-service' route – a period of observation of up to a fortnight, if possible in a variety of LSS environments, – is recommended. A guide to how to use your time identifying what to look for in lesson planning and delivery is available on the web. It is strongly recommended that anyone wishing to work in the sector spends a period of time finding out whether teaching in this sector is what they really want to do. The best way to find this out is to spend some time observing the skills of others. It is recommended that you observe in a variety of contexts (work-based learning, college and adult and community venues) also ensuring that you vary the age focus to encompass 14–16 age learners and the more mature.

An assessment record proforma can be downloaded from the companion website (Web 4)

An assessment record sheet matched against the standards is also available for downloading from the web. It is a working document to be used to record achievement against the standards, records of meetings with your mentors and documentary records of the developmental advice provided through observations of your teaching. The assessment record mirrors the grids provided at the close of each chapter.

Preparing for the training period

1

Before embarking on any course of training it is important to think carefully about the time that this commitment is likely to require. It is important to plan effectively for this by setting aside time in the week for private study. If you have the support of those with whom you live, work and socialise, then this helps. Their understanding that you need Sunday morning alone is worth securing before you embark on a course of study. It can also help if you can form a 'community of learners' with your fellow students. According to Wenger (1998: 18):

> Roles in communities of practice are characterised by both a kind of action and a form of belonging. Such participation shapes not only what we do but also who we are and how we interpret what we do.

Such communities, engaged together in the act of learning and reflecting on their practice, can be very powerful. Some of the benefits provided by this type of association are:

- friendship for the times you may feel a little isolated or homesick
- opportunity to discuss subject content and feel more confident by testing out your understandings with people you feel comfortable with
- clarification on assigned texts and tasks, to clarify and augment your understanding
- feedback from one another before submitting your work for final assessment
- books, texts, videos and other resources to share
- revision support for tests and examinations, especially where one of the group may be a specialist in one area and can support the rest, in exchange for the specialist help of others on a later occasion
- emotional and moral support, guidance, assistance and encouragement
- help when times are difficult, to keep you on track to complete your degree.

Programme support

When you first register or enrol on a course of training to become a teacher, tutor or trainer in the sector you will be given an interview to identify your specific training needs. This will be referred to as an individual learning plan (ILP) and will identify what you need to do first to achieve the initial award and/or QTLS leading to full licence to practise. You may wish to take what you have completed for Task 1.2 with you to this interview, as a starting point in the discussion of your individual learning plan.

An example of an **individual learning plan** can be downloaded from the companion website (Web 5)

This is a tool you will use in your training but will also use with your own learners, designed to help you identify your learning needs and map your personal progress in the learning journey towards full qualification.

As part of your training you will be allocated to a mentor, or learning coach, who will advise you on the general skills of training to teach. Your mentor will be skilled in what is called the pedagogy of the classroom. You will also be given access to a subject specialist coach (this may be the same person as your mentor/learning coach) who will help you develop the skills that are specific to your area of the curriculum. It will be essential that you have access to a number of opportunities to practise teaching and develop your skills. There is an expectation that those completing the initial award will study for a least 30 hours and demonstrate their proficiency through taking part in a number of assessed teaching sessions. Those completing the full QTLS qualification will need to experience eight formal teaching observations, to reflect on the feedback they receive and set themselves targets for improvement, following discussion and critical self-evaluation of their teaching.

Portfolio task 1.3

Write a brief case study scenario describing your position in relation to the new qualification framework. What will you have to do to achieve your aim? Consider your level of competence in numeracy, literacy and ICT. What do you need to do to make sure you are proficient in these core subjects?

Produce a personal action plan targeting the time you will take to complete your qualification and specific periods when you will aim to have achieved your desired ends.

To help you with the above task, and for clarification, a number of case study scenarios are offered below demonstrating how the new qualification framework will impact on the experience of those wishing to gain a qualification.

How can I qualify to teach in the learning and skills sector?

The case studies below describe the old training model and the proposed additional components required for the licensed to practise award.

Case study Michelle

This story begins 15 years ago. Michelle trained to be a nurse and worked in hospitals for many years. She was asked if she could help with some first aid training for the staff. She decided this role fitted much better with the growing demands of her children and applied for a part-time job at the college. While teaching part time in the local further education college she registered for the in-house training course validated by City and Guilds. She completed part one and part two at the college and five years later gained a permanent position in the School of Health and Social Care.

What will be different and why?
It is likely that colleges will still recruit staff like Michelle to teach for a few hours a week on a short-term contract. However, all full-time staff offered permanent appointments after 2001 must have a Certificate in Education/PGCE or agree to complete one within one year of being appointed.

From 2007, for people like Michelle teaching only a few hours a week in a range of areas such as prisons, hospitals, service training organisations, local education authorities and as non-permanent lecturers in further education colleges, the initial award will be a requirement.

Once Michelle increases her teaching commitment she will be required to complete the Certificate of Practice award. The qualification includes the following:

- an initial assessment leading to an individual learning plan
- successful completion of the preparation award (as described in case study Kin below)
- study for the full qualification consisting of large components of practical skills and core units of study.

Once successfully completed:

- registration as a qualified teacher, leading to
- full licence to practise

supported by:

- an annual requirement to complete modules of professional development to secure annual registration with the Institute for Learning (IfL) on a national database of qualified teachers in the learning and skills sector.

Case study Peter

Peter worked in schools for many years as an art teacher. He has a degree and a PGCE so is qualified to teach in schools. He applied to work in his local college as this institution had better facilities for teaching his specialist area of ceramics. He applied for the job and was accepted. Currently Peter would be regarded as qualified to teach post-16 as qualified teacher status, (QTS) is recognised by the DfES in further education contexts.

What will be different and why?

It is not clear in the documentation whether those who already hold qualified status in schools would be required to complete the licence to practise for the learning and skills sector. It may well be that a period of observation, linked to a probation employment period, will be all that is required. Peter will be required to complete modules of continuing professional development on an annual basis, as will all lecturers working in the sector.

Case study Armid

As a prison educator, Armid completed the first phase of a teacher training qualification at a local college. He is now teaching a full timetable at the prison and is working closely with students who have poor basic skills. In the past, Armid would have been encouraged to take the full Certificate or PGCE qualification.

What will be different and why?

Armid will be required to complete the full licensed to practise qualification. As part of his qualification he will complete core modules, designed for all those in training. He will also be able to specialise in modules designed for teachers of basic skills. He will be able, within the new qualification framework, to customise his qualification to suit his specific needs.

Case study Kin

Kin is an accountant who enjoys sharing his skills. He works at his local further education college in the evening, teaching on the accountancy technician course. He currently teaches three hours a week, would like to do more but has no formal teaching qualification.

What will be different and why?

Kin will be required to complete the preparation award that will consist of approximately 30 hours of study in core units of both subject studies and the generic skills of teaching. He will be observed teaching by a qualified observer and given supportive feedback to help him develop his teaching skills.

He will start the programme of study with an initial assessment leading to an agreed individual learning plan to help in the construction of his personal targets. If he can demonstrate competence in skills and knowledge (perhaps his subject knowledge, for example), then this part of the qualification, for Kin, may be given credit and as such recorded as already achieved in his learning plan.

He will be assessed using a variety of methods including: observation, appraisal and reports from others who have observed him in the various aspects of his role.

What will Kin be able to do?

It is in the spirit of the new qualification that all LSS lecturers will be entitled to study modules of continuing professional development (CPD). As Kin's teaching workload increases, he will expected to engage in more study. At the point when he is teaching more than a few hours per week then he will be required to complete a PGCE/Cert. Ed. leading to QTLS.

Case study Phil

Phil graduated in criminal law from Nottingham University, worked as a solicitor for five years but found it depressing, not functional at all in meeting his need to help people. He will apply to do the in-service PGCE at a university near his home in London. To do this he will forfeit his considerable salary and once again become a student.

How will students like Phil gain the licence to practise?

Phil will be able to study full time on a PGCE at one of his local universities. In areas of severe lecturer shortage a fast-route scheme, similar to that used in secondary school shortage subject areas, might be introduced, enabling Phil to earn some money teaching while gaining his qualification. This is yet to be confirmed. However, bursaries of up to £9,000 are available to those wishing to teach certain subjects such as maths, science and basic skills.

Case study Sian

Sian currently runs a number of beauty salons and has made a considerable fortune. She has good managers in place and now wants to do what she loves best: concentrate on training new staff. She has agreed to take on a number of trainees from the local college on the Modern Apprenticeship scheme and has registered her company as willing to be a work-based learning organisation, with her as the provider of training.

How will people like Sian gain the licence to practise?

Sian, as a work-based learning provider, involved directly with the training of her staff, will be encouraged to complete the initial award. A number of changes to the way in which training is currently delivered will have to be introduced, to make it accessible and flexible, but there is a clear commitment in the government paper that all staff should be qualified at least to the initial award.

Case study Farah

Farah completed her PGCE a few years ago but would now like to gain QTLS status.

What will Farah have to do?
Farah will be able to complete recognised modules of CPD which will involve some reflection on her skills as a lecturer and include a record of her engagement in additional development and courses.

Key tips to take from this chapter

- The learning and skills sector is a complex sector governed by statutory requirements and an increasing focus on the qualification level of its staff.
- Government strategy and policy are currently focused on the training of teachers for the sector and many changes are under way.
- The sector is placing a key emphasis on ICT as a tool to drive forward reform. E-learning standards have been designed to underpin the training of staff working in the sector.
- Personal support from your peers and family is crucial.

Assessment grid mapped to the standards

This chapter introduces the knowledge requirements for the areas in scope set out at the start of the chapter. . Completion of the set tasks will provide you with evidence that can be matched to the knowledge requirements, as set out below, for gaining awards in the learning and skills sector.

Task	Summary activity	Level 3 award	Trainer award (level 4)	E-learning standards CPD awards
Task 1.1	The LSS lecturer	AK 3.1	AK 3.1	Pre-award preparation
Task 1.2	Being effective	AK 3.3 (in part only)	AK 3.3 (in part only)	Pre-award preparation
Task 1.3	Professional knowledge, skills and commitment	AK 6.1	AK 6.1	Pre-award preparation
Portfolio task 1.1	Preparing the portfolio	Pre-award preparation AK 6.1	Pre-award preparation AK 6.1	Pre-award preparation
Portfolio task 1.2	ICT strengths and development needs	Pre-award preparation BK 2.6	Pre-award preparation BK 2.6	Pre-award preparation
Portfolio task 1.3	ILP personal needs analysis	Pre-award preparation BK 2.6	Pre-award preparation BK 2.6	Pre-award preparation

2 Professional values
A focus on entitlement, equality and inclusiveness

> **Learning outcomes**
>
> By the end of this chapter you will:
>
> - begin to understand what it means to be a professional working in this sector, having developed an understanding of the professional and statutory frameworks that support staff in this area
> - have considered the implications of professional values for everyday practice
> - have begun to consider the importance of good subject knowledge when training others
> - have explored the concept of the safe learner and its implications for those in training and the already trained
> - be introduced to the concept of personalised learning.

Areas in scope in this chapter in relation to the standards for teachers, tutors and trainers working in the sector are AS 1, AS 2, AS 3, AS 4, BS 1 (in part only).

This chapter considers the professional values and practice expected of those working in the learning and skills sector. The concept of the safe learner is introduced, as is the focus on personalising learning. The debate whether teacher training should focus on how to teach or on how to teach your subject is introduced, to be developed in later chapters.

Training to teach or training to teach your subject

Models of training for those working in the skills sector have traditionally focused on the generic skills of learning and teaching, with a focus on theories about how people learn and the discussion of educational philosophies concerning the atmospheres and cultural approaches which best support that learning. In contrast, training models for secondary teachers focus on teaching a specific subject to the extent that trainees in this sector often criticise their training for a lack of focus on the generic skills of classroom engagement (Teacher Training Agency, 2003).

Interestingly, in trying to predict what schools might be like by 2020, the Teacher Training Agency (now renamed the Teacher Development Agency), has proposed one model of schooling where schools are replaced by learning networks with a diversified workforce providing young learners not with subject-specific knowledge but with skills for the labour market. This model is one of three proposals; the other two take a different view of learning, learners and the institutional frameworks that will support that learning (www.tta.futur99.gov.uk). Each model, however, makes reference to a focus on skills for work rather than the more traditional pursuit of academic knowledge. Chapter 7 of this book explores in more detail proposed curriculum reforms, which also seem to be advocating a curriculum designed much more around the skills for employment than has been advocated in the past.

2

Task 2.1

Consider the statements given below in the light of your ideas about teaching and being a teacher. If you had to prioritise, which statement would you choose as giving the most accurate description of teachers and teaching?

- 'The knowledge requirement of teachers are diverse and complex, constantly changing and developing' (Young, 2005: 20).
- 'Lecturers require subject knowledge, professional judgement and professional knowledge' (Leask, 1999: 15).
- 'Effective lecturers should possess both subject knowledge and pedagogic knowledge' (Morrison, 2002: 56).

Task 2.2

Consider what might be meant by the following terms, used in Task 2.1, when applied to teaching in the LSS: 'knowledge requirement', 'professional judgement', 'professional knowledge', 'subject knowledge' and 'pedagogic knowledge' (a definition of the word 'pedagogy' is given in the glossary at the end of this book). As part of the drive to improve quality in the sector there is an increasing focus on the subject knowledge of the sector skills lecturer such that those providing teacher training are working in partnership with colleges and work based learning providers (WBLP) to redesign the focus of teacher training in the sector. Return to your individual learning plan and consider your levels of knowledge in relation to your subject specialism. Is your subject knowledge current and thorough in terms of the curriculum you will be required to teach?

Task 2.3

Using the outcomes from Tasks 1.3, 2.1 and 2.2, produce a code of practice for lecturers working in the LSS. You may find it useful to think about the code in terms of values and aptitudes within the themes of professional knowledge and expertise; skills and attributes; and commitment to teaching. What will be a priority for you, learning to teach or learning to teach your specific subject? Justify your answer.

Professional values, skills and competences

Tasks 2.2 and 2.3 should have involved you in thinking about your role as a lecturer and helped you to formalise your ideas about what it means to be a teacher. It may be that your ideas about teaching are different from those of your colleagues. There is the potential for debate here about what it means to be professional.

It has been suggested that the term 'professional' in the modern world refers to the desire to strive for excellence in the service of others (McGettrick, 2004). McGettrick (2005: 4) defines professionalism as

> An individual's adherence to a set of standards, code of conduct or collection of qualities that characterise accepted practice within a particular area of activity.

But is this enough for a professional concerned with learning and teaching? McGettrick has called for learning professionals to have the ethical courage to argue that teaching is a more complex set of activities than that which can be simply explained in the form of basic standards. It involves values, ideals and virtues that are honestly focused on the good of all humanity. But, he argues, modern models of training have reduced teaching to a skill-based profession such that the focus on humanity and being human has been lost.

For many like McGettrick the opportunity to discuss what it means to be human and to identify the values that protect humanity is at the heart of what education really is. Such debate involves the search for objective truth, the development of knowledge and an encouragement towards critical thinking. Those who hold this eclectic view of education are concerned that current approaches to education reduce the process to statements of achievement (competences) and as such skew the focus away from what it really means to be professional. In addition, Armitage *et al.* (2002) argue that competence-based approaches lead to a deprofessionalisation of the lecturer's role. This comment is a critique of a competence, or reductionist approach to teaching that describes it in a set of rigid standards which have to be met.

Models of teacher training endorsed by the Further Education National Training Organisation (FENTO), now subsumed under the title LifeLong Learning UK (LLUK) and underpinned by a competence approach (with statements of achievement in the form of standards that lecturers are expected to achieve), have been in place for a number of years. Similar standards that underpin the training of teachers in our schools have been in place even longer. There is still debate, however, among teacher trainers as to how much a training programme can and should be reduced to the competence model. What might be useful at a personal level is for you to examine your philosophy of education to see how your values are reflected in the standards that are set out for teachers working in education today.

It is apparent in the new qualification that the reforms do not represent any retraction from the competence approach to training. However, attempts have been made to broaden the focus away from a tick box achievement mentality to encourage deeper thought, critique and reflection. This book has taken a pragmatic approach to the qualification and, while providing opportunities to demonstrate skills against the criteria, it also encourages what might be referred to as higher-order skills of thinking, reflection, critique and analysis.

In response to McGettrick's call for professional values you may wish to refer to the the General Teaching Council website for teachers in Northern Ireland (www.gtcni.org.uk) which identifies the following as the core values of the profession:

Trust	Honesty	Commitment
Respect	Fairness	Equality
Integrity	Tolerance	Service

Task 2.4

Consider a day in your working life as a trainee teacher or as a student or employee. Can you think of specific examples when you might demonstrate one or more of the core values identified above?

The new standards are introduced with a rationale describing the role of the teacher in this sector as being to 'create effective and stimulating opportunities for learning though high quality teaching'. The standards are set out in seven domains, or areas of interest, namely:

A: Professional values and practice

B: Knowledge and understanding of area of teaching application

C: Planning and preparing

D: Learning and teaching

E: Teaching, monitoring and assessment

F: Supporting access and progression.

The domains are described in terms of key areas of teaching, indicative knowledge and outcomes. These outcomes are not differentiated by qualification aim but they are given a numerical identifier. This identification system is used at the end of each chapter to denote evidence produced, on completion of the tasks, towards each possible outcome.

In addition, the domains are described in terms of values. The first set of standards in domain A 'professional values and practice' require those achieving QTLS to demonstrate that they value:

- the learning goals and aspirations of all learners and the experience they bring to their learning

- equality, diversity and the need for inclusion in relation to learners, the workforce and the community

- the application of agreed codes of practice and the maintenance of a safe environment

- the potential for learning to benefit people emotionally, intellectually, socially and economically and to contribute to community sustainability

- the importance of reflecting on their own practice as teachers, tutors or trainers against the value base of QTLS

- opportunities for professional development as a teacher, as an expert in their own specialist area and in the pedagogy of the specialist area

- collaborative work with other individuals, groups and/or organisations

- appropriate communication with others with a legitimate interest in learner progress and development

- working within the systems and quality requirements of the organisation and commitment to quality improvement.

Domain A underpins, support and informs all aspects of the work of the teacher/tutor/trainer in the sector.

Task 2.5

Review the areas of scope identified above. With which areas do you feel totally competent? Where might you need to improve your knowledge or skills. Return to the front page of your individual learning plan and evaluate your training needs in relation to the domain statements above.

In addition, make a list of five aims for you, as a professional in the sector, specific to creating an inclusive and accepting environment for all. You may find it useful to refer to the *Guidance Notes on Equality, Diversity and Race* at the Learning and Skills Council website (www.lsc.gov.uk).

Portfolio task 1.2

Consider your personal philosophy of education. In no more than 500 words, outline what you think is involved in the act of teaching. In what sort of atmosphere is learning most likely to take place? Why do you want to teach and what standards are you going to set for yourself when performing the role? Consider how you might set out to meet these standards. Think specifically about how you want to communicate with your learners, other colleagues and other professionals with whom you will come into contact.

One of the core professional values expected of teachers in the school context is that of demonstrating awareness and consideration for the social, cultural, linguistic, religious and ethnic backgrounds of the pupils they teach. This description seems to ignore issues of gender and sexuality, which are of equal importance. The LSS has a long-established reputation for great awareness and sensitivity in all areas of diversity, often providing a supportive and inclusive learning environment where other educational institutions have failed. The values of those working in this sector are espoused with a strong focus on entitlement, equality and inclusiveness. This book aims to embrace these values and reflect them in all elements of practice discussed here.

Standards expected of lecturers and trainers

As mentioned above, there are agreed standards expected of all lecturers working in the sector. The original standards that informed the design of teacher training programmes, known as the FENTO standards, were written with further education lecturers in mind. One of Ofsted's recommendations to the DfES in its report on initial teacher training for the LSS was to consider closer links between the current standards for school teachers and those for FE teachers and trainers (Ofsted, 2003: 29). New standards are intended to reflect the increased diversity of the LSS while also aiming to provide greater synergy between the standards expected of those teaching in schools. The standards can be accessed through the IfL website at www.ifl.uk.

A framework for recording your achievement of these standards is available at the end of each chapter of this book.

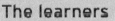

An assessment record proforma can be downloaded from the companion website (Web 4)

Task 2.6

Using the code of practice you devised in Task 2.2, compare your code with the national standards for teachers in the sector. You will need to look at the domain statements for each of the domains A, B, C, D, E and F as set out in the standards.

A link to the **QTLS** standards can be found on the companion website (Web 6)

2

The learners

The LSS provides education for a diverse range of learners. Further education colleges alone attract 27 per cent of their population from the 15 per cent of electoral wards that are recognised as most disadvantaged (HMSO, 2004). Other learners may include retired people learning in community centres, part of our prison population or new immigrants requiring help with using English as their second language. The learning climate is one that embraces difference and welcomes non-traditional learners.

Task 2.7

Complete the following table to indicate which of the following categories of student you might meet as a learner in the skills sector.

Student types	Yes	No
An undergraduate studying for a foundation degree		
Students completing a course leading to university access		
A group of local residents interested in learning a foreign language		
Trainees learning a skill and being paid to attend college on the basis of a weekly programme, which includes set days in work, other days in training		
Adults needing support with basic skills i.e. numeracy, literacy		
A group of 14-16-year-olds studying for vocational qualifications		
Students with learning difficulties being trained in life skills		
A group of adults studying for a teaching qualification		
Young people working in industry receiving training from WBLPs		
Refugees and asylum seekers newly arrived and in need of support		
Young people from a young offenders institution receiving support in numeracy and literacy		
A student studying for a professional qualification such as accountancy, marketing, legal executive		

This is not a trick question, just a warm-up exercise to start you thinking about the diversity of the sector. The answer is provided at the end of the book. A similar activity could be carried out in relation to the curriculum delivered in this sector. A recent LEACAN (Local Education Authority Curriculum Advisers Network) and AoC (Association of Colleges) document, listing all courses approved for funded by the LSC (Learning and Skills Council) is 11 pages in length, and that is just funded provision. The sector opens it doors for training offered at full cost and in some cases for minimal profit, where the provision might meet a regional need. Such events are rare, however, in the current climate of financial rigour and activity-costing models.

The safe learner

The concept of the safe learner and all that it involves has to be a key part of the practice and professionalism of everyone working in the sector. Four key dimensions to the principle are explored below for those training or considering further qualification routes.

The first dimension relates to the statutory requirement for everyone working in the sector to have been subject to a check carried out by the Criminal Record Bureau. The second relates to current knowledge requirements in relation to health and safety regulations that pertain to your subject (such as substance control, workshop/classroom design, use of safe equipment). The third concerns organisational health and safety policy and practice of which you must be aware. Finally, the necessity for risk assessments in relation to everyday activities, extracurricula excursions and work experience activities must be addressed. The concept of the safe learner applies to all learners in the sector but may have particular and greater significance in the training of those working in prisons, adult and community centres and in workplace learning environments.

Portfolio task 2.2

If you are new to teaching, your training organisation or employer will require you to undergo a CRB check. We suggest you keep a copy (or the master if you are able) in your portfolio.

Portfolio task 2.3

A health and safety assessment proforma can be downloaded from the companion website (Web 7)

Access the health and safety policy for your organisation, read it and ensure that you understand the requirements placed upon you. Carry out a risk assessment for an environment you are likely to use (workshop, classroom, salon, training centre). Do you feel that the environment is secure and a safe place for training? If not, it is your responsibility to report your concerns to a more senior member of staff. Keep a written record of the risk assessment and any actions you may need to take. Put a copy of the assessment in your portfolio.

Example 2.1 Risk assessment proforma

Below you will find a copy of a risk assessment proforma. It has been adapted from one used by an organisation which requires its staff to complete risk assessments as part of the planning of every lesson and every activity that is undertaken in the organisation.

This organisation and the staff within it are taking their statutory responsibilities in relation to health and safety matters very seriously. You are urged to take the same approach.

Lesson Plan Risk Assessment					
Faculty/Division:					
Hazards that could occur during the lesson:					
Injured by/from	Yes/No	Injured by/from	Yes/No	Injured by/from	Yes/No
Subject specific		Moving machinery		Falling from a height	
Hand tools		Falling objects		Trapping legs/arms	
Electrical equipment		Moving vehicles		Exposure to dust	
Pedestrian equipment		Fixed or stationary obstacles		Exposure to chemicals or harmful substances	
Manual handing		Slip, trip or fall		Exposure to fire, explosion	

State the pre-lesson preparation you may need to take to ensure a safe working environment is maintained

State the direct precautions you may need to take to prevent an incident or accident occurring

2

Personalisation

Personalisation in the LSS means tailoring services to meet the needs of learners, to shape provision and improve the quality of learner experience within a framework that encourages greater learner independence and learner voice. It requires organisations to listen and support learners, to provide them with clear information about the options that are available to them and encourage an eagerness among the learner to negotiate their learning pathways, seek out information and challenge constructively the nature of the way learning is presented to them. For the teacher in training, this requires understanding of the support systems, professional openness, confidence and the ability to adjust and adopt different teaching approaches leading to a teaching style which encourages learners to adopt a self-discovery approach. This requires great skill, and trainee teachers (as well as the more experienced) will need to develop a number of approaches and strategies and be prepared to change and adapt these to meet individual and group needs.

Portfolio task 2.4

An **assessment record proforma** can be downloaded from the companion website (Web 4)

In Chapter 1 you were advised to set up a portfolio log (an ILP). If you have not done this already, do so now. You should have a number of elements already in your portfolio, namely a completed front sheet, an action plan, an evaluation of your skills, knowledge and practice against the domain statements for domain A, a copy of a risk assessment, a copy of a health and safety check and evidence from other tasks you may have completed (dependent upon your final qualification aim). This task requires you to complete a log sheet to check that you have produced the evidence suggested in the tasks for Chapters 1 and 2.

Key tips to take from this chapter

- There are agreed professional standards expected of those working in the sector.
- These standards place a responsibility on teachers to behave in certain ways.
- One of the key values of those working in the sector relates to respect for diversity and addressing individual need.

Assessment grid mapped to the standards

This chapter introduces the knowledge requirements for the areas in scope set out at the start of the chapter. Completion of the set tasks will provide you with evidence that can be matched to the knowledge requirements, as set out below, for gaining awards in the learning and skills sector.

Task	Summary activity	Level 3 award	Trainer award (level 4) leading to QTLS	E-learning standards CPD awards
Task 2.1	Teachers and art of teaching	AK 1.1 AK 2.1	AK 1.1 AK 2.1	Introductory activity
Task 2.2	Professional knowledge and judgements	BK 1.1 (in part only)	BK 1.1 (in part only)	Introductory activity
Task 2.3	A code of practice	AK 4.1	AK 4.1	Introductory activity
Task 2.4	Core values	AK 1.1 AK 2	AK 1.1 AK 2	Introductory activity
Task 2.5	Inclusive aims	AK 3.1 AK 5.2	AK 3.1 AK 5.2	Introductory activity
Task 2.6	Reviewing the standards	BK 1.1 AK 6.1 AK 6.2	BK 1.1 AK 6.1 AK 6.2	Introductory activity
Task 2.7	The learners	Introductory activity	Introductory activity	Introductory activity
Portfolio task 2.1	Personal philosophy	AK 5.1 (in part only)	AK 5.1 (in part only)	Introductory activity
Portfolio task 2.2	Professional standing (CRB checks)	Essential introductory activity	Essential introductory activity	Introductory activity
Portfolio task 2.3	Safe learner evaluation	AK 3.1 AK 4.1	AK 3.1 AK 4.1	Introductory activity
Portfolio task 2.4	ILP check	Award preparation	Award preparation	Award preparation

2

3 Professional practice

Creating effective and stimulating opportunities for learning

Learning outcomes

By the end of this chapter you will have:

- explored the first principles in the practice of teaching to ensure learning takes place in a safe and healthy environment
- applied first principles to plan a short micro-teaching session
- used, developed and evaluated a range of teaching and learning strategies in a variety of different learning environments
- developed your effectiveness and capabilities as a teacher.

Areas in scope in this chapter in relation to the standards for teachers, tutors and trainers working in the sector are AS 3, BS 1, CS 1, CS 2, CS 3, DS 1, DS 2, DS 3.

This chapter introduces some first principles involved in planning episodes of learning and teaching. It is presented as an introduction to support your skills as a practitioner while at the same time requiring you, through the set tasks, to think more philosophically about the principles involved in learning and teaching. Completion of the tasks will help those new to teaching, tutoring or training to develop new skills in preparation for the initial award. For the newly appointed, the tasks will provide opportunities for the collection of evidence that might be used as part of the licence to practise portfolio. For the experienced, the portfolio tasks will enable you to confirm and provide evidence of your existing experience and expertise.

As a practitioner it is a mistake to think that teaching or training can be reduced to the acquisition of a set of skills or competences which can be learned from copying teachers. There are core skills that trainees must learn in order to manage and organise a learning environment. Skilled teachers/tutors trainers constantly modify their actions and behaviours on the basis of complex thought processes informed by a great deal of practical experience and theoretical knowledge.

Achieving clarity for yourself and your learners

To plan effectively you will need to use and apply the following concepts:

- **Aim** a *general* statement of intent which can have long-term or short-term outcomes that will in principle be infinite (immeasurable or limitless). An example might be: to explore the role of ICT in learning and teaching.
- **Objective** (generally referred to as intended learning outcome): a *specific* statement of what will be achieved. An example might be: by the end of the session students will have used the internet to research government policy on third world aid. Objectives should be SMART: **S**pecific, **M**easurable, **A**chievable, **R**ealistic and **T**ime-bound.

You can see from the definition above there is a great deal of difference between a very broad declaration of intent as set out in an aim and a very specific and detailed expression of the how, what, when and where described in an objective.

Great importance is given to learning outcomes in this text, based on the belief that the more specific the learning outcome, the clearer the focus of the lesson, the better the preparation and organisation of the learning environment. Learning outcomes should be seen as the scaffolding supporting the structure of the whole training session. Once shared with the learner they can ease classroom tensions, motivate and enthuse learners and, more important, provide early evidence that you, as the provider of the learning, are competent, confident and business-like. Providing opportunities for learning is at the heart of what it means to be a teacher/tutor/trainer. The planning of appropriate learning opportunities will be important not only to you as a practitioner, but to other stakeholders as well, namely the learner, your line manager, the examination awarding bodies and Ofsted.

Applying the theory

The principles that inform good teaching should be reflected in any academic study you engage in to achieve the award of licensed teacher. Any course of study should, in theory, reflect the standards for lecturers working in the LSS (see Chapter 1). This may not be made explicit, but implicitly the learning outcomes for your course of study should be grounded in the principles that enshrine the standards. This is achieved through clear articulation of the learning objectives, which you have to achieve, to gain the initial award or award of licensed to practise. An example is provided in Table 3.1. The aim and learning outcomes shown here might form part of lesson delivered by a college lecturer leading a programme of teacher training.

3

Table 3.1 Articulating learning outcomes 1

Aim	To help practitioners define their professional practices and values
Objectives	By the end of this session practitioners will be able to: • explore the ways in which their professional values relate to those of the standards • consider the behaviours and attitudes you would expect to see from practitioners working in the sector • identify ways in which values and professional practice can be demonstrated • reflect on how to resolve conflict in a series of difficult situations • identify how organisations might contribute to this area

A further example uses *The Lord of the Rings* by J.R.R. Tolkein (Table 3.2). Popularised in the film adaptations, the trilogy has ignited the imagination of children and adults alike. The trilogy can be a source of endless teaching material in a range of curriculum areas. The example in Table 3.2 relates to a history session, but the material could equally well be used to discuss film, drama, production, art, the English novel, philosophy, war, the evolution of language, the function of myths and legends, and more.

Table 3.2 Articulating learning outcomes 2

Aim	To explore the environmental themes presented in *The Lord of the Rings*
Objectives	By the end of the session students will be able to: • identify how nature is used to represent good and evil in *The Lord of the Rings* • explore the impact of industrialisation on the ideas presented in the book • discuss the significant key historical events in the twentieth century which influenced the writer, J.R.R. Tolkein, in this epic work

Making objectives more explicit

The examples in Tables 3.1 and 3.2 give rather general description to what is to be achieved. They are, in fact, framed as 'higher-order' or complex objectives, used to describe more academic ways of thinking and understanding. The use of higher-order objectives is not recommended at this stage in your training.

When framing learning objectives for your learners it is advisable to make the objectives specific. The more specific you can make the objectives, the easier it will be for you to measure the effectiveness of the learning. Clearly stated objectives will have a behavioural outcome that can be observed or tested. Non-behavioural outcomes tend to be rather vague and difficult to evaluate. An example of a non-behavioural objective might be:

By the end of the session students will be able to:

• develop an awareness of bias

A behavioural objective, however, would read:

By the end of the session students will be able to:

● list six sentences from the material that illustrate elements of bias

Table 3.3 offers some guidance as to the language which might be used to frame non-behavioural and behavioural objectives.

Table 3.3 Non-behavioural and behavioural objectives

Non-behavioural	Behavioural
to know	to write
to understand	to explain
to be aware of	to demonstrate
to appreciate	to evaluate
to be familiar with	to list
to grasp	to construct

3

Task 3.1

Complete the table below by selecting one topic of subject knowledge from your own subject area. Remember the objectives must be SMART: **S**pecific, **M**easurable, **A**chievable, **R**ealistic and **T**ime-bound.

Aim	
Objectives	By the end of the session students will he able to:

Portfolio task 3.1

Consider how an understanding of behavioural and non-behavioural objectives might influence your lesson planning. Plan a short episode of learning (10 minutes) using behavioural objectives.

Task 3.2

Ask a colleague if you can observe a lesson they are delivering. When observing, consider the following questions.

1 Are the objectives for the session clear to you as a participant?
2 Are they clear to the learners?
3 Are the students engaged in the learning?
4 At the end of the session, what has been achieved?
5 Would you have delivered the session any differently?

An observation log can be downloaded from the companion website (Web 3)

Much of the teaching that goes on in the LSS can be defined in terms of behaviour objectives. However, for those teaching what Bloom (1956) calls 'higher-order skills' then non-behavioural approaches may form the starting point for your planning. The type of teaching referred to here may be in relation to foundation degrees, advanced A level syllabuses (the traditional A levels and Advanced Vocational Certificates), and your study towards being a recognised teacher, qualified to teach in the LSS.

As a point of clarification: objectives should, as far as is possible, be phrased in behavioural terms unless the intended outcome involves specific skills such as the identification of complex types of learning. Complex learning requires demonstration of certain skills and may be described using the following language: understand, recognise, interpret, apply, analyse, synthesis, evaluate. Table 3.4 shows how the language of more complex learning outcomes might be applied (for further reading on learning outcomes visit www.ncgio.ucsb.educ/giscc/format/outcomes).

Table 3.4 Articulating more complex learning outcomes

Aim	To explore the key principles of learning
Objective	By the end of the module participants will be able to: ● demonstrate an understanding of a range of learning theories ● recognise the different needs of learners ● identify appropriate strategies to support learner needs ● evaluate the effectiveness of a planned episode of learning ● demonstrate familiarity with the use of ICT to support student learning

Looking back at Table 3.1 you will see the objectives set out there (linked to a programme of academic study, such as the Certificate to Practise) are couched in these terms. In order to support the achievement of what Bloom (1956) refers to as higher-order skills, Gagne (1985) suggests that periods of learning should be planned using general objectives which are then broken down to be specific. Such an approach supports greater specificity in terms of the outcome that will be achieved and allows complex objectives to be described in terms of behavioural outcomes, as advocated above. Applying the approach would lead to adapting Table 3.1 so that it appears as shown in Table 3.5.

Table 3.5 Breaking down objectives into general and specific

Aim		To help practitioners define their professional practices and values
Objectives		By the end of this session practitioners will be able to:
	General	1. *Understand how their professional values relate to those of the standards*
	Specific	1.1 Construct of list of five professional values appropriate to the role of a lecturer 1.2 Compare these values with those set out in the standards 1.3 Evaluate the similarities and differences between the values expressed in objective 1.1 and those of the IfL standards
	General	2. *Consider the behaviours and attitudes you would expect to see from practitioners working in the sector*
	Specific	2.1 Plan and perform a brief role play to demonstrate appropriate behaviour in a chosen area of professional activity
	General	3. *Identify ways in which values and professional practice can be demonstrated*
	Specific	3.1 Demonstrate your plan to the rest of the group 3.2 Discuss the choice of scenarios and identify the values that are being presented
	General	4. *Reflect on how to resolve conflict in a series of difficult situations*
	Specific	4.1 As a group, explore case study examples where the values expected of a professional are not being practised 4.2 Discuss what action you would need to take in these situations
	General	5. *Identify how organisations might contribute to this area*
	Specific	5.1 Identify what responsibility the organisation might have in the situations you have been discussing 5.2 Explore the role of organisational policies in this context

3

If you compare Table 3.1 with Table 3.5 you will be able to see the benefits of defining, in this case, both general and specific objectives. The use of specific objectives has enabled the lecturer to set out a comprehensive and detailed structure for the session. In some cases the objective is so specific it even identifies the strategy that the lecturer intends to use (role play, case study). Table 3.6 identifies the action verbs which can be used to make general objectives much more specific.

Table 3.6 Action verbs to make general objectives more specific

Knowledge	Comprehension	Application	Analysis	Synthesis	Evaluation
cite	depict	apply	analyse	arrange	appraise
define	describe	demonstrate	appraise	assemble	assess
identify	discuss	dramatise	calculate	collect	choose
label	explain	employ	categorise	combine	compare
list	express	illustrate	classify	compose	defend
locate	locate	interpret	criticise	construct	estimate
match	recognise	operate	debate	create	evaluate
name	report	practise	diagram	design	judge
quote	restate	schedule	differentiate	formulate	justify
recall	review	sketch	distinguish	integrate	measure
record	translate	use	examine	manage	rate
relate			experiment	organise	revise
reproduce			inspect	prepare	select
state			plan	propose	value
underline			question	score	
			relate		
			solve		
			test		

First attempts at lesson planning using objectives to good effect can prove difficult. It is only with practice, determination and the confidence to experiment that lecturers begin to develop their skills and move practice beyond a personal comfort zone into more untried, and exciting, realms of experience.

Achieving your objectives

To achieve your objectives it is necessary to have a strategy. This rather commonsense statement applies to all aspects of our lives and, indeed, to the art of teaching. A strategy might be defined as 'a combination of student activities supported by the used of appropriate resources to provide a particular learning experience and/or to bring about the desired learning' (Reece and Walker, 1999: 32).

The strategy adopted to achieve the intended lesson outcome will vary depending on a variety of factors. These may be associated with the group of learners involved, the resources available (size of rooms, number of staff in support) and the objectives of the session. Objectives also need to be considered in the light of the learners for whom they are planned. Chapter 10 gives focus to the learner and their needs and illustrates the necessity of adapting learning situations to accommodate different learning needs while still managing to establish the intended learning outcomes for the programme.

Domains of learning

The act of learning is often described in three different ways (domains). These are the psychomotor, cognitive and affective domains. Table 3.7 sets out the constituents of each domain.

Table 3.7 **The three domains of learning**

Domain	Key elements
Psychomotor	Concerned with physical skills: playing a sport, lifting an elderly person, operating lighting for a performance
Cognitive	Concerned with knowledge and knowing: explaining how to colour hair, how to design an electrical circuit; explaining the factors which led to the Second World War
Affective	Concerned with feelings and emotions: appreciating a poem, dealing with conflict at work, managing relationships and people

A planned session may need to focus on one or all of these approaches. The novice practitioner may be drawn to work in one domain only. However, it is important to realise that learning may take place in a domain other than the one you might consider most appropriate. There is a need for variety within planning and this can be assured through moving between the three domains.

The starting point for planning an episode of learning is, as has been identified, clear learning objectives. Objectives may be classified under the domains identified in Table 3.7. For example, the objective

to demonstrate the importance of kneading bread dough to achieve edible loaves of bread

would involve a psychomotor skill, whereas

to appreciate Shakespeare's presentation of marriage

would lead to work in the affective domain. Using this principle it is easy to see how objectives might fall into different domains of learning and thus might be better achieved through different approaches or strategies.

Examples of strategies which support the achievement of objectives in different domains of learning are identified in Table 3.8.

Table 3.8 Learning strategies effective within the three domains

Psychomotor domain: objectives concerned with physical acquisition	Demonstration Practice Role play Mini project (e.g. construction of a children's play area)
Knowledge domain: objectives concerned with knowledge and understanding	Research project Investigation Assignment Seminar Question and answer session Written test Lecture Problem-solving activity Group discussion Practical Matching activities (pictures/words in a foreign language) Jigsaws Games Investigations
Affective domain: objective concerned with attitudes and opinions	Poetry reading Analysis of video images and/or pictures Case study Role play Discussion Problem solving

Task 3.3

In relation to Table 3.8, consider the ways in which you were taught at school. Which domain was given the greater focus and why? Consider the implications for learners if you teach your subject solely in one domain?

Differentiated learning objectives

It is important to plan episodes of learning with the needs of your learners as a key focus. Chapters 5 and 10 explore how lecturers might accommodate the needs of different types of learners. Learners whose needs are met in the LSS, more than any other, might require individualised opportunities to demonstrate their skills. Even prior to understanding the specific needs of individuals in a class group it is important to consider how you will provide for different learning needs.

Task 3.4

Consider how you will accommodate the learner who wants to know *how* the computer works and *why* computers have become so influential in education today. Consider the domains of learning that are influencing this particular learner.

Teaching techniques and supporting resources

To provide for the needs of different learners, and to meet the requirements of your role, you may be required to work with large groups, small groups and individual learners. The strategies you select to work with may well be determined by group size, as illustrated in Table 3.9.

Table 3.9 Group size and appropriate strategies

Group size	Strategy/resource
Large group	Lecture Debate Video PowerPoint presentation (see Technology Tip below)
Small group	Role play Discussion Games Field trips Worksheets Online debate
Individual	Set tasks Worksheets Internet research Traditional research: interview, questionnaire, focus group

A focus on group work

The chart below was produced by a group of trainees on a teacher training course in response to a question about the advantages of group work.

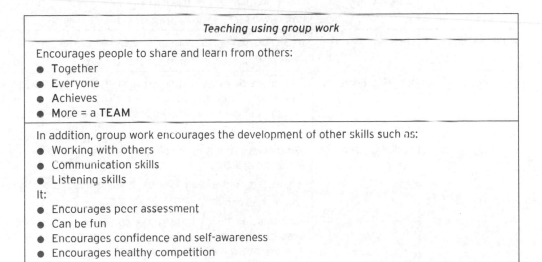

Teaching using group work
Encourages people to share and learn from others: ● Together ● Everyone ● Achieves ● More = a **TEAM**
In addition, group work encourages the development of other skills such as: ● Working with others ● Communication skills ● Listening skills It: ● Encourages peer assessment ● Can be fun ● Encourages confidence and self-awareness ● Encourages healthy competition

There are ways, however, in which many strategies may be adapted and used with different sizes of group. This gives variety to the session, helps maintain concentration and supports learners who will have a variety of learning preferences (see Chapter 5). Table 3.10 illustrates a few examples of how strategies may be adapted; there are many more.

Table 3.10 Different approaches within a strategy

Strategy	Key activity	Adaptations
Lecture	Information given by one individual	Handout: giving structure of the lecturer and asking some key questions Practical tasks: e.g., make a hole in a piece of paper large enough for a person to step through (session on lateral thinking); design a paper aeroplane (use with caution and only when relevant to the lecture!) Discuss with a neighbour: feedback can be taken by sharing 'answers I have had before but what have you to add'? Video: again with a task, a worksheet or discussion questions
Video	Watching and listening	Handout: asking key questions about the sequence you have shown Role play: ask the observers to act out what happens next Group discussion: as a group, discuss the use of colour in the video (set this task prior to showing the sequence)
Demonstration	Observation	Video: record the activity for further analysis
Role play	Group action	Video: record the activity for further analysis Handout: asking key questions about the task
Written assignment	Individual study	Handout: giving a structure plan, or the introductory paragraph to help those new to essay writing Group analysis: participants grade work of other students (anonymous and with permission of the author) to support understanding of the assessment criteria
Debate	Discussion	Write: key points on a flipchart Role play: scenarios that arise from the discussion
Case study	Reading	Group discussion: as a group, discuss key themes Role play: scenarios that arise from the text
Games	Physical dexterity	Memory activity: name individuals or things when the ball is thrown. This may be used as an induction activity or to learn a language, the recipient of the ball being required to translate the language used by the game leader
Project work	Individualised learning	Group tasks: groups given different topics within the main topic area to research Email: carry out research for the topic using local contacts Internet research Electronic portfolios: tasks can be completed and assessed electronically using a learning platform which can mimic the classroom environment (Browne, 2003)

Portfolio task 3.2

Consider the advantages and disadvantages of different methods (questioning, discussion, presentation, small-group work). What are the issues you need to consider? (Think specifically about objectives, domains of learning and the needs of different learners.) Consider the implications of preference for planning. Produce a table to illustrate how and when each strategy might be appropriately used in your curriculum area. Do some subject areas lend themselves to different methodologies or should a variety of methods be applied in all subject areas, discuss this point in detail and give justification for your answers. (200 words)

The examples in Table 3.10 also illustrate how you can move between the different domains of learning within a set lesson (from the cognitive to the psychomotor in the lecture, for example. This fluid approach enables lecturers to appeal to different types of learners (see Chapter 10) and to consider the sequence of the lesson content. The use of different strategies and a planned sequence of events enable session times to be broken into periods of different activity which can then help to maintain concentration.

Portfolio task 3.3

Design three worksheets or handouts for use in a session. Each handout should support a different teaching approach (video, case study, debate, for example). Consider design and structure in the light of the intended group size and the focus of the activity involved. You will also need to think about appropriate and clearly legible content, size of lettering, use of colour and layout.

Technology tip

If you are familiar with using PowerPoint (a Microsoft tool designed for making presentations), you may wish to use one the templates available in the PowerPoint directory of your computer hard drive to structure your handout. The template will provide you with a ready designed format, with headings, access to bullet points and different optional layouts. You may like to design one handout using the PowerPoint facility and compare the result with the others you produce.

Lesson structure and sequencing

As a beginner to the art of teaching it may help if you think of each session rather like a piece of music, with a beginning (or introduction) where some initial themes or phrases are introduced, a development (where these themes are used with greater complexity and variety), a repetition of the key themes, or consolidation, followed finally by a conclusion which brings together and sums up the totality of the musical experience. As a sporting enthusiast you could compare the lesson with a sporting event. The warm-up before the game is the introduction, the game itself is the development (with a repositioning after half-time to refocus the minds of the players); substitutes (or new ideas) might be introduced if things are not going well. The joyous (or demoralising) analysis afterwards concludes the event.

The introduction

This is your first, and possibly only, opportunity as a new lecturer to sound confident and knowledgeable, to gain the attention of the participants and gain control of the session. Gaining the attention and interest of your audience is crucial. Table 3.11 provides you with some ideas on how to do this. Choice of activity will depend on the age of the students, the size of the group, and the topic under study. The chosen activity should obviously be closely aligned to the objectives for the lesson.

Table 3.11 How you might gain the attention of your audience

Activity	Circumstances where useful
Overhead slide summarising the objectives and structure of the session	Large lecture Average-size classroom
Brief test on previous session	Large lecture Average-size classroom One-to-one learning environment
Passing around a number of objects or pictures for examination	Average-size classroom One-to-one learning environment
Showing a small section of video followed by a set of questions	Average-size classroom One-to-one learning environment Can be used to gain the attention of a difficult group
Playing a short piece of calm music from a tape or CD	Often used with students who have a learning disability or who may be tense or nervous
For the very competent and extroverted, with experience of rejection Demonstrating a skill: singing, playing an instrument, miming an activity, modelling a skill or vocational activity (hairdressing, plumbing, etc.)	Average-size classroom One-to-one learning environment

The development

The development is the point where you begin to focus on what you need to achieve. Planned activities need to show some logical sequence with a gradual move from easily grasped concepts to the more difficult. Attempts should be made to meet the needs of a variety of learners (see Chapter 7) and give opportunity for extension and development to the most able. The least able should also feel that they have gained something from the time invested.

The consolidation

At point of consolidation no new concepts should be introduced by the lecturer (although participants may well provide opportunities for extension of ideas and concepts). At this point understanding may be tested. This might be achieved in a variety of ways such as questioning, written tasks, discussions, role play, games and other activities.

The conclusion

The conclusion of the session is as important as any of the others and needs careful planning. Here you have the opportunity to recap on what you set out to achieve, to reinforce the intended outcomes for your learners and give a clear ending to 'the performance'. The clearer you are in bringing the session to an end, the easier it will be to pick up where you left off when you next meet the group.

3

> **Technology tip**
>
> If you are keeping an electronic register of attendees, make a note of absences and be prepared to offer additional help on their return. This can be as simple as a brief recapitulation at the beginning of the next session or keeping extra copies of lecture handouts. Obviously this can be done without the help of ICT: a diary or lesson jotter can be just as useful.

> **Technology tip**
>
> Keep a record of progress made in the lesson, any homework tasks set or key ideas that you think need revisiting. There is nothing more impressive than the lecturer who remembers what has gone before, and nothing less impressive than one who starts the session with the question 'What did we do last week?'

A template for this **lesson plan** can be downloaded from the companion website (Web 9)

Example 3.1 illustrates a lesson plan (some institutions are beginning to use the terminology 'learning plan' to acknowledge the range of venues and settings encompassed by the LSS), showing how a period of learning might be framed. Notice the attention given to timings so that beginnings and endings are neat and clear. Chapter 5 provides an example of a lesson plan that gives attention to the needs of specific learners. For the purpose of this chapter the design has been kept simple.

You may, however, wish to use the format adopted by your institution.

Example 3.1 Lesson plan

Name of lecturer: **Fred**	Course: **Health and Social Care: Intermediate (GCSE) Vocational Qualification: numeracy key skills**
Room: **A21**	Session: **Friday session 4**
Start time: **3.30pm**	Finish time: **4.30pm**
Number of participants: **15**	Significant issues: **This is not a good time for the topic, attendance will need monitoring and activities designed to ensure student enthusiasm is achieved and maintained**

Aims	**To develop students' ability to estimate in varying context using appropriate measuring tools**
Objectives	By the end of the session participants will be able to: ● **Use and evaluate two different systems of measurement** ● **Recognise and apply two different measuring systems to different dimensions of estimation** ● **Recognise the significance of error in estimation**

Time	Lesson content	Method	Resources
3.30 5 minutes	Settle group and clarify objectives Emphasise how functional the session will be in supporting key skill achievements	Link to key skill competence and illustrate how functional the session will be in supporting participants in achieving the skill	Key skills record book for each student Objectives identified on the board
10 minutes	Allocate groups Distribute local maps Set tasks: Identify location of all the nurseries in the region Estimate the walking distance between each one	Mixed ability groupings Small-group activity Worksheet identifying names of each nursery	Maps Record sheet for estimations Record outcomes
5 minutes	Compare outcomes	Large-group brainstorm	Board work
3 minutes	Record agreed estimated distances (metres), in walking time (minutes) and car transport (minutes)	Gapped handout	Paperwork available

Time	Lesson content	Method	Resources
10 minutes	Using a stopwatch send two (trustworthy) students to the onsite nursery and record how long it takes them to return On return compare actual time taken with the estimated time	Remaining students to discuss how long it takes them to travel to their work placements and explore the implications of their method of transport	Stopwatch Discussion sheet
5 minutes	Record outcome of the discussion	Students to compare journey times, external influences that impact on their travel plans	Chart to complete which compares journey times with travel method
5 minutes	Explore the impact of estimated time of journey being much less than actual	Discussion linked to their professional responsibilities as carers	Key questions provided to direct discussion
5 minutes	Collate ideas	Brainstorm and record	Board or flipchart
5 minutes	Individuals to draw up a code for travel when on work placement	Gapped handout	Worksheet provided
7 minutes	Conclusions, revision of activity, key learning points	Return to the objectives	Record achievement, if appropriate, in the individual student key skills record book

3

Notice times, content, method and resources. Those of you who make lists of things to do, your lesson plan will come as a useful tool; others may need to make more effort to commit to writing. The value of such plans cannot be underestimated and there is certainly an expectation with the LSS (monitored through external inspection) that staff will plan all periods of formal activity they engage in with learners.

A template for this **lesson plan** can be downloaded from the companion website (Web 9)

Technology tip

For those of you who are able to use a computer, at this stage of your training it is recommended that you set up a lesson plan template on a disk or on your home/work computer. You can then reuse the template, adapt it if necessary and begin to develop a bank of lesson plans for future use. You do not need to follow the example structure in Figure 3.2; in fact some institutions have templates you are required to use. It might be worth checking this before you design your own.

Schemes of work and course aims

Schemes of work

Schemes of work might best be described as the *grand design* for a set period (term, year, semester). They could be compared with a holiday itinerary in which you plan where you are going to visit in general terms, perhaps with the intention of visiting certain sites, but do not at this stage identify exactly what you will do on each day of your holiday. Reece and Walker (1999: 315) describe a scheme of work as 'a series of planned learning experiences, sequenced to achieve the course aims in the most effective way'.

Schemes of work are long- or medium-term plans designed to ensure progression and continuity in learning over a period of time. They should be 'a working document which summarises teachers' thinking about a course, providing a structure and offering guidelines for more detailed lesson planning' (Balderstone and Lambert, 2000: 69).

Course aims

The starting point in the design of any scheme of work is the course aims. What is the overarching purpose of this course, what areas of the curriculum are relevant and what skills do I want the participants to achieve?

Increasingly, course aims are determined by the external organisations that award the qualification (see Chapter 7 for a discussion of awarding bodies). In many subjects the curriculum is divided into units of study, with the aims of each unit specified in advance. You will need to ensure that your scheme of work matches the course content as set out by the approved syllabus for the programme. You may have some choice over the order in which you address the aims and the way in which you interpret the intended syllabus content, and this is where your experience and training are useful. It is important to plan carefully the order in which you frame each lesson in any time period.

Table 3.12 lists questions to consider when presented with or designing course aims. The questions are designed to help you think about sequencing, planning for learning outcomes and student needs. In other words, using the holiday itinerary analogy, they are the practical questions you need to ask yourself before you set out on your journey.

Table 3.12 Planning to achieve your aims

- What do I hope to achieve in the time available?
- What ideas, knowledge, skills and attitudes do I want to explore?
- What is going to be most helpful for this group of learners?
- What do I need to cover first before the learners can progress to more complex activities?
- Are there any sensitivities associated with the topic for those present? (These might relate to religious belief, ethnicity, health-related topics, political ideas.) If this is the case, consider how well you know the group, how long it might take to build up their confidence and trust before they might be able to tackle potentially sensitive issues.
- Should some material be presented in chronological order to support understanding?
- When can I hope that the group will be confident enough to engage with different teaching strategies such as role play and discussion, and which topics will be best covered using these strategies?

Table 3.12 *continued*

- Are there any safety issues I should address at the beginning of the course? (This might well apply in a workshop or practical situation.)
- Do I need access to any specific resources (when will the computer room or a guest speaker be available?), and how can I sequence the lessons that go before and come afterwards so that the most can be made of these opportunities?
- When will to be best to assess learning?
- How, when and how often should I invite the learners to evaluate the learning experience?

Example 3.2 provides an example of a scheme of work for an advanced leisure and tourism course on the topic of 'The holiday industry'. Notice how the lesson themes are ordered to support learner confidence and develop specific skills.

Example 3.2 Scheme of work for Advanced Vocational Qualification Leisure and Tourism

Topic: *The Holiday Industry*
Based on a timetable of two sessions per week, each of 90 minutes' duration

Key aim	Key knowledge	Key ideas	Skills	Resources	Assessment evidence	Aspects of performance
Week 1 Introduce the industry Ask why we study it? What do we need to know?	Financial role of the holiday industry in the economies of some countries	For many countries the holiday industry is the mainstay of the economy This has an impact on the country's approach to the customer	Understanding of economic principles (numerical skills) Research skills in relation to country and economy Discussion skills (communication of experiences) Enquiry and questioning skills	Maps Chalk and board Photographs Brochures ICT internet searches	List of countries and economic stability Database of information Summary of discussion, key points identified	Understanding of place and function Ability to relate knowledge and experience to demonstrate an understanding of impact
Week 2 Explore the countries which rely most heavily on the holiday industry and why	Specific countries and regions	The importance of the industry to the economy has an impact on client experience	Identify regions and reasons; select one for study Work in a group Distribute tasks Work cooperatively with a team	Internet access Worksheet Holiday brochures	Comparison of brochure image of a selected region with that presented by internet research Tasks allocated for a group presentation	Ability to work in a team Ability to use sources of evidence to present a viewpoint Understanding of place

Key aim	Key knowledge	Key ideas	Skills	Resources	Assessment evidence	Aspects of performance
Week 3 Explore the region in detail in relation to quality of life for the inhabitants Discuss impact of available resources on life experiences	In what ways has the selected region used its resources to support the holiday industry? What other industries entered or exited previously? What impact do they have on the holiday industry?	Key components of the holiday industry (what is on offer) What other industries survive or have declined in recent years? Resources gained from the holiday industry have a key impact on life changes	Research Analysis Enquiry and questioning skills Extracting information from a video	Internet access Holiday brochures Worksheet Video section 'poor kids/rich kids'	Research evidence Analysis of video through a worksheet questionnaire	Ability to use sources of evidence to present a viewpoint Understanding of place Ability to understand the impact of poverty on life chances
Week 4 Identify the implication of findings for the holiday industry	The impact of industrial decline How can evidence of the past be used to enhance to experience of holidaymakers today?	Helping the country visited to exploit its resources to the benefit of all Enhancing the experience of the holidaymaker while providing support to the country	Presentation skills Numerical analysis Team work Independent learning Ethical/ responsibility issues	Group presentation requirements Clear grading criteria previously discussed with the student group	Group presentation Individual report	Ability to work as a team to present a thoroughly researched topic Ability to think critically about the impact of the holiday industry on the selected region

A **scheme of work** template can be downloaded from the companion website (Web 10)

Another example of a scheme of work, using a different template is provided in Example 3.3. This scheme relates to a beginners' session in ICT skills.

The template used for the leisure and tourism session in Example 3.2 has some advantages over the ICT format as it allows space to record opportunities for achievement of certain skills. Where you are required to incorporate key skills into your curriculum, this design will be useful. The integration or otherwise of key skills into curriculum design is discussed in Chapter 8.

Example 3.3 Scheme of work for basic skills in computing

Course title	Qualification aim:			Start date	End date	Course code	ICT/BA 1
Computers for Beginners	Basic skills Introduction equivalent to Learndirect 1st Certificate			8 Nov.	13 Dec.	Course leader	To be confirmed
Target enrolment number	Attendance	Attendance	Number completing	Day of week: **Monday**		Level	Venue
15	15 Nov	29 Nov		Start 9.30 Finish 11am		Basic skills 1, 2 and 3	ICT room 104

Week no. and date	Session title	Content	Activities and skills	Assessment	Resources
1 Monday, 8 Nov.	Introduction to Computers	By the end of the session participants will: • Be provided with details of the course • Have received an introduction to the core computer concepts • Understand turn on and log off facilities • Have explored basic mouse skills • Have understood the importance of saving data	Individuals will learn through: Demonstration • Activity • Practice • Following worksheet directions • Self-practice and exploration	Observation of basic skills Gapped handout to confirm understanding of vocabulary	Whiteboard Handouts A computer per participant Worksheet
2 Monday, 15 Nov.	Consolidation of previous work	Brief test of language and function By the end of the session participants will: • Have practised their typing skills • Know how to save a document • Have used the copy and paste function	Verbal non-threatening questioning Teacher demonstration Practise activities Saving documents to disk	Test understanding and memory levels Discussion Brainstorm Practise sheets Handouts Set homework	Quick test of last week's work Whiteboard Handouts A computer per participant Worksheet Floppy disk per participant
3 Monday, 22 Nov.	Working together	Brief test of language and function By the end of the session participants will: • Understand page set-up • Margins • Tables • Design a template for a menu	Individuals learn through: • Demonstration • Activity • Practice • Following worksheet directions • Self-practice and exploration • Group work	Check progress with homework Discussion Brainstorm Practise sheets Handouts Set homework	Quick test of last week's work Whiteboard Handouts A computer per participant Worksheet Floppy disk per participant

3

Portfolio task 3.4

Construct a scheme of work in your chosen curriculum area. Identify the period for which the scheme is intended (For example 10 weeks, one term), the student group (size, age, membership) and the course aims. Once you have prepared the scheme, provide a commentary to justify your selection and ordering of topic within the scheme.

Key tips to take from this chapter

- ICT can be a great support to you and your learners.
- It is important to set clear aims and objectives that inform your lesson planning; making objectives specific has real benefits.
- Schemes of work are the essential starting points for all curriculum planning.
- Domains of learning need to be considered in lesson planning.

Assessment grid mapped to the standards

This chapter introduces the knowledge requirements for the areas in scope set out at the start of the chapter. Completion of the set tasks will provide you with evidence that can be matched to the standards, as set out below, for gaining awards in the learning and skills sector.

Task	Summary activity	Level 3 award	Trainer award (level 4/5) leading to QTLS (level 5)	E-learning standards CPD awards
Task 3.1	Setting SMART objectives	BK 3.1 BK 2.2	BK 3.1 BK 2.2	
Task 3.2	Lesson observations	BK 1.1 BK 1.2	BK 1.1 BK 1.2	
Task 3.3	Domains of learning	BK 3.1 BK 2.2	BK 3.1 BK 3.2 BK 2.2	
Task 3.4	Learning needs	CK 3.2 (in part only)	CK 3.2 DK 2.2 (in part only) DK 2.1 (in part only)	
Portfolio task 3.1	Behavioural objectives	CP 1.1 (in part only)	CP 1.1 (in part only) CP 1.2 (in part only)	Pre-award preparation
Portfolio task 3.2	Learning preferences	CP 3.2 (in part only)	CP 3.2 (in part only)	Pre-award preparation
Portfolio task 3.3	Designing resources	DP 2.6 (in part only) CP 3.1 (in part only) BK 5.1	DP 2:6 (in part only) CP 3.1 (in part only) BK 5.1	Pre-award preparation
Portfolio task 3.4	Designing schemes of work	CP 1.1	CP 1.1	

4 Professional skills
Planning learning programmes to meet the needs and expectations of learners

Learning outcomes

By the end of this chapter you will:

- have a toolkit of resources to use and questions to ask for every occasion you first meet a new group of students

- have developed your understanding of the function of planning and preparation required to be an effective teacher

- begin to see how you can use ICT/ILT in your teaching and planning

- have explored the role of mentors and subject learning coaches in the LSS and the part they will play in your route to qualification.

Areas in scope in this chapter in relation to the standards for teachers, tutors and trainers working in the sector are AS 5, AS 7, BS 1, BS 2, BS 4, CS 3, DS 1, DS 2, DS 3.

The focus of this chapter is on early beginnings and some of the basics associated with getting started in practical terms. Those new to teaching, tutoring and training will benefit from completing the early tasks. The chapter offers, nearer to the end, more developed portfolio opportunities for those wishing to achieve QTLS. There are also ideas on how to use information and learning technology (ILT) that may be of use to the experienced lecturer. Advice is available for those wishing to achieve licensed teacher status. This relates specifically to the role of subject learning coaches/mentors.

How can I ensure I am effective as a teacher?

The short answer to the above question is that you cannot always guarantee that what you set out to achieve in a session of planned activity is achieved. Teaching is a human activity affected by a range of external factors. You can never be sure that a session you have planned meticulously will work. It may work with one group of learners and not another, on one occasion but not the following week. There are, however, a number of tried and tested things you can do. They do not guarantee success, but they make disasters less likely.

Surviving on your own

Whether you are already teaching or have just joined a course of full-time study to become a licensed teacher, trainer or tutor, you are making a journey that requires preparation, determination and commitment. The issues discussed in this chapter and the advice provided will be useful to new practitioners and the experienced alike.

The word 'survival' has been carefully chosen. In any learning situation it is vital that you, the lecturer are in control of the key activities that are underway. So, at the beginning of every encounter we ask you to be sure that you know what you are going to do, how you are going to do it and what you expect the students to have achieved. Minton (1991) refers to this as the 'who', 'what', 'why', 'how' and 'when' of teaching. In fact each episode of teaching, with a new group of students, can be likened to a criminal inquiry where you, the detective, use all your skills to take control of the situation, to find out about your 'suspects', to try out different methods of working, to bring each case (teaching session) to an effective conclusion. In addition you will be trying to bring about some change in the thinking and/or skills of the students you are working with. Teaching, then, is not just something that you do, and have to prepare meticulously for, it is something that has an intended effect on the participants.

Task 4.1

List the question you will need to ask of yourself, and others, before you can carry out a session of teaching.

If you have not taught at the venue before, then the first questions you will ask relate to buildings, room numbers, resources, your personal space for working. Will you have a desk and a telephone, for example; will the lecture space have IT facilities, video, overhead projector, whiteboard, desks and chairs? Do not assume that every classroom will be fitted out to a high specification. In fact, assume nothing. Other questions will relate to the timetable, the length of sessions, the equipment. The when and where questions, it is hoped, can be easily addressed.

The who questions will fall into two categories: those that relate to your colleagues, and those that relate to the student group. If you are working towards the Certificate to Practise award, then your mentor or subject learning coach will be a key person on your route to success. It is important that you build up a strong working relationship with this person and agree with them at an early stage of your training what you need to achieve and how. The following areas will need clarification:

- How can you contact your learning coach/mentor?
- How often will you meet?
- Can you observe their teaching, and if so, when and how often would they find it appropriate?
- When will they be observing your teaching?
- How will they be making judgements about you? What are their performance criteria?
- Is anyone else likely to observe you at work? If so, what is their role?

It is advisable for all new practitioners to have the opportunity to observe a variety of teachers in a range of different contexts before they are required to teach themselves. Ideally, the launch into managing a whole class should be staged, starting with a period of observation, followed by some small-group work, perhaps a few joint teaching activities (with a qualified and respected role model) and then a whole-class session. This model of training may not, however, always be available, but it is certainly one to aim for.

Some of the questions you will have raised in Task 4.1 relate to what you are teaching (the syllabus or scheme of work), who (the student group) and why (the intended outcomes). You need to glean as much information as you can well before the start of any period of teaching so that you can plan effectively. The how questions are a little more difficult than the wwhen and where questions. Minton (1991: 46) includes the following in his list:

- How am I going to teach?
- How much material should I prepare?
- How will I motivate the students?
- How will I know they are committed and want to learn?
- How will I know if and what they are learning?
- How will I know about past experience, skills, abilities and concerns?
- How flexible does my plan need to be?
- How far can they be given ownership for their learning?
- How do I meet the different needs of a whole class of learners?

Answering the how questions

For those of you engaged in a course of academic study provided by a college or higher education institution, the how questions will be addressed through formal face-to-face lessons, through online computer-mediated activity, or paper-based learning materials. Ideas about how to teach can be spawned from our own experiences of being taught, from trying out different approaches ourselves (practice) and from research theory. For those in training, the early period of your training will involve opportunities to practise teaching (often referred to as micro-teaching) in front of your peers. This should provide the opportunity to test out the theoretical models that inform our ideas about how we should teach. Some of these theories are discussed in Chapter 5 of this book.

Micro-teaching

The role of practice in any performance-related role must not be underestimated. Micro-teaching, or the delivery of small episodes of learning, provides such an opportunity and has long been associated with the training of teachers and lecturers. Micro-teaching provides the opportunity for experimentation and can develop confidence and insight. If used as part of a training programme, with other students who are also learning how to teach, micro-teaching activities can enable your peers to share in constructive advice, discuss the use of different strategies and share in your enthusiasm for your subject. The more you can practise your skills, the better you will be when it comes to the real thing.

Preparing a micro-teaching session

Key advice:

- Keep it simple.
- Make it active – give observers something to do, to examine, to discuss, to think about (possibly not all of these in one short session).
- Think about your audience, who are they, what will be of interest to them.
- Think about beginnings, middles and ends.
- Keep to your time limit.

Example 4.1 A micro-teaching session

As a paramedic, Peter had responsibility for training in his region. He chose a simple first aid activity for his micro-teaching session.

He started the session by explaining what he wanted to achieve (the learning objectives), which were as follows:

- To explore the use of two different methods of pulse monitoring in emergency situations.
- To evaluate the perceived effectiveness of each method.

(**2 mins**) He distributed a brief worksheet to participants setting out his objectives which he then explained. Peter then set a task to observe how a paramedic dealt with an emergency situation in a video clip. The clip related to an incident in a college environment.

(**2 mins**) He then asked the group to comment on what they had observed. His questions were clearly focused and graduated in difficulty, the more challenging at the end:

- What was the emergency that needed attention?
- How did the paramedic respond?
- Was there anything else that you feel should have been done that was not done?

He then asked the participants to discuss, in groups, the circumstances of the emergency in relation to the role of a lecturer who might have been in charge of the injured student, with **5 minutes** only to do this. After **5 minutes** he took only **1 minute** of feedback from the group, having prepared in advance an overhead of the sorts of answers he expected. Finally he gave out pulse-taking equipment for participants to practise on, half using equipment, half using the finger method; **5 minutes** was allowed for practice.

As a closing activity Peter brought the group to order and asked them to reflect on what they had learned from the session. He refocused on the initial objectives that he set for the session to check whether learning had taken place. The session finished after 25 minutes, as planned.

When you plan your micro-teaching session, consider the following questions:

- Have I clarified the purpose of the session to the audience (made the objectives clear)?
- Is there a range of tasks and activities involved?
- Have I prepared enough material?
- Will the session appeal to different student needs? Do I have some practical activities, some discussion, something visual to help the learner? (The need to address learner preference is explored in more detail in Chapters 5 and 10.)

Portfolio task 4.1

Plan a 20-minute micro-teaching activity on a topic of your choice. Think about why you have chosen this subject and what you want the observers to learn. Select the resources you will use, decide how you will divide up the time and what you want the participants to gain from the session. Consider aims and objectives, construct a lesson plan and use a range of strategies to give the session structure and variety.

4

Technology tip

Video technology can be extremely useful for micro-teaching evaluation. It provides an opportunity for you to see yourself in action. It reveals a range of different issues, some of which your peers may not wish to mention but which students will be quick to notice. Do you, for example, appear too relaxed (almost bored by the whole process)? Do you have any annoying mannerisms? Do you appear disorganised, clumsy and incompetent?

Being able to video your performance and reflect critically on your teaching style will be a very useful adjunct to your training as an effective teacher.

Working with a mentor/subject learning coach

It is a requirement of registration for the award of licensed to practise that you have the support of a mentor and/or subject learning coach. Mentoring, according to Meggison and Clutterbuck (2005: 45), is

> A powerful form of learning in which a more experienced individual passes on know-how to someone less experienced.

The mentor role is an important one, and unless you have access to sophisticated electronic communication that can observe all the nuances of classroom interaction, it is not possible to conceive of the mentor role as anything other than one which takes place face to face. This is identified by Meggison and Clutterbuck (2005: 46) in the following way:

> Off-line help by one person to another making significant transition in knowledge, work or thinking.

The mentor should be a qualified and experienced LSS lecturer prepared to spend time with you and take responsibility for your professional development in specified teaching subject areas. Where possible, the appointed mentor should be a subject specialist in the areas in which you will be required to teach.

The mentor should:

- help to induct you into the teaching area and institution
- provide a varied and appropriate programme of developmental experiences for you
- observe, evaluate and review your work, providing you with feedback designed to help you improve
- liaise with others involved in your training (these others may include a university or college tutor or a specially designated licensed to practise tutor qualified to observe you during your training).

Subject learning coaches

In any area of the learning and skills sector, you are likely to come across trained staff with the title 'subject learning coach'. These staff will have responsibility for working with their colleagues to support their subject knowledge and understanding. They will be able to introduce you to some specially designed subject-specific materials that have been developed in a range of curriculum areas. The materials are discussed in more detail in Chapter 6 of this book. The term 'coach' is associated with a style of peer learning where staff work together in an environment of mutual support, to share expertise and skills. The identified subject learning coach may well help you to plan your lessons and work with you, in the spirit of collaboration and sharing. The DfES (2002b) believes strongly that it is through this peer learning approach that standards in teaching, training and learning will be enhanced. If you are interested, once qualified, in supporting your colleagues to become effective teachers/tutors/trainers, then more information is available in Chapter 12 about how to become a trained subject learning coach.

Practising your observational skills

Although we may learn best from trying things out for ourselves in teaching, we can also learn from others. At this point it is recommended that you spend some time assessing a period of learning that has been designed by someone else. Learning occurs in a range of places through a variety of different media, in classrooms, via television documentaries and/or education programmes, and through specifically designed educational CD-Roms, to name but a few of the planned and intended resources for learning.

Portfolio task 4.2

Evaluate four periods of designed learning, each one involving different learners. In defining difference, think about course of study, age of the participants, gender balance of those present and the subject specialism of the lecturer leading the session. Further observations, using a different key focus, are suggested at different stages in this book.

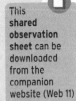

This **shared observation sheet** can be downloaded from the companion website (Web 11)

The table below has been designed to support this activity by addressing some of the components of a successful learning episode. However, you may prefer to design your own table.

You may wish to allocate a numerical grade to the areas identified below, using 1 excellent, 2 good, 3 acceptable, 4 less than acceptable, 5 weak. It is advisable to use this tool on your own. Highly critical evaluation of your mentor's teaching would obviously have a negative impact on your relationship. Remember, you are the pupil in this relationship and do not offer critical comment unless it is invited by your mentor as part of an established reciprocal relationship of peer review. If you are working with a subject learning coach then he or she may be more used to a peer model of learning. However, whatever you do, be tactful in your critique of the teaching of those whose help you will need. It is much easier to observe and recommend than it is to do.

4

Focus area: Grade	1	2	3	4	5	Observations
Clear start to the session, showing attention to time where appropriate						
Effective beginning, gaining the attention of all concerned						
Intended learning outcomes are established at an early stage						
Timekeeping is effectively managed with clear phases of activity						
A variety of teaching strategies are employed						
Learners are engaged in the session						
Instructions are easily followed						
A climate conducive to learning is established						
Opportunities are provided for learners to check understanding						
Instructions are clear						
Checks are made to ensure that learning is taking place						
Flexible approaches are used or alternative strategies made available if the session is not going to plan						
Clear endings draw on the intended learning outcomes to check that learning has taken place						

Portfolio task 4.3

Evaluate the outcome of your observations for portfolio task 4.2. What made each lesson different? Was it the style of the lecturer or group involved? Make a note in your portfolio of the factors that might influence lesson planning. Consider whether the lessons you observed might have been enhanced in any way with the use of different technologies such as video, music or computerised images.

Take one of the sessions you observed and consider whether the session could have been delivered through a CD-Rom or pre-prepared disk linked to an interactive whiteboard. What would have been the advantages to the lecturer and the learner if this had been possible? What might have been the disadvantages?

Reflective practice

One of the key principles that underpin existing models of teacher training is the approach known as reflective practice. This approach is reflected in the standards expected of those for teaching in schools, in higher education and in the LSS sector. For example, standard 1.7, as part of the professional values for those training to teach in schools, states:

> They are able to improve their own teaching, by evaluating it, learn from the effective practice of others and from evidence. They are motivated and able to take increasing responsibility for their own professional development.

Reflective practice is the essence of good teaching and is a process you will, it is hoped, engage in for the rest of your professional life. Reflective practice is based around a cycle of professional development, which involves:

- *Professional knowledge*: gaining experiences and ideas from a wide range of sources about what is effective in the classroom.

- *Professional values*: developing certain attitudes and dispositions which are valued by the profession.

- *Professional practice*: trying things out for yourself in the classroom.

- *Evaluation of practice*: reflecting on what was effective and why, and adding this to your professional knowledge.

In the LSS, reflecting on performance and meeting professional needs are key areas of the standards.

Implicit in the term 'reflective practice' is the idea that the role being undertaken requires constant consideration and analysis. Reflective practice as a learning tool underpins the training of many professionals today: nurses, engineers, lawyers and others all support the principles of lifelong learning. What reflective practice tells us as professionals is that we have many skills to learn, that we never stop learning and that we should always be prepared to adapt and adopt different skills to meet changing needs. In addition, reflective practice is seen a learning process. By reflecting on our own strengths and weaknesses we become more aware of our training needs and can with confidence adapt our teaching styles to try different approaches to meet different student needs.

Reflective action is the opposite of routine action and implies constant self-appraisal and development as well as flexibility, rigorous analysis and social awareness. Reflection is a fundamental part of training to teach and, once applied, should inform the professional practice of every teacher:

> At the heart of becoming a teacher is, above else, being a learner – a lifelong learner. To learn one has to ask questions, of oneself and of others and to know that this process is valued and shared.

(DoE NI, 1999: 82)

One advantage of the reflective process is that learning gained from one experience can be used and adapted to fit another. Reflective learning is cumulative and can be described in cyclical terms. Figure 4.1, adapted from the work of Gibbs (1988), shows the many elements involved in the process.

The model shows that self-awareness, critical analysis, synthesis and evaluation are all necessary for reflection. You will have met these terms in Chapter 3 when thinking about higher-order thinking skills (see Table 3.6); their definitions are provided in the glossary. The cyclical process involves monitoring, evaluating and revising our approaches and practices continuously. To do this, teachers need opportunity and time to think about their skills, to read recent and relevant research, to engage in research themselves leading to evidence-based practice, and to strive continuously to develop high standards in their work. The focus on continuing professional development is demonstrated in the new licensed to practise award, with lecturers expected to undergo, on an annual basis, some form of training or development as a requirement of their continued registration as a qualified teacher (QTLS). It is to be hoped that the model adopted will encourage lecturers in the sector to engage in research that will inform their practice and lead to opportunities for practitioners to influence externally developed frameworks for learning and teaching.

Figure 4.1 **The cyclical nature of the reflective process**

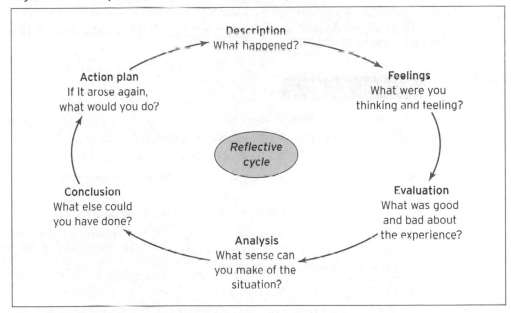

Source: Gibbs (1998)

Portfolio task 4.4

Prepare two lesson plans for different groups of students that you teach. Think about aims, objectives, structure, domains of learning, sequences in the session and strategies to engage learners. Once you have delivered the sessions, prepare a critical evaluation of the strengths and weakness of the session. Present the lesson plan and your critique for assessment in your portfolio.

Portfolio task 4.5

To practise your skills as a reflective practitioner, consider the following questions and produce a brief response to each amounting to no more that 200 words in total.

1 How effective are you at planning a lesson?

2 How effective are you at teaching a lesson?

3 What resources are available on your topic?

4 How do you evaluate lessons that you have delivered?

5 In which areas of lesson delivery do you need more practice and why?

Refer to your ILP and evaluate your position. What are your training needs at this stage?

An example of an **individual learning plan** can be downloaded from the companion website (Web 5)

Further evaluation

How have you developed as a reflective practitioner? Argyris (1991) uses the metaphor of a ladder to evaluate the links between how we interpret situations and shape our future actions. The seven steps of the reflective ladder are shown in Figure 4.2.

It is extraordinarily hard to analyse one's own assumptions and to try to find out where they have their roots.

Portfolio task 4.6

Describe a situation you have recently experienced in the classroom (typically, reflective practice begins with a problem or critical incident).

● Describe what you saw, why you think you adopted this view (perception).

● What meanings did you bring to the situation, based on previous experience and attitudes?

● What assumptions did you make about the meanings you added?

● What conclusions did you draw about the experience based upon the meanings given and your assumptions?

● What are your beliefs following this?

● What action will you take now?

Produce a reflective account of your thoughts in no more than 500 words.

Figure 4.2 **The seven steps to becoming a reflective practitioner**

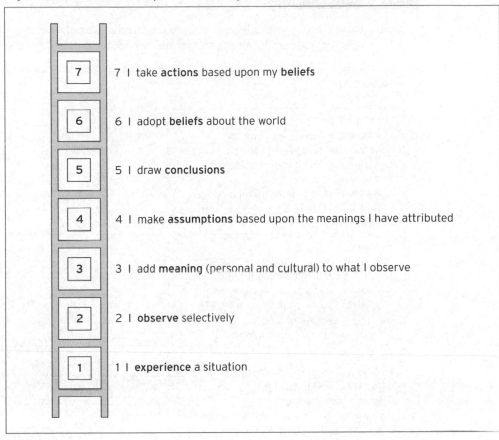

7 I take **actions** based upon my **beliefs**

6 I adopt **beliefs** about the world

5 I draw **conclusions**

4 I make **assumptions** based upon the meanings I have attributed

3 I add **meaning** (personal and cultural) to what I observe

2 I **observe** selectively

1 I **experience** a situation

Source: Argyris (1991)

Technology tip

There are a number of references to subject-specific resources in this text. As you prepare your teaching, you will also be developing a number of your own. It is a good idea to start keeping on file (either on floppy disk, CD-Rom or on your hard drive), resources that you can use for your teaching. It is recommended that you keep a back-up copy of everything you use and design a reference system for each resource so that you can easily locate it should you wish to use it again.

Portfolio task 4.7

Use the table below to evaluate your skills as a reflective practitioner.
Take a further incident in your teaching and carry out the following tasks.

Reporting Describe what happened	
Responding Consider the experience. How did you feel before, during and after the incident? Describe your feelings, thoughts Detail you actions Make observations but do explain or give reasons for these observations, e.g., *I was upset*	
Relating Link what happened to your experience Give the situation meaning for you Recognise what you did well and what you need to develop Identify developmental needs Identify why the incident happened	
Reasoning Link what happened to other experiences, to theory and to concepts in order to understand it better Analyse, question, seek answers and look for alternatives, putting forward your own ideas Create models and stories Actively seek to understand and explain why	
Reconstructing Draw out clear conclusions and apply learning Draw you own conclusions Develop your theories, ideas Make decisions about values, theories, models of practice Take control of your own learning, recognise and act on the personal significance of your learning	

This **reflective practice criteria** table can be downloaded from the companion website (Web 12)

The next section of this chapter offers advice on when and how to use electronic resources. The terms ICT (information and communication technology) and ILT (information learning technology) have been used below to describe the use of the new technologies for teaching. Chapter 6 clarifies what is meant by each term, but for now the terminology ICLT (information, communication and learning technologies) has been used to refer to any use that is made of technology to support the teacher in the act of teaching.

Using ICLT in learning and teaching

The use of ICLT in learning and teaching adds another dimension or strategy to the teacher's toolkit of available strategies and resources. ICLT has the flexibility for use in many different ways. A few are listed below:

- *As part of face-to-face learning*

  in the production of worksheets, gapped handouts, lesson notes, overhead transparencies; through the use of pre-prepared electronic presentations using PowerPoint; through connection to an electronic whiteboard that can transmit pre-prepared lesson material or link up to the internet. This facility also allows you to adapt material as you present it to the student group and to encourage their contributions which can be reproduced on the whiteboard and saved for future reference.

- *As part of individual or group research.* Learners and lecturers can use the internet to search for new information on a specific topic. The research may take part during a session or outside of it, may involve direct interaction with a lecturer.

- *As part of a distance learning course.* Learners may communicate through email or in specially created virtual chatrooms and discuss aspects of their learning. This facility has proved very useful for trainee teachers to seek advice from their lecturers when away from the training base and in need of support at a distance (Browne, 2002a).

- *Using a blended approach.* Planning for learning may involve the use of face-to-face discussion followed by activity using electronic resources.

- *Within a virtually created learning environment.* A virtual learning environment (VLE) is one in which learners and tutors participate in online interaction. It involves a system of communication between learner and tutor, learner and other learners, provides links to resources and enables the tutor to monitor learning electronically.

- *As part of the management of learning in an organisation.* The term 'managed learning environment' refers to the electronic storing of student enrolment details, room timetables, student achievement records and so forth – the whole range of information systems that support student learning.

- *Within a face-to-face teaching session.* The use of electronic whiteboards (where installed for classroom use) provides the opportunity to link, within a set lesson, to a prepared set of materials stored on a disk (or CD-Rom), and to link to the internet for specific resources. It allows the lecturer to record elements of the lesson produced by participants by saving on disk work produced on the whiteboard (or on individual screens). It can be used to record role play, for example (using a webcam facility), and has the potential to be stored for further adaptations at a later date. Material developed in this way, which can be used to support further learning, topic revision, or with a different group of students, is being defined as a reusable learning resource (RLR).

4

Whatever the method adopted, it is important to note that the lecturer has the responsibility to ensure that learning takes place, for monitoring that learning and for providing support to the learner. ICLT is one of the many tools in the hands of the trained teacher; it is not a replacement for their skills. Whether distance or present, teachers/tutors/trainers have similar responsibilities in directing the 'when' and 'how' of the learning experience (Hill, 2003: 55).

Task 4.2

Consider what criteria should be applied to judge whether to use ICT in a period of learning? Think about how activities need to be linked to the learning outcomes. Consider ethical issues, data protection and copyright laws in relation to the storing of information.

Portfolio task 4.8

Prepare a session of teaching in your subject area for a large group of students using PowerPoint presentational tools. Think about your intended learning objectives and design a 10-minute presentation on a chosen topic. Consider pace, variety of student activity (not just reading the overheads), style and format. Present the result in paper and electronic form (i.e. on a disk or CD) in your portfolio. Produce a brief commentary identifying the determinants that influenced your topic choice and timing for the PowerPoint session.

Resource availability

When working in any institution, whether it be your permanent place of work or a work placement to further your experience of teaching, it is worthwhile evaluating the resources that are available to you.

The following questions should be asked to help you plan:

- What hardware and software is available for use and do I have to book specialist rooms in advance if I want to use it?
- Is there a reference list of available resources?
- Has anyone evaluated the resources that are available and made recommendations for their use?
- Is there an institutional intranet, and if so, what does it contain, how can I access it?
- Does the institution have links to the internet, and if so, how can I have access to this facility?
- How is email used?
- Do students have email addresses?
- Who are the IT specialists?
- How is ICT currently used?
- What are the policies, practices and procedures adopted for the use of ICT in the institution?

Portfolio task 4.9

Carry out a small research project by visiting a resource learning centre in a college or university (if this is not possible your local library will do). Once there, collect any free information on the ICT facilities available, including any lists of available CD-Roms, or other electronic resources for teaching. To limit your search you may need to focus on material available in your curriculum subject. Write a report on your findings to include an evaluation of the range of material available and its accessibility for the learner.

Key tips to take from this chapter

4

- The working relationship you form with your mentor or subject learning coach is vital to your success.
- Observing lessons or sessions delivered by others can be very useful as a learning process.
- Even micro-teaching sessions need serious planning and design.
- Being able to reflect critically on your planning and delivery is crucial to becoming a successful and competent teacher.

Assessment grid mapped to the standards

This chapter introduces the knowledge requirements for areas in scope set out at the start of the chapter. Completion of the set tasks will provide you with evidence that can be matched to the standards, as set out below, for gaining awards in the learning and skills sector.

Task	Summary activity	Level 3 award	Trainer award (level 4) leading to QTLS (level 5)	E-learning standards CPD awards
Task 4.1	Preparing to teach	CK 1.2	CK 1.2	B 1 (B 2 and B 3 potentially)
Task 4.2	Using ICT in learning and teaching	CK 3.1 CK 3.5	CK 3.1 CK 3.5	B 1
Portfolio task 4.1	Planning a micro-teaching session	DP 1.1 DP 1.2 CP 1.1	DP 1.1 DP 1.2 CP 1.1	
Portfolio task 4.2	Observe four periods of learning specifically focusing on differentiation	AK 2 AP 5.1 AP 5.2 AP 6.1 AP 7.1	AK 2 AP 5.1 AP 5.2 AP 6.1 AP 7.1	
Portfolio task 4.3	Critically reflect on the four observations in relation to the use of technology	Not essential	CK 3.1 CK 3.2 BK 2.6	B 1 B 2

▶

Task	Summary activity	Level 3 award	Trainer award (level 4) leading to QTLS (level 5)	E-learning standards CPD awards
Portfolio task 4.4	Design, deliver and evaluate two lessons	CP 3.1 CP 4.1	CP 3.1 CP 4.1	
Portfolio task 4.5	Reflective critique of the design, delivering and evaluation of a lesson	AP 5.1 AP 5.2 AP 6.2	AP 5.1 AP 5.2 AP 6.2	
Portfolio task 4.6	Critical incident reporting and reflecting	Not essential	AP 5.1 AP 5.2 AP 6.2 DP 3.1	
Portfolio task 4.7	Reflective practice activity	Not essential	DP 5.1 DP 5.2 DP 5.3 BP 2.4 BP 5.2	
Portfolio task 4.8	Large-group teaching session using electronic resources	Not essential	BP 3.1 CP 3.1 DP 1.2 DP 1.3	B 1 B 2 B 3

5 Theory and practice
Secure knowledge and understanding of what it means to teach

> **Learning outcomes**
>
> By the end of this chapter you will:
>
> - recognise the main theories of learning and be able to draw on these in thinking about episodes of learning and teaching
> - have evaluated the learning preferences of a group of peers and consider the implication of the findings for lesson planning
> - have demonstrated how to plan for effective learning
> - be able to evaluate and justify different approaches to learning.

Areas in scope in this chapter in relation to the standards for teachers, tutors and trainers working in the sector are AS 1, AS 4, BS 2, BS 4, DS 1, DS 2.

This chapter explores some of the many accepted and respected theories that set out to explain how, when and in what conditions learning takes place. The common beliefs and traditions of those working in further education, adult education and work-based learning environments regarding the nature of education are explored. A number of respected theories of learning are presented and evaluated. You are advised to use this evaluation to inform your practice. The use of tools to assess student learning styles is reviewed in the light of research by Coffield *et al.* (2004).

Why theory?

Educational theory, in simple terms, is tried and tested practice that has been shown to work. To use a sporting analogy, a sports coach will be able to tell you the theory associated with the game, the conventions regarding where best to stand on the tennis court, in squash, or when fielding in cricket. There may be a number of theories that may be applied to achieve the best result. In football, for example, the coach may want to place the players in different positions and try out a number of formations, thereby applying known, tried and tested strategies (or theories) about how best to win the game. The same is true of educational theory. Different approaches can be tried in different circumstances depending on the subject, the individuals concerned and other external circumstances. As a practitioner you will want to explore the many theories available. You also need to be aware that individuals learn in different ways and one of the skills of the professional educator is meeting the different needs of the learners we encounter.

Case study Mathew

Mathew has a good range of GCSEs at A*, A and B grades. He was in the first cohort of Curriculum 2000 students to take the new AS (advanced standard) and A levels. At each stage of his education he has been subject to tests to measure his attainment (SATs). In fact, his generation during their years at school were the first to experience the Curriculum 2000 reforms, the first to sit the Key Stage 1 tests in 1989, and the first for all the other SATs which followed. They are the product of the National Curriculum reforms first introduced in 1988. As a result of his educational experience Mathew has a very clear idea about his strengths and weaknesses. He knows he prefers coursework to exams, is good at anything that requires mathematical skills but is less able in linguistic skill. He chose his AS course to match his skills rather than his interests. He now attends one of the top universities where, again, he is applying a strategic approach to his module choice to guarantee success. In the first year he chose maths modules on work he had ready covered at A level. For his second year he has selected the modules that contain statistics (the element of maths he is best at); and in the final year he will again adopt a strategic approach to module choice by talking to other students about which modules will gain him high marks, avoid examination-based assessment and best suit his skills. Mathew will leave university will a good degree.

Task 5.1

Consider the example of Mathew, above. Do you know any students like Mathew? Is Mathew's approach to learning one which the education system encourages? Would Mathew's approach to learning be described as surface learning, strategic learning or deep learning? (See the glossary for definitions of the terminology applied here.) Do you think that Mathew enjoys learning or does he just see education as a means to successful employment? (100 words)

It could be argued that Mathew has reached a level of meta-cognition in his learning. As a student, he understands his own learning, knows how he learns best, and how he learns effectively. He is applying self-reflection to assess his educational journey, and is gaining intrinsic pleasure from his success.

Task 5.2

Think about how you learn. What has been your past experience of education? What are your interests? When, and under want conditions, have you enjoyed learning? How much new information can you learn at any one time about a subject that interests you? How much can you learn about a subject that is of no interest to you? What sort of processes do you go through when you set out to learn something? Record your thoughts in your portfolio. (100 words)

Portfolio task 5.1

Consider Natalie: she is extremely proficient in practical and design-based subjects. Her school reports indicated that she was not successful in academic terms and was considered disruptive. Upon joining a college of further education she has thrived on the NVQ build and construction programme and now wants to study engineering at university. She has applied to Nottingham Trent University to study construction management. In your portfolio, answer the following questions:

1 Why do you think Natalie was considered disruptive at school?

2 Do you know of any students who match Natalie's profile? If so, can you describe them briefly?

3 What are the likely factors that have now enabled Natalie to achieve success where previously she was considered a failure?

4 How can you help your students to feel more successful and engaged with your subject?

Aim for your reflections to run to approximately 200 words, or one side of A4 paper, in total.

5

Meta-cognition

Mathew, the subject of our earlier case study, presented as a learner who was using meta-cognition to achieve educational success in terms of examination results. The theory of meta-cognition as proposed by Flavell (1977) identifies an individual's capacity for self-awareness regarding their potential to learn. Meta-cognition involves the capacity to reflect and evaluate the learning experience and in so doing gain information for future episodes and experiences. Meta-cognition can be encouraged and developed by lecturers when the following strategies are applied:

- Students are encouraged to think.
- Thinking is challenged with developed questioning.
- Criteria for success and failure are made explicit.
- Problems are posed and clear instructions are provided to help the student to reflect on what they achieved well and areas for personal development.

Nisbet and Shucksmith (1986) advocate the use of five specific strategies to encourage meta-cognition:

- *Asking questions*: establishing aims and parameters of a task; linking back to previous work to reinforce memory and understanding; requiring students to reflect on their own learning.

- *Planning*: deciding on tactics and time schedules; setting tasks that are broken down into manageable components; being clear about the skills that are being developed; working through problems visually, graphically.

- *Monitoring*: continuing to ensure that student efforts, solutions and discoveries link to the initial session purpose (as defined in the objectives); conducting debriefings; using groups to give feedback; encouraging cooperative learning; challenging preconceptions; creating disagreements to support greater clarification of ideas; encouraging participants to take their thinking to a deeper level of analysis.

- *Checking*: assessing performance and results; having participants consider all sides of the argument, all issues, pluses and minuses, consequences of, sequels to, additional opportunities.

- *Self-testing*: final review and reflection, by the lecturer, the group and/or individual on whether the objectives have been met.

The principles of meta-cognition underpin the design of this text. As learners progressing through a course of study, you are being invited in the set tasks to think about how you learn, to evaluate what has gone well in clearly defined aspects of your training, to develop skills in reflective practice, and to aim at continual improvement in the way in which you carry out your role as a teacher. Grabe and Grabe (2001) suggest that meta-cognition describes the individual's ability to evaluate, plan for, regulate and adjust their own learning and its characteristics. Training to be a teacher involves just this: evaluation, planning, regulation and adjustment as a continuous cycle of improvement towards competence in the classroom. The journey towards competence involves a certain amount of risk taking, trial and error as you test out what can and does work.

> There is no creativity without risk – the risk of trying a new idea, experimenting with an unfamiliar practice, being prepared to fail or look silly when trying something new, not taking setbacks to heart, being responsive rather than overly sensitive to critical feedback, working with and seeking advice from colleagues who are different as well as colleagues who share one's own convictions, and so on.
>
> (Hargreaves, 2003: 19)

Learning styles

Many educational theorists contend that we know much more about learning today than we have ever known before. The ideas presented through the evaluation and recognition of meta-cognition represent an attempt to help students understand how they learn. There are also numerous tools available to help students diagnose this for themselves. Such tools come with a minor health warning. They are indicators of learning preference; they do not tell the whole story about how an individual may learn. Many of them have not been subject to thorough scientific scrutiny or testing. Research by Coffield et al. (2004) has examined in great detail thirteen of the many models available. While critical of many of the learning style analysis tools that are used, their report recommends the use of learning style inventories for the following two reasons:

- The use of such tools can encourage learners to begin to think about their learning preferences.

- The analysis itself presents an opportunity for discussion between lecturer and student about the act of learning, thus promoting teacher thinking and student awareness (Coffield *et al.*, 2004: 12).

Technology tip

Should you wish to encourage your students to explore their learning style, suggest that they log on to www.metamath.com/lsweb/dvclearn.htm. This particular diagnostic tool, of the many available, is recommended as it was designed for use with college students, identifies different types of learners and recommends how they might adapt their learning to meet individual needs. The four learning styles in the DVC survey are:

- visual/communicative
- visual/non-communicative
- tactile/kinaesthetic
- auditory/verbal.

One of the advantages of applying a learning style approach is the support it can give to teachers when planning to meet the needs of their learners. Ginnis (2002) identifies seven broad approaches to learning styles and the associated inventories (Table 5.1).

5

Table 5.1 **Learning approaches**

Basis of approach	Strategy	Key theorists
Information processing	Defines ways in which different learners perceive and process new material	Kolb Honey and Mumford Gregorc
Personality	Defining different character types	Myers-Briggs Holland Geering
Sensory modalities	Defining different degrees of dependence on particular senses	Messick Bandler and Grinder
Environment	Defining different responses to physical, psychological, social and instructional conditions	Witkin Eison Canfield
Social interaction	Defining different ways of relating to others	Grasha-Reichmann Perry Mann Furmann-Jacobs Merrill
Intelligence	Defining different socially recognised talents	Gardner Handy
Cerebral geography	Defining the relative dominance of different parts of the brain	Sperry Bogen Edwards Herrmann

Source: Adapted from Ginnis (2002: 34).

If you wish to explore any of these approaches and would like more details and links to specific websites, then visit www.universaleducator.com/Learning Style/index.html.

Ellis (2000) describes learners as broadly matching three groups: visual learners, auditory learners and kinaesthetic learners and points out that knowledge about the existence of different types of learners should inform lesson planning. The identification of visual (V), auditory (A) and kinaesthetic (K) learning preferences appears in many of the different learning inventories discussed above to the extent that it is common practice for school teachers to VAK their lessons. This involves designing into each learning episode elements of seeing and looking that might appeal to those who learn best from visual presentation, of sound for the auditory learner and something practical for those who need to engage with learning by using touch and feel.

Task 5.3

Design a lesson plan and do a VAK exercise. Do you notice anything? Is it an easy task in your subject specialism or are some preferences more difficult to design into the lesson plan? Why might this be the case ? Can you do anything about this?

Consider the sequence in Example 5.1. Although it is part of a vocational hospitality numeracy session, the lesson could be adapted to suit a range of vocational contexts by using different everyday items.

Example 5.1 VAK applied to a session plan for vocational hospitality numeracy

Aim: To develop appreciation of how estimation is used in everyday life situations.

Objectives: By the end of the session students will be able to apply estimation to a number of different measuring contexts.

Activity 1: Present the students with a range of different food items (sugar, flour, gravy powder, dried milk, cereal (all in secure packaging and marked with a number).

Activity 2: Students look at the items (observe only) and rate them in order of heaviest first. A worksheet is provided for this activity. **Visual Activity**

Activity 3: Students then handle the items (the weight information on the packet would need to be obliterated) and reassess their estimations. **Tactile, Kinaesthetic Activity**

Activity 4: The actual weights of the items are then revealed.

Activity 5: Through the use of a worksheet the participants are asked to compare their estimates at each stage of the activity. They are then required to discuss their findings. Key questions are provided to guide this discussion: Which was heaviest? Which was lightest? Was it as you expected? Did your accuracy improve once you had touched the items?

Activity 6: A video clip of food storage in a *hells kitchen* is then shown. **Visual Activity** to lead to a discussion.

Activity 7: Implications for storage of items, ordering in bulk, in a specific kitchen environment where shelving is in short supply. Final summary of learning in relation to the importance of estimation in the context of hospitality.

In the example, application of the VAK process – identified in bold print in the lower part of the table – has shifted our thinking from the use of learning styles as a tool to be used by the learner, to learning styles being applied to inform our planning as a teacher. One of the key advocates of this approach is Kolb. His work is categorised in Table 5.1 as an information processing approach.

The work of Kolb has been selected based on the tried and tested experience of those working in the field of teacher education (see Harkin et al. (2001), in particular the chapter by Dawn, for a thorough discussion of Kolb and other theorists). Kolb is a well-known educationalist who links learning styles and strategies in a more developed way than many other theorists. Kolb's work has been influential in the role it plays in encouraging lecturers to plan for different student needs.

For Kolb, learning involves a cyclical process of *concrete experience* (doing it), leading to *reflective observation* (reflection on the experience), the *abstract conceptualisation* (making sense of it), and finally *active experimenting* (Figure 5.1). The learning process is described as a cycle since the learner can be at any stage in this process. For example, a trainee lecturer might plan a new approach to their teaching as an experiment, carry out the session, as an experience, reflect on the process and then decide to make changes before approaching the same subject content in a different way, and so on. In this scenario the trainee would have travelled through all the stages of the learning cycle and, it is hoped, come to some conclusions about their practice as a trainer, for future lesson planning. Using the idea of a cycle of learning highlights the fact that we can travel a great distance using a cyclical process of continuous reflection and action. Teaching is just this: a constant journey of trying, testing and discovering new ways to reach different learners.

5

Figure 5.1 Kolb's cyclical model of learning

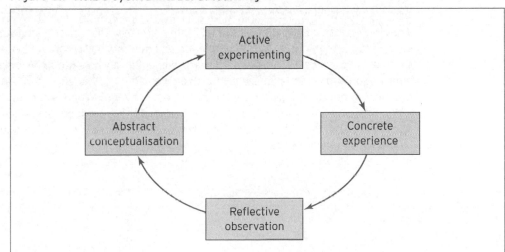

Kolb has identified four types of learners who inhabit the four elements of the learning cycle. They are:

- *Reflector*. This person seeks out different ways of approaching a task (the divergent thinker who likes to be personally involved in the task). The reflector is adaptable and able to use their imagination to think about different ideas and approaches. They learn by listening to others but are good at generating new ideas.

- *Theorist (or converger)*. This person tries to gather all the facts and is well organised, reviewing alternatives and calculating probabilities, working independently, learning from past experiences. This learner would prefer to be given research activities or investigative tasks to explore topics on their own.

- *Pragmatist (or assimilator)*. This learner is keen to test out new ideas, thrives on problem-solving activities and is able to process information either on their own or with the help of others. The pragmatist takes a very logical approach to tasks and works well when mathematical or scientific concepts are involved.

- *Activist (or accommodator)*. This learner thrives on risk, is happy to share their views with others, engages in the task and relies on feelings and emotions to drive their actions. The accommodator is likely to be action oriented, working quickly to set goals, carry out plans and become involved.

Example 5.2, taken from the Magical Methods website (www.magicalmethods. org.uk), shows how a session may be planned to accommodate a number of learners with different learning preferences.

Example 5.2 Planning a session to accommodate different types of learners

A2 Politics

Group consists mainly of Reflectors but also some Pragmatists

Methods: Workshops, role play, private study

Resources: Intranet, laptop, projector

Activity: A session looking at the UK legislative process. This is a session that allows students to take part in a debate on hunting and hunting legislation. An initial workshop session allows students to research into the subject as a whole group by looking at information and links previously set up on an intranet site. Students then take part in a role play where the Pragmatists will debate from pro-hunting and anti-hunting viewpoints and the Reflectors act as observers and then give feedback. A question and answer session then allows students to start to plan for an essay which is supplemented by a private study session.

Task 5.4

Redesign the session described in Example 5.2 to include activities for all types of learners. A suggestion is provided in the example answers section at the end of the book.

The sequencing of the above session mirrors the four stages identified in Kolb's cycle. Consider this cycle when completing portfolio task 5.2.

Portfolio task 5.2

Describe the learning preferences of three colleagues or friends. Analyse these preferences in terms of a least two theories of learning discussed below. Consider how you might design a teaching session to meet the needs of the four different approaches to learning as identified by Kolb. (350 words)

Kolb's ideas about learning might be categorised as part of a cognitive approach that describes learning through a study of strategies to support the learner. Such theories acknowledge that at the heart of effective learning is the learner. Theories that might be categorised as experiential learning theories take this one step further and focus on personal discovery through the activity of learning. Such approaches are located within the constructivist or social constructivist school of theories, as shown in Table 5.2.

This chapter introduced learning theories by focusing on meta-cognition. Meta-cognition is a relatively new approach to learning and teaching. If we were to take a chronological approach to categorising known theories, meta-cognition would be located alongside approaches identified as constructivism whereby the learner constructs meaning for themselves rather than passively accepts knowledge as a given. This rather simplified assessment hides a complex shift in thinking from ideas in the past that adopted a behaviourist approach, through to theories about knowledge and cognition, to current approaches which focus on individual learners and their abilities to discover learning for themselves. Table 5.2 presents a simplified view of the differences between these schools of thought.

Table 5.2 **Learning theories**

	Behaviourist	*Cognitivist*	*Constructivist*	*Social constructivist*
Learning	Stimulus and response	Transmitting and processing knowledge and strategies	Personal discovery and experimentation	Mediation of different perspectives through language
Type of learning	Memorising and responding	Memorising and application of rules	Problem solving in realistic and investigative situations	Collaborative learning and problem solving
Strategies	Present material for practice and feedback	Plan for cognitive learning strategies	Provide for active and self-regulated learning	Provide for support in the learning process
Key concepts	Reinforcement	Reproduction and elaboration	Personal discovery generally from first principles	Discovering different perspectives and shared meanings

Source: Hung, D. (2001) Theories of learning and computer-mediated instructional technologies, *Education Media International*, vol. 38, no. 4 pp. 281–287. Taylor & Francis Ltd. http://www.tandf.co.uk/journals

A number of theories are presented in more detail below. Focus is given initially to cognitive theories before the ideas of constructivism and social constructivism are explored.

Information processing theory

George Miller's human cognition theory identified the limitations of the working memory through the study of individuals and their ability to use memory in learning (Miller *et al.*, 1960). Miller advocates 'chunking' knowledge as he maintains that the short-term memory has a limited capacity to hold only 5–9 chunks of information (a chunk was defined as a meaningful unit, digits, words, chess positions, people's faces, and so forth). Miller believed that the mind was like a computer and could only perform a variety of functions on the data it received, namely to change the data's form and content to aid memory, to store and locate for retrieval when necessary. These ideas led Miller and other information processing theorists to advocate the following learning principles:

1 Make sure students understand the task.

2 Help them make connections between new information and what they already know.

3 Provide for repetition and review of information.

4 Present material instructions in a clear and ingrained way.

5 Focus on meaning, not memorisation, of information for understanding.

Sousa (2001) has studied the working of the brain and identifies what are referred to as prime times: the first part of the lesson is prime time and, as such, presents the best opportunity for student learning. The longer the session the more the brain switches off. The key, then, is to plan lessons as sequences with short and focused periods of activity or, in a long session, to change the activity during the session with an eye to keeping the pace and momentum of the session.

Research has also identified which teaching strategies are most likely to support knowledge retention. The learning pyramid in Figure 5.2 shows how passive learning and one way transmission lead to low levels of knowledge retention, whereas involve-

Figure 5.2 **The learning pyramid**

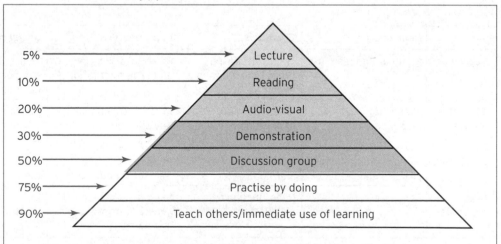

Source: Sousa, D.A., *How the Brain Learns*. Copyright 2001 by Corwin Press, reprinted by permission of Corwin Press, Inc.

ment with others and the application of learning lend themselves to very high retention (Sousa, D.A. [2001], in Cohen *et al.*, 2004: 175).

A template for this **lesson plan (ii)** can be downloaded from the companion website (Web 13)

Task 5.5

Plan a teaching/training session - think about different types of learners, periods of learning, opportunities for experiment, bite-size chunks and so on. Produce a structured lesson plan giving full attention to variety, pace and change. Produce a short paragraph discussing your choice of activity in relation to the specific learners you may have in mind.

Constructivist theories

5

Drawing on the ideas of the cognitive approaches, constructivist theories focus on the role of the learner in the learning process.

One of the key advocates of constructivist theory is Bruner. The major theme of his work is that learning is an active process in which learners construct new ideas or concepts based on their current and past knowledge (Bruner, 1990). In this model the learner selects and translates knowledge to give it meaning. This supports understanding of what is being presented. Bruner's work has developed from the cognitive theories proposed by Piaget and Vygotsky whereby the teacher sets up the learning situation and promotes that learning through scaffolding or support.

Bruner's ideas are simplified below.

Application

Instruction must be concerned with the experiences and context that make the student willing and able to learn (this idea underpins our thinking about vocational education).

Key principles

1 Instruction should be structured so that it can be easily grasped by the student.

2 Instruction should be designed to encourage further exploration and self-discovery.

Developing from these ideas, Rogers (1951) has been the theorist most associated with experiential learning. The view is that learning that is applied to a practical situation is more significant and therefore more likely to engage the learner. Experiential learning requires personal involvement, learner initiation and evaluation. For the lecturer this involves:

- Setting a positive climate for learning.
- Clarifying the purpose for the learner.
- Organising and making available relevant resources.
- Balancing intellectual and emotional elements of learning.
- Sharing feelings and thoughts with learners.

Key principles

1 Significant learning takes place when the subject matter is relevant to the personal interests of the student.

2 Learning which is threatening to the self (new attitude or perspectives) is more easily assimilated when external threats are at a minimum.

3 Self-initiated teach is the most lasting and pervasive.

Conditions of learning

Similar in many ways to the ideas of Bruner, and located within the constructivist school, the ideas of Gagne (1985) identify different types or levels of learning. The significance of these ideas is that different types of learning require different types of instruction. Gagne identifies five major categories of learning:

- Verbal information
- Intellectual skills
- Cognitive strategies
- Motor skills
- Attitudes.

Different internal and external conditions are said to be necessary for each type of learning to thrive. For example, for cognitive strategies to develop there must be a chance for learners to practise developing new solutions to problems. To learn attitudes, the learner must be exposed to a credible role model or persuasive argument.

Gagne suggests that learning tasks for intellectual skills can be organised in a hierarchy according to complexity:

- Stimulus recognition
- Response generation
- Procedure following
- Use of terminology
- Discriminations
- Concept formation
- Rule application and problem solving.

The significance of the hierarchy is to identify prerequisites that should be completed to facilitate learning at each level and to provide a basis for the sequencing of instruction. The theory outlines nine instructional events and cognitive processes:

1 Gaining information (reception)

2 Informing learners of the objective (expectancy)

3 Stimulating recall of prior learning (retrieval)

4 Presenting the stimulus (selective perception)

5 Providing learner guidance (semantic encoding)

6 Eliciting performance (responding)

7 Providing feedback (reinforcement)

8 Assessing performance (retrieval)

9 Enhancing retention and transfer (generalisation).

(Gagne, 1992: 27–35)

Key principles

- Different instruction is required for different learning outcomes.
- For learning to occur, specific conditions for learning need to be present.
- The specific operations that constitute instructional events are different for each type of learning outcome.

Gagne uses the following example to illustrate a teaching sequence corresponding to the nine instructional events for the objective Recognise an equilateral triangle:

1 Gain attention: show a variety of triangles.

2 Identify objective: pose question 'What is an equilateral triangle?'

3 Recall prior learning: review definitions of triangles.

4 Present stimulus: show a picture constructed using only equilateral triangles.

5 Guide learning: show how to create an equilateral triangle.

6 Elicit performance: ask students to create a picture using five equilateral triangles.

7 Provide feedback: check examples are correct.

8 Assess performance: show outcome and identify examples to the group.

9 Enhance retention/transfer: test knowledge by asking students to draw a variety of different triangles, identifying those which are equilateral.

Situated learning

Lave (1988) argues that learning as it normally occurs is a function of the activity, context and culture in which it takes place (i.e. it is situated). Social interaction is a critical component of situated learning with learners becoming involved in a 'community of practice'. The approach acknowledges that new learners can benefit from the experienced, that group learning can support the weaker student and enhance the confidence of the stronger.

Key principles

1 Knowledge needs to be presented and learned in an authentic context, that is, settings and applications that would normally involve that knowledge.

2 Learning requires social interaction and collaboration.

Hokanson and Hooper (2000) contend that our approaches to education have moved from a focus on instruction and representation to more personal approaches to learning, where learning is about problem solving, communication and the ability to evaluate and apply information. The role of the lecturer in such a climate is to develop in learners a range of thinking skills and strategies.

Peer-assisted learning

Peer-assisted learning (PAL) is a relatively new and not, as yet, well-researched approach advocated by the HEFCE for students working on complex concepts at undergraduate level, and offered here to support those working on foundation degrees.

PAL is an active student-centred learning method where students on conceptually complex courses are trained to facilitate the learning of students in the following year of a programme. Facilitation involves encouraging discussion to enhance comprehension. The role of the facilitator is to ask questions which guide discussion, not to give explanation or answers.

Purpose

● To bring about more student-centred and deeper learning opportunities.

● To enable students 'to learn how to learn'.

● To enhance students' skill development within the curriculum, (this applies to both those doing the facilitation and those being facilitated).

● To develop more responsible, independent, autonomous and lifelong learners.

In America this scheme was adopted to reduce student dropout on difficult courses and to increase student grades.

Engagement theory

Developed by Schneiderman (1994), engagement theory addresses the theoretical approaches underpinning effective electronic and distance learning environments. The fundamental idea underlying engagement theory is that students need to be meaningfully engaged in learning activity through interaction with others and worthwhile tasks. Engagement theory provides a conceptual framework for technology-based learning and teaching.

Principles

1 All activity involves cognitive processes such as problem solving, reasoning, decision making and evaluation.

2 Learning occurs in a group context (collaboratively) through the need to relate with others (this can be achieved electronically though email or in specifically created electronic café's).

3 Learning is a creative, purposeful activity. Students need to define an area of interest through project work and focus on the application of their idea in a specific context.

4 Being able to share ideas and make a contribution to the study community is a key component of collaborative online learning.

An example of how ICT might be used for collaborative learning is provided in Example 5.3.

Example 5.3 Collaborative learning

A group of business students is required to plan and execute a recruitment evening for local employers. Group members meet face to face only once a fortnight, the course being delivered mainly through electronic means. The first task, then, would be to set up email communication links and allocate tasks to the individuals concerned: project co-ordinator, secretary, finance officer, marketing manager, and so on.

In applying the principles of collaborative learning the students in the above example will need to work as a team, to communicate effectively, to share ideas and monitor the progress of the project.

Since collaborative methods may be novel to many students there is likely to be a high level of uncertainty at the beginning of such projects. Students will need guidance in working together, including help with project management, scheduling, time management, leadership and consensus building. The skills required by the lecturer involve monitoring, encouraging and supporting where necessary. Collaborative learning is not an easy option, as it involves the ability to give responsibility to the student group while at the same time maintaining the control necessary to ensure that the project reaches the desired outcome within the realms of safety and financial viability.

Portfolio task 5.3

Consider an aspect of the curriculum content in your subject that might lend itself to collaborative learning using ICT/ILT. When considering the task, explore what would be involved in the effective monitoring of such an activity. The task could be as simple as a short activity involving pairs of students, or it could be a lengthy term project.

Key tips to take from this chapter

- There are a number of respected and well-tried theories and methods available to support the teacher/tutor/trainer.
- It is advisable to develop a repertoire of approaches to plan and deliver your subject.
- Technology can be a great support to enable you to work 'smarter', rather than harder.

Assessment grid mapped to the standards

This chapter introduces the knowledge requirements for the areas in scope set out at the start of the chapter. Completion of the set tasks will provide you with evidence that can be matched to the standards, as set out below, for gaining awards in the learning and skills sector.

Task	Summary activity	Level 3 award	Trainer award (level 4/5) leading to QTLS	E-learning standards CPD awards
Task 5.1	Consider a learner and their learning needs	AK 1.1 DK 1.1	AK 1.1 DK 1.1	
Task 5.2	Evaluate episodes of learning in respect of meeting different learner needs	AK 5.1 DK 1.1	AK 5.1 DK 1.1	A 2 B 1 B 3 D 1
Task 5.3	VAK a lesson	Not essential	DK 2.1 DK 2.2	
Task 5.4	Plan for different learners and critically evaluate the outcome	Not essential	DP 2.1 DP 2.2 DP 2.4 DK 2.4 DK 2.6	
Task 5.5	Planned lessons for specific learners	Not essential	DP 2.1 DP 2.2 DP 2.4 CP 3.2	
Portfolio task 5.1	Evaluate learner success	DK 1.1 DK 1.3	DK 1.1 DK 1.3	
Portfolio task 5.2	Analyse learning preference and design a lesson to meet individual needs	Not essential	DK 1.1 DP 1.1 CP 3.2	
Portfolio task 5.3	Use ICT/ILT to meet the needs of different learners	EK 1.4 (in part only) DP 5.1 DP 5.2	EK 1.4 (in part only) DP 5.1 DP 5.2	C 1 C 2 C*1 (potentially) C*3 (potentially) F 1 (potentially) F 2 (potentially)

6 The new technologies for teaching
Using ILT as an enhancement to learning

Learning outcomes

By the end of this chapter you will have:

- developed an awareness of how ILT can function as a tool for learning and teaching
- explored a range of technological resources available in your specific areas of interest
- evaluated different ways in which IT can support you in your role
- explored how ILT can support the needs of the learner and provide opportunities for greater learner autonomy, individualisation and stretch.

Areas in scope in this chapter in relation to the standards for teachers, tutors and trainers working in the sector are CS 1, CS 2, CS 3, DS 1, DS 3.

It will be a requirement of those gaining a licence to practise that they are competent users of technology. Those aspiring to the initial award qualification will gain much from engaging with this chapter as well. Throughout this text, reference has been made to ways in which technology may be used in the learning and teaching process as a support for those in training and for those already in role. This chapter develops still further the debate about the use of ILT as a tool for the effective practitioner in the twenty-first century.

ICT competence

In Chapter 1 you were advised to complete a brief audit of your IT skills to identify any developmental needs. Chapter 2 provided advice on where to go for additional help if needed. This chapter assumes that progress, if necessary, has been made in your skill level and that you are now well prepared to use the tools explored below.

The focus on technology in this text is a response to the policy agenda. In addition, training in the use of ICT has been given high priority in the newly framed qualification for those working in the LSS sector. Those wishing to gain the full QTLS qualification will be expected to demonstrate their ability to use technology in the skills tests. In addition, new standards for the application of ICT to teaching and supporting learning in the sector have been devised. These have been prepared to provide a national benchmark for the educational application of ICT in the lifelong learning sector.

A new e-learning CPD framework is under development which can be accessed as part of the continuing professional development credit award framework discussed in Chapter 12.

A link to the **ICT standards** can be found on the companion website (Web 14)

Clarifying the terminology

The model depicted in Figure 6.1 illustrates the various terms used to describe how technology is being used to support the learning process. (The terms are defined below.) The diagram presents rather like a whirlpool with information technology (IT) at the core, the influence of which can be felt across all dimensions of learner experience.

The use of technology to enhance the learning environment is complex. In order to simplify matters it is useful to define the terminology. There is much debate about how the terms 'information technology' (IT), 'information and communication technology' and 'information and learning technology' (ILT) might be applied (Hill, 2003). For the purposes of this book, the term 'IT' is applied to discuss the physical equipment: computer, desktop, laptop, printer, that is, the computer infrastructure or what is called hardware and software. Once the technical equipment is used in a connecting way, with the keyboard set up to *talk* to other computers, such as in the use of the internet, intranets, emails, blogs, websites and so on, then the term 'ICT' applies. In the teaching environment this tool for communication can then produce shared worksheets, graphs and data to show, across the institution, information such as attendance records. The definition also includes email communications to colleagues about room changes, policy decisions and forthcoming meeting dates. The term 'ILT' refers to the next stage, the point at which

Figure 6.1 **Technology and the learning process**

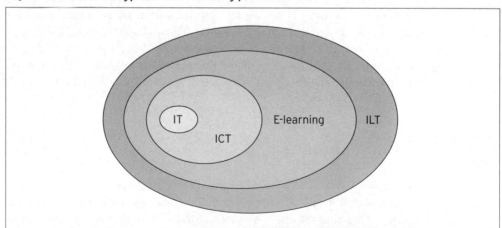

Source: This figure is reproduced with the permission of the Institute for Learning. At the time of publication initial teacher training is in a period of significant change with the implementation of *Equipping our Teachers for the Future*. Within its remit for advancing the teacher professionalisation agenda the Institute for Learning is developing a new model of professionalism which supersedes this figure. For the latest information on the professional development agenda please visit www.ifl.ac.uk

the computer does more than just enable communication: it enables, enriches and supports the core activity of the educational experience. Here it becomes a tool in the hands of the learner and the practitioner to stimulate and encourage learning. At the point when the term 'ILT' is applied, the definition has moved from the use of the technology to support planning and operational issues in education to its use to provide opportunities for the learner to direct their own learning experience. Here it supports the learner's search of knowledge, investigation and thinking, and becomes a powerful medium for growth, intellectually and cognitively, rather than just a tool. The term 'e-learning' has a central role in the Figure 6.1. This is a term used to describe the use of technology in course provision both as a structured support or platform for learning and as a descriptive explanation of what takes place through the use of technology in educational situations.

Task 6.1

Consider all the ways in which you use or envisage students using the five technologies listed in the table below. List each of the uses that you have thought of in one of the columns according to the definitions given above.

IT	ICT	ILT
Computer		
Electronic whiteboard		
Website		
Access to the internet		
Access to the organisation's intranet		

An example answer is provided at the end of the book.

Additional skill development

The ICLT e-learning standards (LLUK, *Skills for Learning Professionals*, 2005: 2) propose six components (as identified in the standards) for the effective use of technology in the sector. They are:

1 Encouraging learners to manage their own learning.

2 Planning to use ILT as part of a learning programme.

3 Facilitating learning on-site using ILT.

4 Facilitating learning online (using the intranet or internet).

5 Developing and adapting ILT materials.

6 The assessment and tracking of learner achievements.

A link to the **ICT standards** can be found on the companion website (Web 14)

Task 6.2

In relation to your work environment or work experience placement, what is your initial evaluation of the amount of use being made of technology to support the six areas of activity outlined above? Produce a brief paragraph summarising your findings for each activity.

The six areas of activity are described in more detail below.

Encouraging learners to manage their own learning

Technology can be a powerful tool to enhance the experience of the learner. In many institutions you will see technology in the form of digital cameras and videos to create exciting opportunities for students to capture fieldwork, take images for inclusion in portfolios and design multimedia presentations. In the area of individual research, a college intranet (or access to the external internet) can encourage learners to be investigative, to research topics using the World Wide Web for set assignment tasks and investigate ideas for presentations. In this case, technology can be a source of knowledge, to supplement that available in books and other more traditional resources. The flexibility and accessibility of technology can allow remote learning, any time, anywhere, enabling access to materials away from the traditional boundaries of the classroom environment. It can support the teacher in meeting the needs of different learners, as it can allow learners to proceed at their own pace as part of a group following the same programme. Through effective use of technology, individual learners who have ability can have their skills and knowledge enhanced while the less able learner can work at a pace and level appropriate to their needs.

There is much debate in educational terms about what is being called the *personalisation agenda*. The term describes a government-supported philosophy which encourages learner autonomy with the aim that individuals can understand themselves better as learners and so take greater control of and responsibility for their learning. Technology is advocated as one of the tools to promote this approach.

A simple example might be using the CD-Roms, such as those provided free by Learndirect, to help practitioners assess their literacy, numeracy and ICT skills. Here the completion of an initial assessment encourages the learner to identify their strengths and weaknesses, thus encouraging more personal responsibility for development needs. There are more active ways in which technology can support the personalisation agenda since the use of interactive technologies free the act of learning from the traditional boundaries of time, pace and place and allow learners far greater autonomy to manage their own learning.

Planning to use ILT as part of a learning programme

ILT can be used to give presentations using software such as interactive whiteboards. Whole sections of a lesson may be pre-prepared on disks, CD-Roms or be downloaded directly from the internet. Learners can be supported in their own skill use of ILT through encouragement to give presentations. This can help learners meet the communication key skills requirements and those associated with the use of technology. An approach known as blended learning might be adopted (see Table 6.1 below). Some institutions use internal 'learning zones' where course materials can be made available to students electronically to encourage independent learning. Consider the example session plan in Example 6.1, adapted from the Magical Methods website (www.magical-methods.org.uk).

Example 6.1 Session plan for GNVQ Intermediate Leisure and Tourism

Methods: Simulation, ICT discovery, presentation and discussion, demonstration

Resources: Learning zone materials, digital camera, PowerPoint resources

Aim: To introduce learners to information resources

Objectives: by the end of the session learners will have:

- evaluated existing material and suggested areas for improvement
- been actively engaged in producing electronically formatted materials that could be made accessible to a wider audience
- reviewed the resources produced by others and made recommendations for their improvement.

As an introductory session the students are required to produce some marketing resources which will then be critically evaluated. This activity forms the introduction to a larger assignment. Working in small groups, using the learning zone materials students evaluate the existing information about leisure facilities available in their institution. Using technology they are required to take a series of photographs and video clips of the institutional facilities. These are then edited and compiled into a PowerPoint presentation and presented to the rest of the class. A group discussion then allows the learners to discuss problems encountered and possible solutions.

Note: This task not only supports independent learning but also provides a variety of activities to meet the needs of different learning styles. In addition, learners who complete the task will have achieved a number of the requirements for demonstrating competence in key skills (see Chapter 8).

Facilitating learning on-site using ILT

Through the increased use of CD-Roms, posted on a shared site or intranet, groups of learners may use ILT to work through a scheme of work. This is the next developmental stage from the idea of a language lab, where individual learners worked through audio-tapes to improve their language skills. In this case, CD-Roms, available on a wide range of subject areas, can be made available to learners within an IT/resource-based learning environment. A number of available resources are listed at the end of this chapter.

Although expensive to produce, there is an increasing use being made of reusable learning objects (RLOs) in some branches of training. Such objects are commonly used in medical education where technologically enhanced models (body parts) may be used to practise resuscitation, for example. Some are so sophisticated that they can be programmed to mirror human responses and give feedback to the practitioner, thus enhancing learner experience. Through the use of technology within the formal learning environment the classroom setting can be enhanced.

Facilitating learning online (using the intranet or internet)

In this scenario, the formal boundaries of the classroom are removed. Here learning takes place at a distance from the author/lecturer and the participant may never interact face to face with other learners or, indeed with the teacher/trainer. In these situations, communities of learners are encouraged and developed through virtual chatrooms and cyber-conversations. The sort of material available might be an exemplar test, quizzes to test understanding, gapped answer worksheets for revision purposes and learning materials written specifically for courses or subjects. Useful websites to visit are www.ccm.ac.uk and www.sheffcol.ac.uk/links.

Developing and adapting ILT materials

This refers to the specialist skills of producing or modifying resources for use with learners. It may involve modifying existing materials or creating new ones. Materials may include CD-Roms or RLOs (reusable learning objects).

The assessment and tracking of learner achievements

It is possible to use technology to record student achievements either in the form of keeping a personal register of marked work or as part of a college-wide mapping of progress. In addition, students may submit work electronically in the form of assessment tasks, electronic portfolios and written assignments. There are a number of sophisticated technological tools available to enable the practitioner to set tests, virtual assimilation and examinations. Some of these tools are explored in Chapter 9 on assessment.

Supporting the achievement of key skills

Technology can be used to enable learners to achieve evidence of competence in the key skills (see Chapter 8). Table 6.1 illustrates the many ways in which this might be achieved.

The rest of this chapter explores the use of resources and tools developed specifically for an educational purpose to support both practitioners and learners.

Resources to support teaching and learning

The main central resource for ideas about teaching and learning practices in the sector is the national learning network at www.nln.ac.uk. Here you can access a tool to support you and/or your organisation towards greater use of e-learning. In addition the Resources

Table 6.1 Supporting the achievement of key skills

Technology	Description
Remote learning	Any time anywhere, enables access to learning material via the internet and work at a distance to record Key Skills achievements
Anytime learning	Enables Key Skills learners to access some or all of the key skill resources whenever college is open and work independently (one of the key skills)
Differentiated programme	IT can enable the planning and delivery of an individual learner programme. This is specifically relevant to key skills that can be tracked and delivered using technological means
Differentiated pace	The use of ILT can enable learners to proceed at their own pace within a group following a common programme. IT can support tracking of progress
Blended learning	IT can support learning when used in conjunction with traditional resources. For example, students might be introduced to an assignment via written brief in a classroom setting. They could then do research on the internet and word-process a first draft, perhaps including images (IT key skills) This could be emailed to the tutor who can give email feedback. A chatroom can be set up to encourage the learners to develop a virtual discussion group and share resources
Traditional teaching tool	ILT can be used to give presentations using software, interactive whiteboards, word-processed handouts and other documents. Learners can be supported in their own skills by giving presentations (Communication key skill) and use the technology to prepare these (IT key skills)
Supporting learning	ILT can provide opportunities outside scheduled learning time that complement or support the main programme of learning

Source: Adapted from http://ferl.becta.org.uk.

Discovery Network (RDN) is a free national gateway to internet resources for the learning, teaching and research community. It contains 100,000 resources accessible via a number of subject-based information gateways or hubs and can be found at http://www.rdn.ac.uk.

There are a number of general and subject specific resources available for use to support lesson design and enable students to work independently. It would be impossible to list them all. In the following sections you will find reference to some useful sites that will help you in your lesson preparation. This is by no means an exclusive list and only a small range of specific subject material is listed. If you still need help to find more information on your topic, follow the advice below on search engines.

Search engines

There has been a rapid growth in resources available online accessible through what are called search engines. Search engines are tools that allow you to enter keywords and then search databases for matching or linked terms. If you have access to a computer connected to the internet your internet service provider (ISP) generally has a search engine.

If you do not have a specific site in mind you can use a search engine such as www.yahoo.com to help you. When entering a search term try to be as specific as possible. Websites may date and/or change. The following search engines may be useful:

www.altavista.com

www.ask.com

www.google.com

www.yahoo.com.

You may also wish to use *web crawlers* and *mega-search engines*. These search tools are more powerful and work by searching the indexes of other search engines and may produce better results. Try, for example:

www.onlysearchengines.com

www.metacrawler

www.webcrawler.com.

If you want to find out more about using the web search tools and improving the quality of your search results the following may be useful:

www.brightplanet.com/deepcontent/tutorials/search.

If you are working in an educational institution, that institution may have an intranet for access to internal resources. It also useful to explore what is available there as well.

Help with evaluating the quality of websites

Some websites are of better quality than others. In order to locate one that will be useful to you, look for:

- *Accuracy*. Can the information be verified or cross-checked? Are the sources of information acknowledged and referenced?

- *Authority*. Does the information herald from a known source? Is the author named? Who is sponsoring the page? Are they likely to be of good reputation?

- *Timeliness*. Is the information current? When was it last updated? Is the information likely to be useful to a student group or to yourself as a teacher?

- *Bias*. Is the information source likely to result in bias? This may not distract from the quality of the information but you will need to be aware of it when you consider the perspective that is being presented.

- *Accessibility*. Does the site take a long time to download? Is the material presented in a way that it can easily understood? Are there clear links to other sites? Is there a site directory to help you find what you need? Is the site attractive, using appropriate graphics and clear text? Does the use of colours and fonts enhance the usability of the site?

Task 6.3

Using the guidance provided above, evaluate three websites that might be of use to you in your role as a teacher/tutor/trainer. There are a number of references to different sites throughout this book. Evaluate each site in terms of its suitability for supporting the subject-specific knowledge and skills associated with your specialism.

Starter guides

The following references relate to starter guides for those interested in using online learning. They have been prepared as a support for teachers who wish to use the technology to enhance learning (ILT). They contain information on using the web as a research tool, designing learning opportunities facilitated by internet communication (this is known as virtual learning or computer-mediated learning) and using ILT in assessment.

Four starter guides, of which there are eight in total, are listed below:

*Using the World Wide Web in Learning
and Teaching*

Virtual Learning Environments

Computer-mediated conferencing

*Using Computer Assisted Assessment to
Support Student Learning*

They can all be accessed on the e-learning resource section of the Higher Education Academy site at www.heacademy.ac.uk/1775.

Other sources

There are a number of websites – many of them government sites – designed for educationalists and those interested in learning. These are:

www.dfes.gov.uk	Government department for education; for access to policy changes, research opportunities, national curriculum initiative, sector skills initiatives
http://ferl.becta.org.uk	Further Education Resources for Learning (FERL) is the information service for all staff working in the LSS. It aims to support individuals and organisations in making effective use of ILT. It achieves this through a web-based information service, conferences, publications and other events. The FERL website is large and contains a wealth of resources
www.lsneducation.org.uk	Learning and Skills network website for information on research and educational initiatives. It contains support and advice for lecturers in the LSS
www.niss.ac.uk	Information about education
www.nln.ac.uk	National Learning Network, covers a wide range of vocational subjects with access to free materials
www.jisc.ac.uk	An information source for those wishing to explore the use of ICT/ILT in learning and teaching
www.rdn.ac.uk	Resource discovery site with resources available in a range of subjects
www.teachernet.com	Contains links to lesson plans

6

www.bbc.bitesize.co.uk	Teaching materials and guides for a range of GCSE subjects
http://curriculum.becta.org.uk	Website of the British Educational Communications and Technology Agency supporting the use of ICT in learning and teaching
www.nfer.ac.uk	National Federation for Educational Research

Below you will find a number of general resource sites linked to specific vocational and academic areas of study.

- Useful websites for media studies:
  www.cineweb.com/cineweb
  www.teleport.com/-cdeemer/scrwriter
  www.communicator.com/toppage
  www.axisartists.org.uk
  www.trilt   a television and radio index for learning and teaching

- Useful websites for film and video resources:
  www.rtvf.nwu.edu/links
  www.rmplc.co.uk./eduweb/sites
  www.bfi.org.uk

- Useful websites for construction:
  www.emap.com
  www.euroad.com
  www.hss.co.uk
  www.blackanddecker.com
  www.dulux.com
  www.blw.co.uk
  www.buildingonline.com

- Useful websites for business and economics:
  www.bized.ac.uk   for business information
  www.euromonitor.com   for global market and company information

- Useful websites for geography/sociology, human sciences:
  www.census.gov.uk   population data
  www.euromonitor.com   global market and company information
  www.humbul.ac.uk   humanities website
  www.knoweurope.net
  www.data-archive.ac.uk
  www.westminster.watch.co.uk

- Useful websites for health-related subjects:
  www.omni.ac.uk
  www.nmap.ac.uk

- Useful websites for the physical sciences:
  www.nhm.ac.uk   the Natural History Museum
  www.sparkseducation.co.uk

- Useful websites for English:
  www.naturegrid.org
  www.go-ed.com
  www.brownless.org/durk/grammar/punct
  www.shakespeare.com

- Useful websites for modern foreign languages:
  www.becta.org.uk/supportproviders
  www.en.eun.org
  www.cortland.edu/flteach/methods

- Useful webites for learning disability issues:
  www.ipsea.org.uk
  www.deafworldweb.org
  www.hood.edu/seri/serihome

- Useful websites for mathematics:
  www.teachingideas.co.uk
  www.bbc.co.uk/education/megamaths
  http://mathsgoodies.com   resource website
  www.mathsnet.com

- Useful websites for legal matters:
  www.safety.ngfl.gov.uk
  www.dca.gov.uk

6

Portfolio task 6.1

Access three websites that provide specific information for your subject. Evaluate their usefulness and identify ways in which you might incorporate their content into your schemes of work and/or lesson plans. Use the resource in your teaching and evaluate the outcome in terms of meeting the needs of a variety of learners.

Java applets

Applets are small programs which are often used to provide interactive features or animations. Access the following website to see an animation of light rays passing through lenses or reflected from mirrors:

http://surendranath.tripod.com/Applets.html

Select the **Applets** menu, then **Optics**, followed by **Spherical Mirrors and Lenses**.

Task 6.4

Access an interactive resource or a static resource (map, picture) and use it interactively with a group of trainees by using interactive whiteboard technology in a learning situation. If your teaching training space has no access to whiteboard technology, consider other ways (perhaps using a laptop) in which you might set a small-group task using a resource you have accessed from the internet or intranet.

Image libraries

An image library is an online repository of visual presentations, images and pictures.

WebQuests

WebQuests were invented by Bernie Dodge, professor of educational technology at San Diego State University in Calafornia. A WebQuest may best be defined as a tool to support educational research carried out by learners who are involved in enquiry-oriented activity. There are two types of WebQuest:

- **Short-term WebQuests**. The goal here is a limited period of time spent searching for new information. It is designed to be completed in one or two sessions and involves using material from the internet, optionally supplemented with video conferencing or commentary, to create a virtual project.

- **Long-term WebQuests**. These aim to enable a learner to extend and refine their knowledge, analyse information and create some form of paper-based or electronic presentation to which others can respond.

The stages involved in constructing a WebQuest are as follows:

1 An introduction sets the stage and provides some background information.

2 A task is set. It must be achievable and interesting.

3 The learner is provided with a set of information sources needed to complete the task. The sources might include web documents, the contact details of available experts (or a tutor), books, journals. These pointers prevent wasting time searching the web for hours and becoming distracted.

4 A description of the process the learners need to engage with, or an activity they need to complete.

5 Guidance is given on how to organise the information acquired: produce a mindmap, timeline, quiz, cause-and-effect diagram.

6 Conclusion. The learner is supported in evaluating what they have achieved.

Advantages of WebQuests

WebQuests can be used to support the development of the following skills:

- Compare and contrast
- Classify into groups
- Analyse errors and make corrections
- Search for patterns or contradictions
- Discuss personal views and perspectives (debating)
- Look for consequences and possible rules or generalisations.

Example 6.2 shows one section of a WebQuest designed by Torbay Library which focuses on a villain called John Lee. Designed as part of investigation into local history, the researcher is guided through a range of tasks.

Example 6.2 Section from a WebQuest

Now that you have chosen the other reporter that you are going to work with, you need to get on with your research.

You will need to find out the answers to these questions:

Where and when was John 'Babbacombe' Lee born?

Where did he work?

Why was he famous?

Where did Emma Keyse live?

How did she die?

Emma painted a picture that now hangs in Torre Abbey. What was the picture of?

What happened on the night of 15th November 1884?

Who arrested John Lee?

What was John Lee's sentence?

What happened next?

Note: This example uses paired working to show that electronically mediated learning can be adapted for individuals working alone or with others.

6

To find out more about WebQuests go to: http://stagenlnonline.ngfl.gov.uk or www.rdn.ac.uk.

Blogs

The word 'blog' is shorthand for 'weblog', which is defined as a diary or journal kept on the web and updated periodically. Some institutions have set up blogs as a way of communicating with their students, reminding them about homework, exam timetables, deadlines and forthcoming events. Figure 6.2 is a copy of a weblog found at http://www.chemistry.blog-city.com.

Another example can be found at http://aceuk.blogspot.com. This blog was written by Theresa Welch, a former IT tutor who uses it to review and share (free of charge) IT resources for adult education. Figure 6.3 is taken from the blogspot. It contains a useful tip for distributing photos on a CD.

SmartGroups

SmartGroups is the generic name for the conversations that people might have in virtual space. Free software is available at www.smartgroups.com which will enable the creation of a electronic (or virtual) conversation group. SmartGroups can be created using the email and the internet and allow people to keep in touch, share information, organise events and make group decisions.

Figure 6.2 **Example of a chemistry weblog**

HOMEWORK - DUE TUESDAY 8TH NOVEMBER
« H » email link

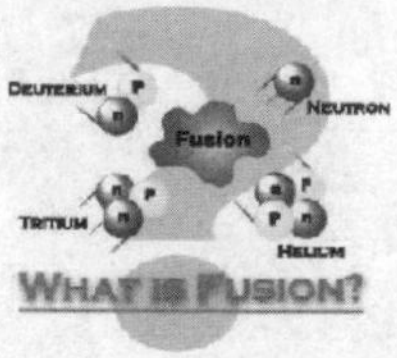

WHAT IS FUSION?

This week your homework, which is due on Tuesday 8th November, is to make some notes on the following:

(1) **Outline the formation of elements in stars by nuclear fusion processes**

(2) **The use of radioactive tracers**

As well as any other sources of information the two Salters textbooks will help you with this research.

Tips

- Minimum 1 side of A4
- include equations where you can when explaining fusion
- try and find at least 3 different examples of the use of radioactive tracers

You may find these links interesting and useful (though you may well find better ones)

http://fusioned.gat.com/

http://en.wikipedia.org/wiki/Nuclear_medicine

http://www.chem.duke.edu/~jds/cruise_chem/nuclear/agriculture.html

Some interesting background information on the science of stars http://www.bbc.co.uk/science/space/stars/twinkle/index.shtml

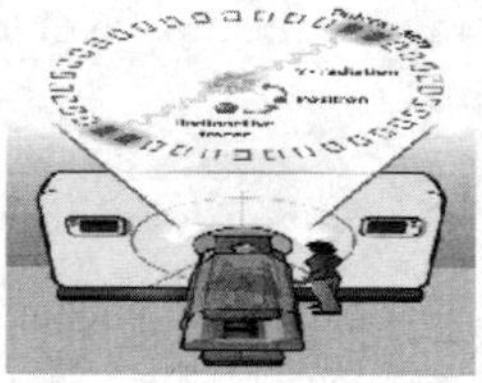

posted Saturday, 5 November 2005

Source: http://www.chemistry.blog-city.com

Figure 6.3 A blogshot

Online Tip - Distributing Photos on a CD

This article has a really good tip for distributing photos on a CD, complete
with a built in slide show and a customized photo CD cover (using free
software called Picasa.) It's really easy to do and allows you to create a
really professionally packaged CD in a matter of minutes. I tried it earlier
and it really is simple yet effective. The article itself explains how it's done.

But as well as creating gift CD's you can also use Picasa to:

- **Make picture collages.**
  Select a group of pictures, and Picasa will create a collage of them
  like the quick one I've included above.

- **Turn your photos into a movie.**
  Select your best shots, adjust the delay time, sizes, and video
  compression settings. That's it. Picasa will render a movie that you
  can play and share.
- **Make a personalised desktop picture or screensaver.**
  Pick a favourite photo as your desktop picture or add several into
  your screensaver rotation. What better way to enjoy your
  photographic genius at your desk?
- **Create a poster.**
  Picasa can tile any picture you select, allowing you to print each
  part and reassemble them at poster size – up to 1,000% larger
  than the original.

(John, whose photos I shared last week, loved the editing features
Picasa has for fixing your images up and 'turning those grey skies into
picture perfect days'.) But whether you're into photo editing or you're not,
the gift CD feature and all of the others listed above do make this a very
useful piece of software – which, let's not forget is also free!

To give it a whirl yourself, you can download Picasa here or find out more
in a tour here.

via Quick Online tips

Source: http://jcouk.blogspot.com

6

Task 6.5

Obtain the email addresses of the learners in one of your groups who are willing to share them and set up a group list on your email account. Post a message to the group reminding them about the preparation needed for the next session, encourage debate and discussion. Reflect on the outcome with the group when you next meet.

Using electronic methods to meet learners' needs

E-learning approaches can enhance the focus on individual learners and support individual learning needs. Example 6.3, illustrates how e-learning approaches can support differentiation.

Example 6.3 Using e-learning approaches to support different types of learners

English Language GCSE

Group consists of Activists and Reflectors

Methods: Group work, tutorials, online learning

Resources: Camcorder, VLE, bulletin boards

Activity: This activity looks at persuasive communication techniques and developing listening comprehension skills. In groups, students play a game where they take it in turns to talk on a variety of situations in which they have to use persuasive language and other techniques to effectively communicate their point of view to an audience. These presentations are filmed using a camcorder which can then be reviewed later in a tutorial session to emphasise and reinforce key points. For homework, students will complete a written assignment using online learning. They will have access to resources and links through the VLE [virtual learning environment] (including a National Learning Network materials module). They will also use an electronic bulletin board to facilitate further discussion about the topic. Differentiation is provided by producing a series of cue cards that the teacher can use with students during the activity to help them if required. These can be varied according to the level.

Portfolio task 6.2

You are required to deliver one module or session of your teaching programme by virtual means. Decide how you will do this: which module, which group of learners and the specific tool (blog, CD-rom, RLO, whiteboard, internet research project). Experiment with this as far as you are able. Ask learners to evaluate the experience. As in Example 6.3, consider how you have met the needs of individual learners. Write a report for your portfolio of the outcome (500 words). Include evidence of the virtual media you have produced.

Portfolio task 6.3

Revisit your ILP and consider your training needs in terms of ILT. Reassess your requirements for staff development and training as, and if, required. Record your findings in your portfolio by updating your ILP.

Plagiarism

6

The education press often identifies issues around plagiarism and the anguish this can cause. Research by Brown and McDowell (1998) has shown that just telling your learner about the dangers of plagiarism is not enough: you need to show your learners how to paraphrase work and cite sources. The Joint Information Systems Committee website (www.jisc.ac.uk) contains a number of plagiarism detection tools that can be used. Using technology to detect plagiarism helps learners to see that one of the most powerful benefits of technology is the way it enables us to share ideas and thoughts.

Students should be encouraged to investigate, discuss, explore and share online. Useful sources of information in the library or on the web should be shared. That is what makes a learning community. However, with the benefits come a number of problems. The crucial point is that the work that your learners produce for assessment must be entirely their own, written by them, in their own words, and containing their interpretations, ideas and approaches. If they use other people's words or major ideas, then they should state clearly where that material come from. If they use diagrams or photos from published works then they should state where the diagrams or photographs came from and add their own caption or footnotes to it, not those of the original source. In other words, it is quite easy to avoid plagiarism while also being a learner who shares with others and supports the creation of learning communities. The same applies to you in your assignments and set tasks leading to the award of licensed to practise.

Key tips to take from this chapter

- Technology can be used to help you to work smarter not harder. It can save you time in planning.
- Reusable learning objects enable the use of lesson materials on more than one occasion.
- Technology can help you to keep in touch with your learners in between set contact times, to encourage greater learner involvement and commitment.

Assessment grid mapped to the standards

This chapter introduces the knowledge requirements for the areas in scope set out at the start of the chapter. Completion of the set tasks will provide you with evidence that can be matched to the standards, as set out below, for gaining awards in the learning and skills sector.

Task	Summary activity	Level 3 award	Trainer award (level 4) leading to QTLS (level 5)	E-learning standards CPD awards
Task 6.1	Defining the terminology	CK 3.5	CK 3.5	B 1 C 1 D 1 E 1
Task 6.2	Evaluating the use of technology	CK 3.5	DK 5.2	Potential for elements of A, B, C, D, E, F
Task 6.3	Evaluating three websites	Not essential	CP 3.5 CP 4.1 CK 3.5	B 1 B 2 D 1 D 2 (potentially)
Task 6.4	Using electronic resources for teaching	DK 1.3 CP 3.5 CK 1.1	DK 1.3 DP 5.1 CP 3.5 CK 1.1	D 1 D 2 (potential)
Task 6.5	Using technology to communicate with your learners	Not essential	BP 5.1 BP 5.3	D 1 D 2 D 3 D 4
Portfolio task 6.1	Evaluate the effectiveness of three websites to support the needs of individual learners	Not essential	BP 5.1 BP 5.2	

Task	Summary activity	Level 3 award	Trainer award (level 4) leading to QTLS (level 5)	E-learning standards CPD awards
Portfolio task 6.2	Design, deliver and evaluate an episode of learning using technology	Not essential	CP 3.1 CP 3.2 CP 3.5	B 1 C 1 C 2 C 3
Portfolio task 6.3	Revisit your ILP and evaluate your training needs, taking action where necessary to ensure you address any skills gaps	AP 6.1 AP 6.2 AK 6.1 AK 6.2 CK 4.1	AP 6.1 AP 6.2 BP 3.4 AK 6.1 AK 6.2 CK 4.1	

6

7 The curriculum contextualised
Secure knowledge and understanding of the subject and curriculum

> **Learning outcomes**
>
> By the end of this chapter you will:
>
> - have explored the influence of policy and philosophy on curriculum design
> - have identified opportunities to access support for teaching/tutoring/training in a subject-specific way
> - have developed an understanding of the current debates surrounding curriculum design and delivery
> - be aware of the role of validating bodies and external stakeholders
> - have applied a theoretical model to identify the complexities of curriculum design and delivery.

Areas in scope in this chapter in relation to the standards for teachers, tutors and trainers working in the sector are AS 2, BS 1, BS 2 BS 3, CS 1, CS 3, DS 1, DS 2, DS 3.

The curriculum is deeply influenced by the society we inhabit, the ideology of the powerful and by the way it is interpreted and presented by those responsible for its delivery. This chapter provides an overview of the current education agenda in relation to curriculum reform and explores the policy, ideology and practice that prevail. A number of government policies are discussed and the values that underpin their conception are explored.

What do we mean by the term 'curriculum'?

Kelly (1999: 5) defined the term 'curriculum' as:

> All the learning which is planned and guided, whether carried on in groups or individually.

This definition is very practice-oriented and makes the word sound active, seeming to imply that the teacher and the learner have some freedom to design and develop curriculum content. It reads as if the curriculum is an active relationship between the learner and the designer/director of the learning. What the definition ignores is the stage before the curriculum reaches the learning environment: the stage at which it is constructed or designed.

How is the curriculum constructed?

The curriculum is much more than what goes on at the point of learning. The content of what is taught, the level, the subject and the eventual outcome are often not the decision of the teacher or trainer but are dictated externally by government policy, current philosophy and intended practice.

> The physical text that pops through the school (college) letterbox does not arrive 'out of the blue' – it has an interpretational and representational history – and neither does it enter a social or institutional vacuum. The text and its readers and the context of response all have histories.
>
> (Ball, 1994: 15)

Some recent history

One of the key challenges in writing this book has been the need to keep abreast of the many reforms impacting on the LSS. In the area of curriculum this has been particularly difficult. For example, the Tomlinson Review of 14–19 curriculum reform (DfES, 2004a) following the introduction of Curriculum 2000 suggested the abolition of the A level qualification and its replacement by a diploma. One year later, a government White Paper (*14–19 Education and Skills*) appeared to ignore this recommendation, with the statement: 'We will keep both GCSEs and A levels' (DfES, 2005c).

This example illustrates not only that

- the curriculum is strongly influenced by policy and public opinion, and
- the curriculum is strongly influenced by philosophy,

but also that (and this is where you do have an impact)

- the curriculum is influenced by practice, that is, the way we interpret the content and how this is presented to the learner.

To explain this is more detail, this chapter is presented in three sections: curriculum policy, curriculum philosophy and curriculum practice.

Curriculum policy

Policy decisions are not made in a social vacuum. They are influenced by the views that prevail at the time and the values and political stance of the government and policy makers of the period. Attempts to trace different curriculum policy to its embryonic root and map all the factors that have influenced it are both complex and interesting. There are a number of theorists you may wish to read who write critically about curriculum policy. They ask specific questions about who influences policy, what motivates their interest and in whose power interests they operate. *Pedagogy of the Oppressed* by Freire

7

(1972) is particularly interesting. If you are interested in the impact of policy on social mobility you may also like to read Giroux (1994) who identifies the impact of power, status and prestige on emerging ideas about pedagogy.

There are a number of stakeholders who will have influenced decisions before any idea is articulated as a policy. The policy associated with the importance of a curriculum area will be subject also to regional and local influences. In holiday resorts such as Bournemouth and Poole, Scarborough and Brighton, for example, the local colleges offer extensive courses in hospitality and catering. You might like to think about the influences that have shaped the curriculum you deliver. First, however, it will be interesting to examine a few of the current policy initiatives impacting on curriculum design.

Overview of current policy

Government policy is increasingly advocating 14–19 education as a single phase of studying in which individuals can undertake a range of qualifications. The current landscape of available provision is complex. This complexity will increase rather than decrease during the rest of this decade as reforms to the whole qualification framework are introduced. Changes will be introduced gradually, with many of the qualifications listed below remaining to be replaced using a phased approach over time. This means that the newly trained and those in post will need to keep abreast of the changes and be prepared to adapt their schemes of work to meet the changing curriculum landscape. The phased and staged approach to curriculum reform means that the complex range of qualifications will exist for many years.

The curriculum currently offers the qualifications described below.

Entry-level qualifications

Certificates that can be taken in over 200 subjects, including basic skills (see Chapter 8). These are aimed at students with learning difficulties and disabilities, those for whom English is a second language or those who may have been out of education for some time. This policy reflects government concern about a group it refers to as NEET (not in education, employment or training), and gives focus to skills for employability and personal fulfilment.

GCSEs

GCSEs (General Certificates in Secondary Education) include the newly introduced vocational GCSEs which replace part 1 of the General National Vocational Qualifications (GNVQs).

GNVQs

GNVQs (General National Vocational Qualifications) are to be phased out. They are traditionally taught in colleges of further education at three levels: foundation, intermediate and advanced. The advanced level was replaced in the Curriculum 2000 reforms by the Advanced Vocational Certificate, due for another redesign as part of the White Paper reforms suggested in 2005 (see vocational A levels discussed below). GNVQs will be replaced by diploma qualifications using a phased approach leading to full implementation. Fourteen new diplomas are due to be in place by 2013.

Key skills

Key skills can be studied in six areas which can be taken as a qualification in their own right but which are usually taken alongside other qualifications. When taken with other subjects the key skills are assessed as an integral part of the core curriculum (as part of an A level syllabus, for example).

NVQs

NVQs (National Vocational Qualifications) are available in over 700 different subjects: construction, hairdressing, business, aromatherapy, management, administration, plumbing, and so on.

A levels

A-levels (General Certificate of Education – Advanced Level) consist of AS (the first half of an A level as a self-standing qualification), and A2 which completes the qualification. In the proposed reforms (DfES, 2005c) these qualifications remain, but with a reduced number of assessment points (from six down to four). These qualifications may be dis-aggregated into two separate awards.

AEAs

AEAs (Advanced Extension Awards) designed to stretch talented A level students. The aim is to allow able students to demonstrate their skills and aptitude more fully, with opportunities available for them to complete modules of university work at an early age.

7

VCEs

Vocational Certificates in Education (VCEs, also known as vocational A levels) are available in a range of subjects, such as business and leisure and tourism, as progression from vocational GCSEs. Given the title 'applied A level', these qualifications, launched in summer 2005, have replaced advanced vocational provision, the intention being that employers and higher education institutions will accord the applied A level the same respect as given to A level qualifications. The Learning and Skills Development Agency has produced a series of guidance booklets to help lecturers prepare for the external assessment requirements that accompany these qualifications.

PELTS

The Qualifications and Curriculum Authority has developed a draft single framework for personal, employment, learning and thinking skills (PELTS) for all learners aged 11 to 19. This framework combines the study of functional English, mathematics and ICT, and is designed to equip young people with the skills they need to be employable and to achieve success in life.

For further details see www.nc.uk or www.vocationallearning.org.uk. More information about the White Paper *14 19 Education and Skills* is available on the DfES website at www.dfes.gov.uk. Here you will find a summary of the main points of the reform and an implementation plan. You will need to access this for the last part of task 7.1.

Task 7.1

Explore one of the dimensions of the curriculum for which you have a responsibility and complete the table below. Identify the timescale for the 14–19 reform agenda impacting on your subject area. An example is provided to demonstrate the type of response you might make.

Name of course	Intended qualification	Rationale	Impact of the reform
Hospitality and Catering	GNVQ 3	To support the local hotel industry by providing qualified staff	Qualification to be replaced in 2009 Redesign of content influence by industry requirements Integration of functional skills as part of the core

Portfolio task 7.1

Explore current government thinking (in terms of a recently published White Paper) by considering the focus of the proposed policy, the target group under consideration and the possible key motivators for the proposed change. In addition, consider what impact this policy will have on you and your role in your organisation. (300 words)

Curriculum philosophy

Two particular philosophies seem to underpin current thinking about the curriculum, with a third gaining momentum very quickly. These are:

- A *liberal humanist tradition* with a focus on subject where the curriculum is seen as knowledge centred. This view promotes the systematic study of a subject with clear knowledge in a defined area of discipline. Evidence for this approach can be seen in the policy decision to keep A levels, the Ofsted inspection framework which inspects the quality of teacher training of the basis of how it prepares teachers to teach their subject (rather than focusing on the generic skills of teaching as a professional activity), and the production of learning materials on a subject-by-subject basis, to support the *Success for All* strategy (DfES, 2002b).

- *Instrumentalism*. This view enables us to see the curriculum as having a specific product, namely producing a skilled workforce for economic and social stability. It focuses on the importance of skills as required for economic stability and global competitiveness. In this view, knowledge acquisition is somewhat refined in terms of its relevance for twenty-first-century Britain:

> Investment in and reform of education and training is central to our vision for a fair society and successful economy.
>
> (Tony Blair, quoted in DfES, 2005d).

- *Personalisation.* This approach is present in the 14–19 reforms where the focus is on individual choice, individual pathways and progression from one stage to the next, not on the basis of cohort but on when (and only when) the individual has demonstrated competence at the first level of skill (in all areas).

Current philosophy seems to present a perspective focused on knowledge acquisition (as proposed in the liberal humanist tradition) and a skill development focus (central to the instrumentalist school of thought). As part of the focus on knowledge acquisition there is a desire to give greater status and prestige to what have traditionally been labelled 'vocational' subjects. In an attempt to give equal status to all forms of knowledge, work is under way to bring together all qualifications in the LSS under one umbrella, in a unifying framework, thus reflecting the liberal humanist tradition. The Qualifications and Curriculum Authority (QCA) has confirmed that the fourteen curriculum areas will form the curriculum frameworks for the future and give equal focus to all areas irrespective of whether in the past, they have been defined as 'academic' or 'vocational'. See www.qca.org.uk for more details.

In addition, the concept of personalisation can be described as a new philosophy impacting on curriculum design. The 14–19 reforms will result in a major review of the curriculum, with a focus on entitlement and learner choice. The new curriculum philosophy places the individual at the centre of the curriculum, in receipt of skills and knowledge that are required by society. There is almost a contractual relationship described here, whereby the learner, in gaining certain skills, is offered an environment in which their skills are used and valued. Personalisation means learner autonomy, learner engagement and the promise of social inclusion and economic prosperity. Personalisation is the new approach to equality and opportunity, driven by curriculum reform.

Part of the contract for equality, contained within the personalisation agenda, is the attempt to give equal status to vocational and academic knowledge and skills as reflected in the two proposed changes set out below impacting on vocational and work-based education and training. To drive this desire for equity the use of the word 'vocational' will disappear, to be replaced by the term 'applied', when the new diploma qualifications are introduced.

Improving vocational education

Two White Papers (DfES, 2005a, b) give a commitment to improve the credibility and status of vocational education.

> The quality of vocational training for young people and adults has been a persistent weakness in this country.
>
> (Tony Blair, quoted in DfES, 2005b)

The proposals are for dramatic reform of the current system (with around 3,500 separate qualifications) to be replaced by diplomas in 14 broad sector areas. The first four diplomas are expected in ICT, engineering, health and social care, and creative and media, and are due to be ready for 2008, with four more subjects following by 2010.

The 14–19 curriculum reforms will result in a new National Curriculum founded upon qualification entitlement with learner choice. Individuals will be able to pursue general qualifications including a new general diploma awarded for those achieving the equivalent of five A–C grade GCSEs (to include GCSE English, maths and ICT) and the new specialist diplomas.

All learners will be required to achieve the functional skills (namely the ability to use basic English, maths and ICT). The new specialist diplomas will be developed at three levels, with individuals expected to master the functional skills in order to achieve either the general diploma, the specialist diploma or an apprenticeship-related qualification. Designed by sector skills councils (made up of representatives from the industry for each vocational area), the diplomas place a strong focus on skills for employability.

Subject specificity remains

The aim of the reforms is to give greater parity to the vocational curriculum, with a focus on a subject-based curriculum remaining in proposals for fourteen diploma strands which appear to be designed around defined subject boundaries with distinctive elements of subject knowledge. The rationale for this approach is based on the belief that knowledge is subject-specific. Alexander et al. (1992: 17) argue that subjects are 'some of the most powerful tools for making sense of the world which humans have ever devised'. Having placed the subject at the centre of curriculum design, the LSS curriculum offer also adopts an integrated focus to what are described as key skills (for those working at levels 1, 2, 3 and above), or basic skills (for those in need of additional supporting the introductory elements of numeracy, literacy and English as a second language). These are discussed in more detail in Chapter 8.

The context

It is important not to forget that the context in which the curriculum is delivered can have a major impact on how it is delivered. One of the major strengths of vocational learning has been its close alignment with the world of work and business. Close links with the world of work, with extended periods of work experience for the learner, have been at the heart of vocational qualifications since their conception. This approach is likely to be strengthened as the LSS builds stronger links with employers through the formation of sector skills councils (DfES, 2002b). Curriculum delivery in association with industrial/work placement adds an interesting dimension to curriculum design, with issues of health and safety and regulatory requirements being given a high focus in many syllabi.

The LSS curriculum is also delivered in venues other than colleges or work-based learning environments. It is also delivered in prisons and in community centres throughout the country. Curriculum reform will have a major impact on the educational services provided in such areas and a number of reviews, particularly of prison education, are currently under way. The government paper entitled *Reducing Re-offending through Skills and Employment* (HMSO, 2005) has identified the need to increase the quality and effectiveness of learning and skills delivered to offenders and to introduce employment contracts to encourage offenders back to work. The Learning and Skills Development Agency (now the Learning and Skills Network) has produced a text called

Just Learning? which includes a number of case study exemplars of how to improve offender education and training.

If you are interested in reading more about curriculum ideologies, Armitage et al. (2002) contains an excellent chapter on this topic. You may also like to access the website, http://www.infed.org/biblio/b-curric.htm.

Curriculum practice

Here we move to consider the curriculum as a product to be designed and interpreted by those who engage with it. Unfortunately, we are still not able to move immediately to the level of the practitioner and the learner: we need to be aware of such things as 'awarding bodies'. It is the awarding bodies (EdExcel, City and Guilds, RSA, to name but a few), who determine in broad terms the content of what is taught, namely the syllabus.

The first step, then, for the practitioner, in working with a group of learners, is to make sure they are working towards the current syllabus, specific to the date when the learners are likely to be assessed. This may seem obvious but, unfortunately, the pressures of external change and internal organisational difficulties can mediate to make this crucial component of your teaching difficult to obtain. The websites of the most commonly used awarding bodies are listed below so that you can check the most recent information on the syllabus with which you are working.

ACCAC	www.accac.org.uk
AQA (previously City and Guilds)	www.aqa.org.uk
CCLA	www.ccla.org.uk
EdExcel (previously B.Tec)	www.exedcel.org.uk
OCR	www.ocr.org.uk
WJEC (a Welsh awarding body, previously JWEB)	www.wjec.org.uk.

The syllabus, then, is the first part of the teacher/tutor/trainer's toolkit for designing the curriculum in terms of it practical application.

Task 7.2

Obtain a copy of an up-to date syllabus for the subject specialism you teach. Identify the key components of content and complete an audit of your knowledge against the requirements of the course. Produce a list of subject content you feel competent to deliver identifying areas where you are less secure. Consider how you will improve your knowledge, where you have gaps and identify what action you will take, by when, to ensure you have the knowledge required to deliver the syllabus.

Regional context

Regional variations, employer needs and context will influence the curriculum focus in many institutions. Basic skills training is given high status in offender education. Adult and community education centres are renowned for providing access to IT training in remote areas. The curriculum will also be influenced by regional focus, regional need and the existing local provision. A major shift in curriculum focus in preparation for the Olympic Games in 2012 is currently under way in London, with the regional Learning and Skills Councils using European Social Fund grants to develop training opportunities linked to a range of vocational and basic skill developments specific to the skill-base required to make the 2012 Games a success.

A model for curriculum practice

In order to help you translate government policy, curriculum philosophy and the requirements of awarding body syllabi into reality, a model for practice is proposed below. The model is based on work carried out by the Kellogg Foundation, whose aim is to:

> Help people help themselves through the practical application of knowledge and resources to improve the quality of life and that of future generations
>
> (www.kelloggfoundation/logicmodel)

The Kellogg Foundation has developed what it calls a Logic Model to provide a picture of how something works. This knowledge is then used to support practitioners in their planning, design, implementation and analysis of all aspects of the work they do. The Logic Model is applied here to curriculum delivery, but it could be used to analyse your organisation or be applied to a specific project in which you are engaged.

The Logic Model has five stages:

1 Resources or inputs

2 Activities

3 Outputs

4 Outcomes

5 Impact.

Table 7.1 illustrates how the Logic Model (somewhat simplified and adapted) might be applied to curriculum practice. The first two boxes, 'resources' and 'activities', focus on your planned work and include all the resources you need to implement your programme and what you want to do. The next three boxes refer to your intended results.

A **Logic Model** template can be downloaded from the companion website (Web 15)

The model is offered here to show that work started on schemes of work in Chapter 4 offered only a brief introduction to the complexities of curriculum planning. By applying the Logic Model it is easy to see that schemes of work cannot be seen in isolation, are complex documents that require much planning and need to be designed in the light of intended outcomes and eventual impact.

Table 7.1 The Logic Model applied to curriculum practice

Resources or inputs	Activities	Outputs	Outcomes	Impact

• Government policy
• Curriculum philosophy
• The course syllabus
• The learning environment
• The faciltities
• Learners':
  - previous knowledge
  - skills
  - abilities
  - needs
	• Scheme of work
	• Planned activities
	• Objectives
	• Diagnosis of needs
	• Adjustments to meet specific learner needs
	• Organisation of the learning experience
		• Learner involvement
		• Learner activity
		• Evidence that learning has taken place
		• Determination of what to evaluate and of the ways and means of doing it
			• Intended changes in knowledge, skills, understanding and/or level of functioning
			• Learner achievements
			• Qualifications achieved
			• Conversation, evaluation and thinking
			• Critical assessment of process, leading to thinking in action
				Long-term impact on:
				• Learner achievements
				• Learner views
				• Workforce
				• Industry

The model illustrates that curriculum planning involves more than just organising the activities and timings of an episode of learning. It requires you to think more specifically about the learner, their needs, their previous experience, knowledge and skills, and how individual needs might be addressed. This leads to the development of more complex lesson plans which require the practitioner to consider a wider range of issues than were raised earlier in this text.

Back to the lesson plan

In Chapter 3 you were introduced to a lesson plan activity to illustrate how episodes of learning need to be designed and planned in clear sequence, with regular activity change and variety. The lesson plan exemplar, which focused on a session in health and social care (refer back to Table 3.12), used different tasks, a variety of organisation (group work, whole-class and individual tasks) and a range of resources (visual, auditory and kinaesthetic) to meet the needs of different types of learners. Example 7.1 repeats the lesson plan but adds in a section which identifies specific learning needs (coloured grey). This demonstrates how the curriculum can be adapted to meet the specific needs of the learning group.

Example 7.1 Lesson plan identifying specific learner needs

Name of lecturer: **Fred**	Course: **Health and Social Care: Intermediate (GCSE) Vocational Qualification: numeracy key skills**
Room: **A21**	Session: **Friday session 4**
Start time: **3.30pm**	Finish time: **4.30pm**
Number of participants: **15**	Significant issues: **This is not a good time for the topic, attendance will need monitoring and activities designed to ensure student enthusiasm is achieved and maintained**

Specific learner needs:	**Jo has some reading difficulties so needs to be paired with Mary. Ali is in a wheelchair and would enjoy us estimating his journey time compared with someone who walk to college**

Aims	**To develop students' ability to estimate in varying context using appropriate measuring tools**
Objectives	By the end of the session participants will be able to: ● **Use and evaluate two different systems of measurement** ● **Recognise and apply two different measuring systems to different dimensions of estimation** ● **Recognise the significance of error in estimation**

Time	Lesson content	Method	Resources
3.30 5 minutes	Settle group and clarify objectives Emphasise how functional the session will be in supporting key skill achievements	Link to key skill competence and illustrate how functional the session will be in supporting participants in achieving the skill	Key skills record book for each student Objectives identified on the board
10 minutes	Allocate groups Distribute local maps Set tasks: Identify location of all the nurseries in the region Estimate the walking distance between each one	Mixed ability groupings Small-group activity Worksheet identifying names of each nursery	Maps Record sheet for estimations Record outcomes
5 minutes	Compare outcomes	Large-group brainstorm	Board work

Time	Lesson content	Method	Resources
3 minutes	Record agreed estimated distances (metres), in walking time (minutes) and car transport (minutes)	Gapped handout	Paperwork available
10 minutes	Using a stopwatch send two (trustworthy) students to the onsite nursery and record how long it takes them to return On return compare actual time taken with the estimated time	Remaining students to discuss how long it takes them to travel to their work placements and explore the implications of their method of transport	Stopwatch Discussion sheet
5 minutes	Record outcome of the discussion	Students to compare journey times, external influences that impact on their travel plans	Chart to complete which compares journey times with travel method
5 minutes	Explore the impact of estimated time of journey being much less than actual	Discussion linked to their professional responsibilities as carers	Key questions provided to direct discussion
5 minutes	Collate ideas	Brainstorm and record	Board or flipchart
5 minutes	Individuals to draw up a code for travel when on work placement	Gapped handout	Worksheet provided
7 minutes	Conclusions, revision of activity, key learning points	Return to the objectives	Record achievement, if appropriate, in the individual student key skills record book

7

Task 7.3

Using the new template with additional detail required, design a lesson plan for a group of learners you know. Think specifically about how individual needs can be met. Information about specific and defined learning needs is provided in Chapter 10. Share you plan with your mentor/coach and ask them for advice and comments on the design and structure you have adopted.

A template for this **lesson plan** (iii) can be downloaded from the companion website (Web 16)

The national transformation project and the focus on teaching and learning

In Chapter 1, mention was made of the *Success for All* agenda with four goals for sector reform. Reforms to teacher training which have resulted in this text are part of goal 3. As part of goal 2 'Putting teaching and learning at the heart of what we do', a major national transformation project has been launched. This has involved government investment in what have been identified as three enablers, namely:

- The production of materials in subject areas seen as key to the agenda designed to transform teaching and learning in this sector. The first rollout of materials covered construction, business, entry to employment (e2e) and science. This was closely followed by mathematics, land-based subjects, and health and social care. The third group of resources cover adult and community education and will be available in 2007.
- Regular networking events for practitioners to meet and share good practice and ideas for teaching and learning.
- A professional training programme for subject learning coaches.

Focus is given here to the curriculum resources as a source of ideas and innovation for the practitioner. Teaching resources have been sent to every provider. The ideas that underpin the tasks presented in these resources are transferable across subjects and well worth investigation. Below is a list of some of the activities available in just a few of the subject boxes. It is recommended that you seek these resources out and use them in your teaching.

- Matching activities
- Crosswords
- DVD and video clips
- Resources file
- Quizzes
- Activity sheets.

The resources for health and social care contain materials for addressing health and safety issues, activities around the theme of client confidentiality and whole-class discussion topics. The resources include lesson plans, schemes of work and photocopy-able materials. The schemes of work are mapped against the achievement of the key skill of communication, number and ICT (see Chapter 8). One interesting approach to achieving number skills in this subject domain suggests the use of data collection from a quiz that tests learning from a taught session. The scores are then analysed in a variety of ways by the participants to demonstrate skills in data handling. These data are then logged on to a spreadsheet to demonstrate achievement of the ICT skills. As a developmental task that would link in easily with the requirements for monitoring data and keeping records, the same approach could be used for client information and record keeping, thus making the resources and the approach transferable across a number of subject domains.

In the business resources, learners can access a Bingo activity which is good for tackling legislative issues. In Science there are useful resources on videos and CD-Rom.

The resources for mathematics are exemplars of approaches to teaching and learning which have worked with a range of learners. The underpinning rationale for the resources is to improve teaching and learning, and to this end the resources include materials not only for teachers to use with their learners but for training colleagues as well (the CPD box encourages discussion, reflection and active learning).

The session materials are differentiated by level of challenge, ranging from A to D. Each session also includes suggestions for differentiated activities to support various needs. Many of the session materials can be adapted for use at higher or lower levels. Resources are provided for the full range of abilities and grouped by levels of challenge, as shown in Table 7.2.

Table 7.2 Rationale for the level of challenge descriptors applied to session materials

Level of challenge	Rationale
A	Adult Numeracy, Key skills Application of Number, level 1 GCSE grades E to G
B	Adult Numeracy, Key skills. Application of Number level 2 GCSE grades D-F
C	Key skills Application of Number level 3 GCSE Level 2 A-D grades
D	AS, A2

Example 7.2, taken from the resources index, illustrates how the materials are presented. This particular example is from a section entitled 'Mostly shape and space'.

Example 7.2 The mathematics resources index

Title	Description	Level of challenge
Understanding perimeter and area	Learners work together to investigate areas and perimeters of rectangular shapes	A/B
Dissecting a square	Learners work together to calculate areas as fractions of wholes. Learners then create their own questions Links are then drawn between areas, fractions and percentages	B
Interpreting frequency graphs, cumulative frequency graphs, boxes and whisker plots	Learners interpret multiple representation of large distributions: frequency graphs, cumulative frequency graphs, box and whisker plots	C
Using binominal probabilities	Learners explore binominal probabilities and make generalisations about the symmetries of cumulative binomial probabilities	D

Source: DfES, 2004b.

Portfolio task 7.2

Gain access to the subject material resources either in your subject area or one that might be closely aligned. Select one task available from the menu, adapt the requirements for your subject area (if necessary) and test out the activity with a group of learners. Ask your learners for feedback on the activity. Critically reflect on the outcome. Produce a report on your findings for your portfolio. If you are not able to access these resources then it is suggested that you evaluate another prepared training pack, perhaps from one of the websites identified by Huddersfield University (see below).

The Standards Unit resources have been designed to address issues of differentiation and learner need. They represent clear attempts at a focus on subject pedagogy in the LSS. In addition, they can help those undergoing teacher training to address the requirements of the minimum core. The materials have been designed to support all learners and to help practitioners identify barriers that might be restricting learners (such as past educational experience, personal association and socio-cultural factors) that limit opportunities for some learners. These learners are considered in more detail in Chapter 10.

The resources discussed above do not encompass all subjects covered in the sector. Staff at the University of Huddersfield have been working with other universities interested in supporting subject specificity in training by setting up online resources to establish subject-by-subject online communities. You can contact those responsible at http://ASSOCiate.hud.ac.uk to contribute and join in resource-building activity, which includes the following subject areas:

1 Health and public services and care

   1.1 Medicine and dentistry

   1.2 Nursing and subjects allied to vocations allied to medicine

   1.3 Health and social care

   1.4 Public services

   1.5 Child development and well-being

2 Science and mathematics

   2.1 Science

   2.2 Mathematics and statistics

3 Agriculture, horticulture and animal care

   3.1 Agriculture

   3.2 Horticulture and forestry

   3.3 Animal care and veterinary science

   3.4 Environmental conservation

4 Engineering and manufacture techniques

   4.1 Engineering

   4.2 Manufacture technology

   4.3 Transportation, operation and maintenance

5 Construction, planning and built environment

   5.1 Architecture

   5.2 Building and construction

   5.3 Urban, rural and regional planning

6 Information and communication technology

   6.1   ICT for practitioners
   6.2   ICT for users

7 Retail and catering enterprise

   7.1   Retail and wholesale
   7.2   Warehouse and distribution
   7.3   Service enterprises
   7.4   Hospitality and catering

8 Leisure and tourism

   8.1   Sports, leisure and recreation
   8.2   Travel and tourism

9 Arts, media and publishing

   9.1   Performing arts
   9.2   Crafts and creative art and design
   9.3   Media and communication
   9.4   Publishing and information services

10 History, philosophy and theory

   10.1   History
   10.2   Archaeology
   10.3   Philosophy
   10.4   Theology and religious studies

11 Social sciences

   11.1   Geography
   11.2   Sociology and social policy
   11.3   Politics
   11.4   Economics
   11.5   Anthropology

12 Language, literature and culture

   12.1   Language and culture
   12.2   Other languages

13 Education and training

   13.1   Teaching and lecturing
   13.2   Direct learning support

14 Preparation for life

   14.1   Foundation for learning and life
   14.2   Preparation for work

15 Business, administration and law

   15.1   Accountancy and finance
   15.2   Administration
   15.3   Business management
   15.4   Marketing and sales
   15.5   Law and legal services

7

Summary

This chapter set out to explore some of the complexities associated with the curriculum. It has identified the influences that impact on course design and delivery. The key components of policy, philosophy and practice have all been discussed. It is important, however, not to forget the learner, who is central to whole process. The next chapter explores the issue of individual needs in rather more detail. Figure 7.1 illustrates in diagrammatic form the curriculum influences discussed so far.

Figure 7.1 **Factors influencing LSS curriculum design**

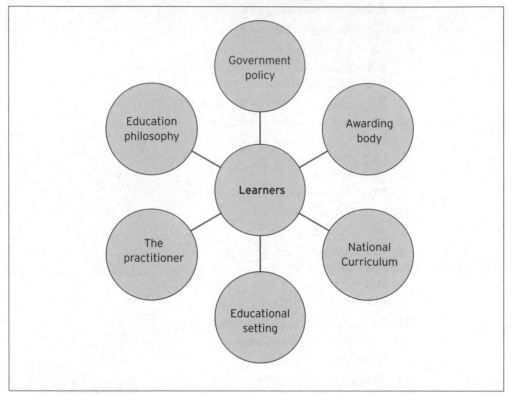

Portfolio task 7.3

Name of awarding body for one of the qualifications you are teaching. Carry out an internet search for information about that body. Search for additional resources on the Net which might be useful to support you in your teaching of the topics involved. Download some teaching resources that you might use or adapt. Write a paragraph (500 words) about how you would use these resources to support your teaching and session planning.

Portfolio task 7.4

Gain a copy of the syllabus for your topic and plan a scheme of work for ten weeks. Identify areas where you feel professionally competent to cover all the topic and areas where you might need to refresh your subject knowledge. Produce a 500-word justification for your scheme of work, why you have chosen to cover topics in that order, what you think participants will learn easily, what will be more challenging. Identify your areas of personal development (refreshment) and clarify how you will deal with these. In relation to the Logic Model described earlier in the chapter, consider your intended outcomes for those participating in the programme of study.

Technology tip

As the curriculum content for the new diploma qualification in your subject area becomes available, you will be able to access information and set aims and objectives from the QCA website www.qca.org.uk. Regular reference to this website is advised.

Key tips to take from this chapter

7

- Government policy and philosophy impact on curriculum design and curriculum change.
- External issues need to be considered before a scheme of work or lesson plan can be constructed.
- Curriculum models can be used to support the understanding of the complexities of curriculum design.
- A number of resources are becoming available to support subject knowledge in the learning and skills curriculum.

Assessment grid mapped to the standards

This chapter introduces the knowledge requirements for the areas in scope set out at the start of the chapter. Completion of the set tasks will provide you with evidence that can be matched to the standards, as set out below, for gaining awards in the learning and skills sector.

Task	Summary activity	Level 3 award	Trainer award (level 4/5) leading to QTLS	E-learning standards CPD awards
Task 7.1	14–19 reform	Not essential	BK 1.1 CK 1.2 CK 4.2	
Task 7.2	Subject knowledge audit	AK 3.1 AP 6.1 CP 1.1	AK 3.1 AP 6.1 BP 1.1 BP 1.2 CP 1.1 CK 4.2	
Task 7.3	Planning to meet individual needs	AP 2 AP 5.2 AP 6.1 BP 2.1 BP 2.2	AP 2 AP 5.2 AP 6.1 BP 2.1 BP 2.2 BP 2.3 BP 4.1 DP 2.2	D 1 (potentially)
Portfolio task 7.1	Policy influencers	Not essential	BK 1.1 BK 1.2 BK 2.7	
Portfolio task 7.2	Evaluate subject-specific resources	Not essential	BP 1.1 BK 2.1 BP 2.2 BP 2.3	D 1 (potentially)
Portfolio task 7.3	Using subject resources in a session	Not essential	BP 2.3 BP 5.1	
Portfolio task 7:4	Design a scheme of work in your subject area	CP 1.1 CP 1.2 CP 1.4 CP 2.1 DK 1.4	CP 1.1 CP 1.2 CP 2.1 DK 1.3	D 1 (potentially)

8 Skills for the twenty-first century
Using the learner's experience as a foundation for their learning

Learning outcomes

By the end of this chapter you will:

● be aware of the focus on skills in the LSS curriculum

● begin to design lesson plans which facilitate learner development in the required skills

● have considered how you might support different types of learners, engaging the less able while also stimulating the gifted

● understand the concept of the safe learner and be aware of its implications.

Areas in scope in this chapter in relation to the standards for teachers, tutors and trainers working in the sector are AS 1, BS 1, BS 2 BS 3, BS 4, DS 1, DS 2, DS 3.

The attention given to education and skills in government policy is based on a deeply held belief that education is the route to social transformation. It is through a skilled and adaptable workforce that we will achieve economic stability and social cohesion. Individuals with the skills required for the world of work can live independent of state funding and be productive, thus boosting the economy. This chapter explores the current focus on the skills required by the learner to succeed in the world of work. These skills are common to all subject areas and should be seen as an essential ingredient of all LSS teaching.

National strategy and its impact on the curriculum

As implied in Chapter 2, learners in the sector present a diverse picture in terms of subjects studied. For many years the sector has been know for its variety and complexity but recent legislation has extended this further. Increased flexibility projects have led to more 14–16-year-olds accessing programmes of learning in the LSS (DfES, 2002b). A focus on lifelong learning (DfES, 1995) is producing an expansion to the welcome offered to mature students intent on learning new skills. In addition there has been increased awareness of the need to support those who have not developed functional capability in numeracy and literacy as well as those for whom English may be an additional language (ESOL learners). It was the Moser Report that identified the need to support those who have limited skills in the basic subjects of numeracy, literacy and ICT (DfES, 1999).

The focus on the individual learner and their needs means that the lecturer working in the LSS will need to be mindful of the National Curriculum frameworks, will be required to understand the basic skills needs of specific students and be able to provide extension opportunities for the talented student in the vocational and/or academic context. The focus on what are known as key skills, namely numeracy, literacy, ICT (the hard skills) and the soft skills of problem solving, working with others and improving own learning and performance, is also increased.

Requirements for staff

There is an expectation that an individual lecturer will need to be competent themselves in working with the key skills at level 2 as a minimum. Within the new qualification structure for lecturers in the sector, opportunities will be made available on an annual basis for training and development to support those needing to address different curricular requirements at different times in their careers.

Those studying for the initial award are expected to be able to function at least at level 2. To gain full QTLS, lecturers will be required to pass the skills tests in all three key skill areas (numeracy, literacy and ICT) at level 2. The level descriptors are given in Table 8.1.

Table 8.1 Level descriptors for the key skills award

Framework level	Level indicators	Examples of qualifications
Entry	Entry-level qualifications recognise basic knowledge and skills and the ability to apply learning in everyday situations under direct guidance or supervision. Learning at this level involves building basic knowledge and skills and is not geared towards specific occupations	Qualifications are offered at entry 1, entry 2 and entry 3, in a range of subjects
Level 1	Level 1 qualifications recognise basic knowledge and skills and the ability to apply learning with guidance or supervision. Learning at this level is about activities which mostly relate to everyday situations and may be linked to job competence	NVQ 1; Certificate in Plastering; GCSEs grades D–G; Certificate in Motor Vehicle Studies
Level 2	Level 2 qualifications recognise the ability to gain a good knowledge and understanding of a subject area of work or study, and to perform varied tasks with some guidance or supervision. Learning at this level involves building knowledge and/or skills in relation to an area of work or a subject area and is appropriate for many job roles	NVQ 2; GCSEs grades A*–C; Certificate in Coaching Football; Diploma for Beauty Specialists

Framework level	Level indicators	Examples of qualifications
Level 3	Level 3 qualifications recognise the ability to gain and, where relevant, apply a range of knowledge, skills and understanding. Learning at this level involves obtaining detailed knowledge and skills. It is appropriate for people wishing to go to university, people working independently, or in some areas supervising and training others in their field of work	Certificate for Teaching Assistants; NVQ 3; A levels; Advanced Extension Awards; Certificate in Small Animal Care
Level 4	Level 4 qualifications recognise specialist learning and involve detailed analysis of a high level of information and knowledge in an area of work or study. Learning at this level is appropriate for people working in technical and professional jobs, and/or managing and developing others. Level 4 qualifications are at a level equivalent to Certificates of Higher Education	Diploma in Sport and Recreation; Certificate in Site Management; Certificate in Early Years Practice
Level 5	Level 5 qualifications recognise the ability to increase the depth of knowledge and understanding of an area of work or study to enable the formulation of solutions and responses to complex problems and situations. Learning at this level involves the demonstration of high levels of knowledge, a high level of work expertise in job roles, and competence in managing and training others. Qualifications at this level are appropriate for people working as higher-grade technicians, professionals or managers. Level 5 qualifications are at a level equivalent to intermediate higher education qualifications such as diplomas of higher education, foundation and other degrees that do not typically provide access to postgraduate programmes	Diploma in Construction; Certificate in Performing Arts
Level 6	Level 6 qualifications recognise a specialist high-level knowledge of an area of work or study to enable the use of an individual's own ideas and research in response to complex problems and situations. Learning at this level involves the achievement of a high level of professional knowledge and is appropriate for people working as knowledge-based professionals or in professional management positions. Level 6 qualifications are at a level equivalent to bachelor degrees with honours, graduate certificates and graduate diplomas	Certificate or Diploma in Management
Level 7	Level 7 qualifications recognise highly developed and complex levels of knowledge which enable the development of in-depth and original responses to complicated and unpredictable problems and situations. Learning at this level involves the demonstration of high-level specialist professional knowledge and is appropriate for senior professionals and managers. Level 7 qualifications are at a level equivalent to masters degrees, postgraduate certificates and postgraduate diplomas	Diploma in Translation; Fellowship in Music Literacy
Level 8	Level 8 qualifications recognise leading experts or practitioners in a particular field. Learning at this level involves the development of new and creative approaches that extend or redefine existing knowledge or professional practice	Specialist awards

8

Currently, qualification titles such as 'certificate' and 'diploma' are not indicators of the level of a qualification, but this will change as the implications of 14–19 curriculum reform become apparent.

The rationale behind a clarification of these levels has associated links with the personalisation agenda, which proposes that learners will progress through these levels at their own pace, moving on once they have achieved each level, at the time they are personally ready to progress rather than at the currently artificial stage determined by their chronological age. In addition, learners will not be allowed to progress to the next level of operation until they have achieved functional ability in their current level (DfES, 2005c). Lecturers will need to take into account the needs of their learners at a functional level in numeracy, literacy and ICT, and monitor their developments through the student ILP process. Target setting in ILPs is discussed in Chapter 10.

The key skills qualification

Key skills can be completed at a number of levels from level 1 to level 4, as described above. They may be offered as part of an existing qualification or studied for as part of a key skills award. In this case they are offered as part of an A level curriculum as one key skill qualification (when all components are present at level 3 or above).

High focus is given to the key skills in the areas where learners might be engaged in a work experience element of their studies, if working towards a Modern Apprenticeship for example, studying for their qualification on a part-time basis or incorporating elements of work experience into their programmes.

Example 8.1 is taken from a leaflet produced by the LSDA, to be used with Modern Apprenticeship students for whom work experience is a major part of their qualification. Its focus is key skills within the Modern Apprenticeship programme and contains advice on how to achieve the skills as part of training provided.

Example 8.1 Key skills in Modern Apprenticeships

What are key skills?
Key skills are part of your Modern Apprenticeship. They are the skills used in all jobs and industries. There are six key skills. They are:

Communication
Application of number
Information technology
Working with others
Improving own learning and performance
Problem solving

'Key skills go across the board – they're in every job.'

People who work well in groups, are well organised and can solve their problems are the people who get on best at work and get promoted. For example:

- it's no good being a brilliant engineer if you can't communicate with clients and colleagues
- you won't get far as a chef if you can't manage the kitchen budget
- no one wants to work with someone who can't be part of a team.

The point of key skills is that you use them in your work. Look out for chances to practise and develop them in your day-to-day work, as well as in training sessions or at college.

Your training provider will also have planned how they will make sure that key skills are part of your learning and assessment.

Source: LSDA, 2002.

The key skills qualification structure

The skills are set out in units that describe what needs to be known and achieved. There is one unit for each key skill at each different level. The communication unit at level 1 is:

- take part in discussions
- give a short talk
- read and obtain information
- write different types of documents.

The unit is then broken into three parts:

- *Part A* of the unit spells out what the learners need to be able to do so that they can feel confident about applying their communication skills and producing evidence.
- *Part B* identifies what must be done and describes the skills that have to be demonstrated. Learners need to have evidence in their portfolios to demonstrate that they can do all the things listed.
- *Part C* gives ideas for developing and practising communication skills and examples of the sort of evidence that learners might put into their portfolio.

Every key skills unit has the same structure, with Parts A, B and C as set out above. The key skill level is differentiated in the following ways:

- *Level 1* describes the skills that people use in routine situations and tasks that occur regularly at work.
- *Level 2* asks people to take more responsibility for some of the decisions about how to apply key skills.
- *Level 3* has more complex activities that involve reasoning and more personal responsibility for organising and carrying out tasks using key skills.
- *Levels 4 and 5* are generally for people with management or strategic responsibilities in an organisation.

These levels equate with the level descriptors given in Table 8.1.

8

Task 8.1

Obtain a copy of the key skills curriculum and carry out a personal audit of your skills against each area. Produce a personal action plan to identify skills you wish to develop in each of the key skill areas. Update your ILP at this stage and review you progress. Identify when and how you will address any areas of outstanding competence that you still need to achieve.

The six key skills

Application of number

The application of number key skill involves working with and applying numbers to a work context in terms, for example, of handling money, calculating sales figures, measuring, calculating costs or understand graphs or charts. It is not just about doing sums; it is about using mathematics in practical situations that are relevant to the work environment, for example applying percentages to work out discounts or VAT.

Some examples of key skill tasks incorporated into a work situation are:

- Calculate the cost of ordering packed lunches for 20 children in the nursery if each meal costs £4.50. If the parents are charged £5.00 for the service, how much profit does the nursery stand to make in one week?
- Reduce the cost of all stock by 10 per cent as part of a New Year sale. How much will the following items, currently charged a £5, £10 and £100, now cost?
- Measure a room or area and draw a floorplan, e.g. for a new display area or to plan storage.
- Price a job or prepare an invoice.

Communication

Communication skills are important to all organisations. They can be practised in the work or college context in relation to activities that require learners to talk to colleagues and managers, follow instructions and read documents such as reports, health and safety information and so on.

The communication key skill is about receiving the right messages from written and spoken communication and being able to transmit that message to others. It includes spelling, punctuation, grammar use and being able to use these skills appropriately as part of a job.

Some of the activities that might be carried out as part of the evidence towards meeting the key skill requirements are:

- reading health and safety instructions about a product or piece of equipment
- discussing how to tackle a task with a work colleague
- writing a business letter or report.

Working with others

One of the most important qualities that employers look for is the ability to work with other people. Employers know that good teamwork is a major factor in business success and that people who can work together to achieve objectives make a big contribution to this.

Working with others involves being clear about responsibilities and how these fit in with the organisation and the work of other people. It is about working cooperatively, asking questions to find out what others need doing, and carrying out tasks accurately, safely and on time. It also means asking for help or advice when needed.

Some of the activities that might be carried out as part of the evidence towards meeting the key skill requirements are:

- organising an event or group project
- agreeing what needs to be done and working cooperatively with other people
- planning and doing a job for a customer or client.

Information technology

Successful businesses make good use of new technology – and they want the people who work in them to be confident about using computers and other kinds of information technology.

The information technology key skill is about using IT to find, input, reorganise and present information. It means being able to find what you want on the internet or in a database, sending emails, entering information on to a computer and presenting information using word processing or graphics programs. As with all the other key skills, the emphasis is on using IT skills in a practical situation.

Some of the activities that might be carried out as part of the evidence towards meeting the key skill requirements are:

- find information for a project or your work from the internet or a database
- using a spreadsheet to keep track of your personal finances or a project budget
- writing a letter, report or presentation using a word-processing program.

Problem solving

Problem solving requires individuals to work autonomously and find ways to resolve a problem. It will probably entail testing out theories to find the optimal solution.

The problem solving key skill involves identifying when there is a problem and thinking of different ways of tackling it. You then need to decide on a course of action, carry it out and check that it has worked. The problem won't necessarily be a major issue – if it is, the right course of action would probably be to tell a colleague or your supervisor. It is more likely to be something like running out of supplies, equipment failure or making changes to a plan that isn't achieving your intended result.

Some of the activities that might be carried out as part of the evidence towards meeting the key skill requirements are:

8

- arranging an end-of-term event with a limited budget
- ordering fresh supplies for the workplace salons when stock is running low
- identifying an opportunity to reduce waste or costs
- reorganising group work when team members are absent.

Improving own learning and performance

Organisations are always looking for ways to improve their products and services, and they want staff to help them to do this. They need people who are keen to learn, are able to set and agree their own targets, and able to find ways of improving their performance at work.

This key skill is about doing more and performing more effectively in a planned way. It is about setting targets, taking opportunities to learn and reviewing learning and achievements. The evidence for this skill may come from home or leisure activities as well as from work.

Some of the activities that might be carried out as part of the evidence towards meeting the key skill requirements are:

- planning to learn a new skill at work or a hobby and deciding how you will go about it
- keeping a record of what you have learned
- reviewing your progress with your trainer or tutor.

The skills do not have to be seen as separate entities achieved only through different tasks, it is possible to meet a number of skill areas in one activity. For example:

- When dealing with a problem, learners will use communication and problem solving skills.
- If they prepare a report and produce it using a word processor, they are using communication and IT – and application of number as well if the report has charts or figures in it.

Below is an example taken from a work experience project where a number of skills are being practised simultaneously. In this extract, Carly, an apprentice, is describing her work in the office of a dental equipment company:

> I'm working on a new pricing system. We weren't making a profit from our sub-contracted engineers so I've been looking at how much is charged by the engineers for callouts, how much we're charging and the profit on each job. I might follow it up with a survey of our customers to find out how much they'd be prepared to pay as a standard callout fee. When I've got all the information I'll write a report for my boss with recommendations about what we should do.
>
> (LSDA, 2002)

The challenge for the lecturer or workplace tutor is to provide the opportunities for learners to practise and achieve the key skills. Example 8.2 is a scheme of work which shows how opportunities to meet the key skills can be incorporated into a lesson plan. Additional examples are available on the key skills website www.keyskills4u.com. The example has been developed from specifications for a module from the Edexcel programme in sport. The focus is on work experience. This focus is deliberate given the added commitment to assess employability skills that underpins the design of the new diplomas. The example related to sport could be amended to meet the requirements of other vocational work placements.

Example 8.2 Incorporating key skills into a scheme of work

Work experience

Assignment Information

This assignment relates to Unit 13 from the **First Diploma in Sport** - Work-based Project in Sport (**Edexcel** specification).

Assignment background

Students will develop an awareness of the employment opportunities available in the sports industry and develop an understanding of the requirements to work in that industry. They will assess risk factors involved, write letters requesting a placement, review advertising literature, identify health and safety hazards and carry out calculations in relation to their planned activity. Finally, they will participate in a period of work experience and present their findings to various audiences.

Key skills coverage

Evidence   Students will have opportunities to provide appropriate evidence for the following key skills:
- Communication   (L2)
- Application of number   (L2)
- Information and communication technology   (L2)
- Working with others   (L2)
- Problem solving   (L2)

Practice   Students will also have opportunities to practise aspects of the following key skills:
- Communication   (L2)
- Application of number   (L2)
- Information and communication technology   (L2)
- Working with others   (L2)
- Problem solving   (L2)

Learning outcomes

By the end of this assignment students will have
- understood the nature and purpose of a range of sports facilities
- designed a health and safety check list for themselves should they gain employment in the industry
- explored existing marketing material
- calculated travel times, routes and cost implications
- evaluated their experience and
- presented their findings to an audience.

Work to be submitted by students
- Their work for Tasks 1-5.

8

▶

Preparation and delivery

Read these teaching notes and the student handout, and review the key skills that naturally arise from the activity. Ensure students have access to the internet.

Task 1   **Introduction and preparation**

Distribute the worksheet and Task 1 sections of the handout.
Explain to the students the role of work experience within their qualification and how their experience will be assessed towards their intended qualification outcome.

Task 1

Students, in groups, to brainstorm all the local sports facilities they can remember. This completed they will be given access to computers and
Com2.1   marketing materials and will be required to access the websites of the
ICT2.1   identified places and if necessary search for more.
ICT2.2   Individually they should produce a database of key information about each
ICT2.3   location – place, address, telephone contact, resources available, costs of
PS2.1   faciilities and accessibility.
Each student will be required to set up a file for work experience, referenced and saved on the system for future use.
PS2.1   In groups, students to identify what they hope to achieve during work
WO2.1   experience and begin to think about how they will record their experiences.
Students will be required to set up a work experience diary on the computer
Each template and the front cover must contain the following information:
- centre number
- centre name
ICT2.1   - student's name
ICT2.2   - student's number
- specification code and title
- unit code and title.

Task 2   **Initial investigation**

C2.1   Refresh the work from the previous session. Students to access saved files
N2.3   and begin to explore placement opportunities in more detail. Using a route
WO2.2   finder internet function they should locate, print and save a map of those
N2.3   places located nearest to their place of residence. This information should
WO2.2   be used to perform a number of calculations in terms of distance, travel
PS2.1   opportunities and likely costs.
A work sheet will be provided requiring the students to complete a number of calculations.
This task involves individual work, work with partners, and work with the rest of the class.

Task 3   **Experience preparation**

Students receive information about their placement attachment.
Encourage students to think about questions they need to ask on the
C2.2   first visit.
N2.1   How will they travel to the place, what will the weekly costs be, what other
N2.3   costs will be incurred?
ICT2.1   Students in groups prepare a list of initial questions for their first
ICT2.2   placement visit.
WO2.1   Individually they will word-process a letter of introduction to take with them
WO2.2   on their first visit.
WO2.3   Confirm the time for the initial visit and/or arrange for the students to
C2.2   make their first contact with the intended placement organisation.
ICT2.1   Students to be prepared for health and safety issues and area of risk
ICT2.2   identified and explored. Show health and safety video.

Task 4   **Placement experience**

C2.3   Students will be required to keep a daily diary while on placement to record
PS2.1   what they have achieved, when and where. They will be encouraged to
PS2.2   identify learning experiences and evaluate the benefits to them of a period
PS2.3   of work experience. Any problems they encounter should be recorded and
C2.3   examples given to show how they dealt with their concerns.

Task 5   **Negotiating the most from the placement**

C2.1
C2.2   In groups, students identify targets to identify what they hope to achieve
N2.1   from work experience.
WO2.2   Student to set up an electronic diary or blog to record their experiences
ICT2.2   against the target identified above.
C2.1b   A number worksheet will be given to the students asking them to calculate
C2.2   likely take-home pay after deductions, to deduct living costs and travel and
N2.2   itemise how they will spend any left over money.

Task 6   **Events management**

C2.1   As a group plan a 'thank you' event for those who have helped you in your
C2.1   work experience. Calculate the costs of providing light refreshments, the
ICT2.2   venue and other expenditure.
PS2.1   Design the invitations, draw up a guest list and plan the event.
C2.1a   Ensure that your diary or electronic blog material is available for public
C2.1b   view, plan the event and evaluate the outcome.
ICT2.2

8

▶

Task 6	Events management
C2.1	In Task 7, students write a thank you letter.
C2.3	
ICT2.3	Discuss the requirements and purpose of the letter and what it should
PS2.3	include.
C2.1	Students produce their word-processed letter and final report on their experiences.
C2.3	
ICT2.3	

Suggested timescale

For this assignment, 150 hours of which half is spent in a work placement situation.

A template for the extended scheme of work can be downloaded from the companion website (Web 17)

Task 8.2

Review the scheme of work in Example 8.2. Can you identify ways in which further evidence towards achievement of the key skills might easily be incorporated into the plan? Design a scheme of work in your subject area to last ten weeks that provides the same detail as that set out above.

The personalisation agenda

You will need to ensure in your planning that you meet the needs of all learners by providing opportunities to stretch the most able and support those most in need.

The rest of this chapter explores individual needs, with specific focus on those requiring extension and stretch and those who need additional support. It is important, however, to remember that all learners have support needs of some sort or another.

Stretching able learners

A number of strategies might be adopted to support the able and gifted learner. Table 8.2 suggests some tactics to consider in your lesson planning which should focus your attention on reaching and stretching the most able.

Table 8.2 Ways to extend learner thinking and develop higher skills

Tactic	Examples
Withhold judgement	Respond in a non-evaluative fashion: 'Mary thinks . . .', thus inviting a further response or clarification: 'What do others think?'
Invite the contributor to elaborate	'Can you say more?'
Cure alternative responses	'There is no right answer' 'What are the alternatives?' 'Who's got a different point of view?'
Challenge the suggestion	'Tell me why'
Contribute your own thoughts or experience	'I remember when' 'I think that'
Use thinking-pairing and sharing	Allow thinking time Discuss with a partner, then in a group Pair so they can discuss (possibly in their own first language for mixed language groups)
Allow rehearsal of responses	Test out the answer in your head and try to think of another further response Try your answer out on your partner
Invite group responses	'Would anyone like to ask Ahmid a question about that?'
Use thinking aloud	Model rhetorical questions: 'I don't quite understand. Tell me more'
Ask learner to invite a response	'Ali, will you ask someone else what they think?'
Don't ask for a show of hands	Expect everyone to respond

8

Portfolio task 8.1

Observe another practitioner using questioning and extension skills. Evaluate the outcome. Test out some of the strategies in your own teaching and evaluate the outcome. Have your questioning skills improved as a result of this exercise? What has been the outcome? Try out three questioning of techniques. Consider the age, ability, subject and appropriate use of the technique with each group of learners. Critically evaluate the outcome. (500 words)

The strategies listed in Table 8.3 will encourage your learners to be more involved in questioning.

Table 8.3 **Strategies to involve learners in questioning**

Activity	Details
Topic questions	In groups, devise questions to ask of another group on a given topic
Reading/study review questions	As a revision exercise, ask individuals to set three questions for the group to answer, providing brief model answers
Hot seating	Learners take turns to choose to be a character from literature, history, sociology, psychology, politics. The group prepares questions to ask of them
Question game	Learners choose an object, person or place; others have 20 questions to find out what it is. Only yes or no answers are allowed. Only three direct questions permitted. Set up in groups of six (two choose, four ask). Have some starter ideas ready to set the game going
Question and answer	Learners devise questions to fit a given answer (person, place, thing, or poem, famous saying, piece of literature)
Any questions?	Learners write a question (empirical, conceptual or value related). Each question is then given to an 'expert' partner to answer
Interview	Decide on someone to interview (imaginary visitor, MP, TV character). Learners devise, share and evaluate the best interview questions
Questions on the environment	Prepare pictures of environmental damage, weather change, etc. to promote questioning
Questions on a specific topic, e.g. citizenship issues (homelessness)	Devise, write and display questions to stimulate thinking and discussion about objects, pictures or texts in our classroom. Record the questions posed
Keep a questions box, board or book	Collect any interesting or puzzling questions to stimulate thinking and discussion. Create a place to write, store or display questions to stimulate thinking and discussion about objects, pictures or texts in your learning environment. Record the questions posed. Some learners may wish to take the questions home, or swap questions with another group of learners
Meta-cognitive questions to assess learning	Display some meta-cognitive questions to encourage learners to assess and reflect on their own learning, such as: What have I learned? What have I found hard? What do I need to learn next. What would help me to do better? Discuss these in a plenary session
Introduce artefacts that may be new to the learner	Examine artefacts (e.g. range of cooking implements from different cultures). Give time for learners to explore them and ask questions about them. In language classes for ESOL, encourage participants to bring an artefact to discuss

Web references to support extension activities

www.nrich.maths.co.uk   maths-solving problems

www.murderousmaths.co.uk

www.channel4.com/learning

www.sciencemuseum.org.uk   excellent extension activities in a range of
appropriate curriculum areas

Task 8.3

Consider:

- How are your teaching strategies developing higher-order thinking?
- How can you use questioning to extend the thinking and challenge all participants?
- Which skills provide appropriate opportunities for independent learning and extension?
- How can you motivate learners to be more creative?

Supporting those with additional needs

Learners will experience different needs at various times on their learning journey. There are some groups of learners who have been given priority attention by the LSS. They are identified below:

- Parents
- Adults receiving benefits
- Low-skilled workers, public sector employees
- People living in disadvantaged communities
- Prisoners and those on probation
- Other groups at risk of exclusion, for example, homeless, refugees.

Any of these people may also be:

- People with disabilities and ill health
- People with learning difficulties, including dyslexia
- Older people
- People who do not speak English as their first language.

8

Portfolio task 8.2

Produce three case study exemplars of three different learners (each one to cover one of the three key learning barriers of language acquisition, literacy and numeracy). In each case study address the following issues:

- Personal factors affecting the acquisition and development of language, literacy and number skills.
- The impact of limited acquisition in the skill area on the individual's ability to participate in society.

Identifying need and providing support

Skills for Life is the national strategy for improving adult literacy and numeracy in England. The government invested £1.6 billion between April 2003 and March 2006 with the target of helping 1.5 million adults improve their skills by 2007. The Skills for Life Strategy Unit (formerly the Adult Basic Skills Strategy Unit) within the DfES is responsible for the strategy's implementation and is overseen by a Cabinet committee across all the relevant government departments. The Skills for Life strategy includes new national standards for adult literacy, numeracy and language learning, a National Curriculum within each major strand, new entry-level qualifications and national tests.

In order to support the aims of Skills for Life, more focus has been given to the training of teachers who can support this initiative. Chapter 12 shows how additional strands of study may be incorporated into teacher training to increase the supply of qualified teachers of basic skills. You may also wish to become a qualified teacher of basic skills as part of your programme of continung professional development.

Linked to Skills for Life are some specific programmes designed to improve adult literacy levels among those most at risk:

- The *Step into Learning* programme trains staff in the early years and childcare workforce to help them identify parents and carers with literacy, language or numeracy skills needs and encourage them to improve these skills to the benefit of both parent and child.

- The *Link Up* project recruited volunteers to help support adults with their language, literacy and numeracy skills in twenty-one of the most deprived communities in England. The project was funded by the Adult Basic Skills Strategy Unit (now the Skills for Life Strategy Unit) and the Active Community Unit, and delivered by the Basic Skills Agency.

- The *PLUS Programme for literacy and numeracy* is the Youth Justice Board's literacy and numeracy strategy for young people in the youth justice system.

- *Skills for Families* is a joint initiative of the DfES and the Learning and Skills Council, delivered by the Basic Skills Agency, which aims to further develop effective strategic approaches around family literacy, language and numeracy.

- *Move On* is a national project aimed at helping adults pass the national tests in literacy and numeracy. Move On aims to reach higher-level learners, who often may not think of themselves as needing help. It gives them an opportunity to brush up their skills, gain a national qualification and move on.

For more information on Skills for Life and the Strategy Unit visit www.dfes.gov.uk/readwriteplus. For the framework for understanding dyslexia, visit www.dfes.gov.uk/readwriteplus/understandingdyslexia, and for the Basic Skills Agency, visit www.basic-skills.org.uk.

Portfolio task 8.3

Explore the provision available in your institution to support those with basic skill needs. Consider the following:

- How is this provision advertised?
- Is there a special department supporting these learners?
- Are courses free to all applicants?
- Are the learners made welcome and encouraged to participate?
- Do they receive one-to-one support for their needs?

In addition:

- Do you know what to do if you have a learner in your classroom or workshop who would benefit from extra support?
- Who would you contact?
- How would you encourage learner participation? (See Chapter 10 for a discussion about the induction of new learners and the assessment of their skills.)

Produce a brief guide to the support services available to your learners.

The safe learner

Chapter 2 introduced the concept of the safe learner in respect of your responsibilities. You also need to consider how you can encourage your learners through the curriculum you deliver, to be aware of their safety and gain an understanding of health and safety legislation. This topic is often part of the taught curriculum in a specific vocational area. It is important that in all areas of the curriculum your learners develop a set of safe behaviours so that they can play an active part in the many learning experiences available to them. Health and safety awareness should be the starting point for all learners when they join an educational environment. For those engaged in work-based learning in Modern Apprenticeship schemes, for example, a staged approach is recommended:

Stage 1: Pre-work experience briefing

Stage 2: Workplace induction

Stage 3: Early supervised practice

Stage 4: Safe learning at work – assessment of understanding

Stage 5: Lifelong commitment to health and safety learning.
(www.eastberkshirecollege.ac.uk)

The standards unit resources, discussed in Chapter 7, contain numerous activities associated with raising awareness of health and safety issues. For example the resources for teaching construction contain a CD-Rom on safety signs (with a click-and-drag game); a card activity using common words and their definitions; cards with common abbreviations to be matched to their definitions; preventing accidents cards; quizzes on working with electrical power; a safety quiz; an activity entitled 'being safe at work'; a video to alert learners to accidents; a fire activity; and an activity to do with noise pollution. Although designed for the construction world, some of these activities can be used in other curriculum areas. In general, you will be able to adapt subject-specific material from the different areas to meet the needs of your learners. Issues of health and safety have legislative backing and should not be ignored. You have a responsibility to ensure the safety of your learner and instil in them the need to be conscious of their own safety and that of others at all times.

Figure 8.1 extends Figure 7.1 to include even more components that influence the LSS curriculum.

Figure 8.1 **Factors influencing LSS curriculum design – extended**

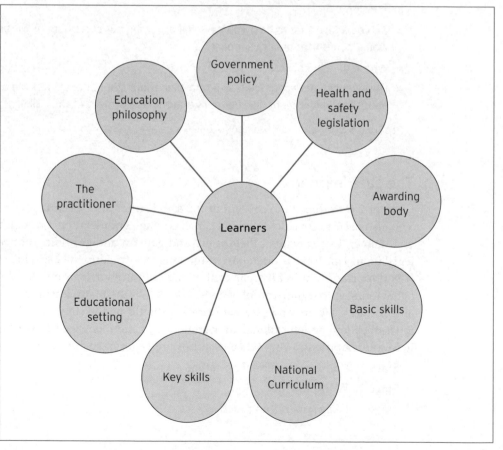

Personalising learning

Research carried out by Demos, a well-respected and independent think tank, has identified good practice in the sector in creating a personalised learning journey for individuals by helping them to articulate, work towards and achieve their goals (Demos, 2006). In the research Demos identified examples where 'person-centredness' was part of the ethos of the whole organisation.

> Putting the person at the heart characterised learners' every interaction with the institution. It was the mission of everyone from principal, to receptionist to caterer.

Working in the sector requires a commitment to adopt this ethos, where every learner matters and every learner's learning needs should, if possible, be accommodated.

Technology tip

There is a great deal of advice available on a number of websites about how best to integrate key skills into the curriculum. Entering the term 'key skills' into a search engine will produce some interesting resources, including not only the official key skills site but also resources produced by practitioners like yourself. Remember to evaluate the site, however, before using the resource (see Chapter 6 for a website evaluation tool).

Portfolio task 8.4

Select two courses which fall within your curriculum area and determine how key skills *and* basic skills are incorporated? Describe the course-awarding body, level, expected delivery time, etc., for the two courses. What is the likely learner profile for the group? Compare the two courses in terms of curriculum models and ideologies. How are these reflected in the choice of content? (1,000 words)

8

Key tips to take from this chapter

- The current focus on key skills, basic literacy and numeracy skills requires you to consider the needs of individual learners when planning your teaching.
- You will meet learners with different needs. All will require your support and help, whatever their ability, to reach their full potential.
- Institutions provide additional support and guidance for learners who may have specific needs. It is your responsibility to be aware of the support available.

Assessment grid mapped to the standards

This chapter introduces the knowledge requirements for the areas in scope set out at the start of the chapter. Completion of the set tasks will provide you with evidence that can be matched to the standards, as set out below, for gaining awards in the learning and skills sector.

Task	Summary activity	Level 3 award	Trainer award (level 4/5) leading to QTLS	E-learning standards CPD awards
Task 8.1	Personal evaluation against key skill criteria	DP 3.1 DP 2.5	DP 3.1–3.2 DP 2.1	
Task 8.2	Design a scheme of work to incorporate opportunities to demonstrate key skills	Not essential	BP 3.3 BP 3.4 BP 4.2	E 1 (potentially)
Task 8.3	Teaching strategies for extension and creativity	CP 1.2 CP 1.4 CP 2.2	CP 2.1 DP 2.1 DP 2.3	
Portfolio task 8.1	Observation of questioning technique, personal practice and critique	DK 3.1 DK 3.2	DK 3.1 DK 3.2 DP 3.1 DP 3.2	B 1 (potentially) B2 (potentially) B3 (potentially)
Portfolio task 8.2	Produce three case studies exemplifying the impact of basic skill deficiencies in three different learners	Not essential	EP 1.1 AK 4.2	F 1 (potentially)
Portfolio task 8.3	Planning to support those with additional needs	DP 2.3-DP 2.5	DP 1.3 BP 3.2	E 1 (potentially) E 2 (potentially)
Portfolio task 8.4	Evaluate two courses in terms of curriculum ideology and their suitability for incorporating key skill and basic skill requirements	Not essential	BK 5.2 BP 5.2	D 1 (potentially)

9 Assessment
Using feedback as a tool for learning and progression

Learning outcomes

By the end of this chapter you will:

- have explored the role of assessment in teaching and learning
- know the distinction between assessment for learning (formative assessment) and assessment of learning (summative), and understand the characteristics of each form
- have identified how, when and why diagnostic assessment may be used
- be aware of the range of assessment evidence
- appreciate the importance of good feedback and record keeping.

Areas in scope in this chapter in relation to the standards for teachers, tutors and trainers working in the sector are AS 7, DS 3, ES 1, ES 2, ES 3, ES 4, ES 5.

This chapter has been designed with two purposes in mind: first, to explain different types of assessment, and second, to encourage you to consider different types of assessment practice from the perspective of both the student and the lecturer.

A rigorous and quality-driven approach to assessment is central to effective teaching and learning. Those engaged in theorising about assessment believe that good assessment practice is at the heart of the student learning experience (Jenkins, 2000). The most important outcome for any student participating in a programme of study will be the opportunity to say they have achieved in the assessed task and gained credit for their work. In the current climate of accountability there can be serious implications for you as a student on a teacher training programme and as a qualified teacher/tutor/trainer if the word 'fail' appears too often on any mark sheet. Appropriately designed assessment is crucial to a quality assessment process and outcome. But do we give it enough attention?

The function of assessment

Assessments should be designed to provide evidence that the learner has benefited from the learning experience and now understands what the teacher/tutor/trainer set out to teach, in other words the learner has achieved the intended learning outcomes. Unfortunately, the testing of achievement can often feel artificial and contrived. It is also the case that some assessment practices are far from fair, accurate or reliable. Good assessment practice should increase student motivation, provide useful support for improvement and give an objective judgement of the work under discussion. There are assessment methods that favour different types of learners; others, if inappropriately selected, may not accurately measure what has been achieved. This needs to be considered when planning any course of work.

Presenting evidence for assessment

Within your course and in your own teaching/tutoring/training you will meet a variety of different ways in which evidence is presented for assessment purposes. Basically, there are five broad presentational categories:

- oral evidence (for example, debates)
- written evidence (for example, essays)
- graphic evidence (for example, sketches)
- observable practice (for example, a session plan)
- products (for example, models).

Task 9.1

Consider what other types of evidence might be collected within each of the five categories above. Compare your ideas with those of people teaching subjects different from your own. Are there similarities and differences? Discuss some of the problems and issues that might arise in using the sources you have identified as assessment evidence. Compare your answers with those given in the table below.

Method	Strengths	Weaknesses
Oral work	Develops the skills you will need in the workplace There is the potential for instant feedback It is seen as a powerful learning experience	The focus on presentation can lead to superficial coverage of the content If feedback is not immediate it may have minimal impact on learning
Written literature and/or research-based assessment	Valuable where students need to show developed intellectual skills such as research, application of theory, evaluation, etc. Provides an effective way of focusing student study in particular areas of interest	The assessment can dominate the learning and those who 'know how' may be advantaged Students can cheat easily. This is particularly problematic with the increased use of the internet

Method	Strengths	Weaknesses
Written assessment within a set time limit	Develops your skills to work under pressure Addresses breadth and depth of learning Limits the time spent on assessment Appears to be fairer (more objective) than other methods	May encourage 'surface' learning Tests your ability to remember and pass exams, rather than the understanding of ideas and concepts Benefits those who can work under pressure
Graphic assessment	Allows those with artistic skills a chance to demonstrate their talent	Benefits those with graphics skills If the assessment is completed elsewhere it is difficult to confirm the identity of the author
Observation of practice	Allows demonstration of skills	Is useful when associated with a training period External dimensions may impact unfairly on the learner (resources, nature of the group involved, support from others)
Products	Provides an opportunity for creativity to be demonstrated and assessed	Learners may have access to different resources to the extent that some may become disadvantaged

9

What is assessment?

The definition quoted below was written some years ago and goes some way to describing assessment:

> Assessment in education is the process of gathering, interpreting, recording and using information about students' responses to an educational task. At one end of the dimension of formality, it involves the teacher reading a students' work or listening to what he or she has to say. At the other end of the dimension, the task may be a written, timed examination which is read and marked according to certain rules and regulations. Thus assessment encompasses responses to regular work as well as to specifically devised tasks.
>
> (British Educational Research Association, 1992)

The definition provides a broad view of assessment methods in terms of what teachers might do but fails to consider how the assessment decision may be used to inform the planning of further teaching or help to identify the needs of a specific learner. Definitions of assessment written today tend to focus far more on the purpose of the assessment as an identifier for appropriate developments towards the next stage of learning. Today, assessment is considered much more as an activity for the learner, as well as one providing information to the teacher.

When asked why we assess work, a group of trainees produced the mindmap shown in Figure 9.1. Mindmaps are useful tools to use in teaching/tutoring/training. They were developed by Tony Buzan (see Buzan and Buzan, 2000) whose mindmap tool can be accessed from the Buzan company website (www.mindmap.org). Mindmaps can be used for notetaking, to structure your thinking processes, to help you present your findings in a logical manner and to produce summaries for others.

Types of assessment and their purpose

Broadly speaking there are three types of assessment:

- *Diagnostic assessment* to identify your skills and abilities and to highlight areas which need support. This form of assessment is often used to assess ICT skills.

- *Formative assessment*, which checks on learning carried out during the course, such as a term test or assignment which may be graded but not necessarily count towards the final grade for the year.

- *Summative assessment* used as part of the final classification of achievement against set

Task 9.2

Consider how the assessment types given above might best be employed. Draw up a table for each assessment method using the headings provided below.

Type of assessment	Explanation	Function
Diagnostic assessment		
Formative assessment		
Summative assessment		

To give you an idea of what you might consider, an example answer is provided at the end of the book.

Figure 9.1 Assessment mindmap

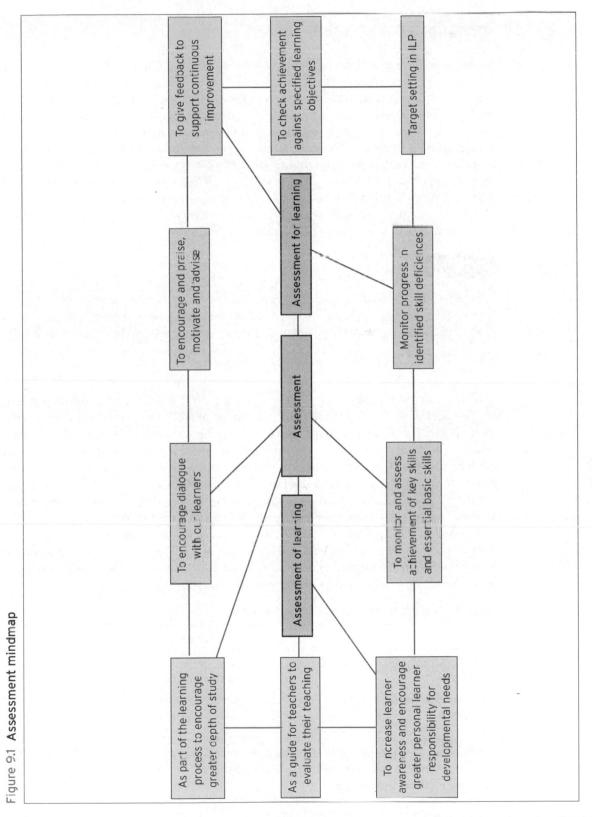

9

Designing assessment tasks

As part of a drive to maintain and improve the quality and fairness of assessment, while also assessing the achievement of more learners, teachers/tutors/trainers are increasingly exploring different ways in which to assess potential. These ways might include group presentations, an assessment of newspaper reports, the production of a reading list on a specified topic, or designing a website to include an evaluation of a process in terms of strengths and weaknesses. Students of A level law may be asked to take part in a mock court case (or moot), whereas those studying the sociology of religion may be required to visit and report on a variety of religious buildings. Students of the performance arts may demonstrate their practical skills, and complementary beauty students may run salons offering different therapies to external fee-paying clients. Those on work-based courses will be assessed, under supervision, on their competence in real work situations.

Task 9.3

Consider the curriculum specific to your subject specialism and design an innovative assessment task that would enable the student to demonstrate a range of skills. Discuss your thoughts with your coach/mentor or someone from a similar study background to your own.

Most vocational programmes currently offered in the LSS require participants to create a portfolio of evidence to illustrate the range of work they have completed during their course. If you are a student yourself, studying for a teaching qualification, then you too will be required to prepare a portfolio to illustrate your competence in certain predefined areas. Throughout this text there are suggestions for activities that you can complete and that may be used at a later date towards assessment for a qualification. Creating a portfolio of evidence provides a means of assessing CPD in a range of professional contexts. In your specific case, if working towards qualification as a teacher, it is expected that the portfolio of evidence will include lesson plans and evaluations that both you and those observing you will have completed. The evidence used to illustrate achievement can be varied. Table 9.1 illustrates how evidence can be presented when a portfolio is used as all or part of programme assessment.

Table 9.1 Assessment evidence for a portfolio

Task	Assessment evidence
Prepare a micro-lesson on a subject of your choice	Lesson plan Written evaluation from an observer
Evaluate the resources available on a set subject	A critical review of a number of texts, CD-roms, articles, etc.

You will see from the table that the assessment may be written, visual or take the form of a witness statement from a person observing the activity. Short written tests may also confirm knowledge.

Portfolio evidence as a means of gathering evidence to be assessed is common not only in teacher training courses: you will meet this assessment method on programmes leading to Advanced Vocational Qualifications (AVCs), National Vocational Qualifications (NVQs) and key skill awards. This is illustrated in Example 9.1, where a motor vehicle engineering student is required to prepare a workshop for the daily activity. It will be apparent to the reader that this task could be adapted to any vocational area such as complementary health, childcare, business, or sports and leisure studies.

Example 9.1 Assessment task for motor vehicle engineering

Task	Assessment evidence
Prepare a room for a practical session ensuring that all the equipment is of an acceptable standard	A photograph and/or a signed statement from a superior confirming that the resources were as required

During your training you will be assessed using a variety of different assessment methods. An example of the assessment methods or 'assessment mix' used on a training programme is given in Example 9.2.

Example 9.2 Assessment mix used on a training programme

Module	Module title	Assessment task
M 01614	Learning and Teaching in FE	Practical assessment
M 01615	ICT in Education	Design a website, and review a range of subject-specific ICT resources
M 01616	Initial Teaching Practice	Learning diary and reflective log plus two observation reports completed by a mentor
M 01617	Teaching Practice 2	Portfolio of evidence to include four observation reports completed by a mentor and reflective commentary from the learner
M 01618	Classroom Management	3,000 word assignment
M 01619	Teaching Practice 3	Portfolio of evidence to include four observation reports completed by a mentor and reflective commentary from the learner
M 01610	Curriculum Planning	Group presentation and report on a curricular change issue
M 01610	Support and Guidance in FE	Written presentation of three case exemplars to illustrate different support mechanisms in operation

9

The choice of assessment approaches needs to made with a number of considerations in mind, the most important being whether the assessment task fits the purpose and is an accurate measure of what needs to be assessed.

Task 9.4

Consider the methods of assessment employed in the programme in Example 9.2. Do you feel that the strategies employed are reasonable, balanced and fair? Be prepared to justify your answers.

Appropriateness of assessment task

Awarding bodies that confer a qualification have a responsibility to ensure that assessment decisions are fair and that some logical connection can be seen between what the student is expected to learn and how this is assessed. The content of a programme of study is commonly described as a learning outcome (see Chapter 3). Tables 9.2 and 9.3 (taken from a Certificate in Education programme) illustrate an appropriate assessment of the defined outcomes and an inappropriate one, respectively.

Table 9.2 **Example of an appropriate assessment task**

Learning outcome	Assessment task
Develop and create activities to support the delivery of key skills in an education environment	Prepare a set of teaching materials (to include a scheme of work and lesson plans for 10 weeks) for the delivery of key skills in a defined education setting

Table 9.3 **Example of an inappropriate assessment task**

Learning outcome	Assessment task
Develop and create activities to support the delivery of key skills in an educational environment	Produce a 3,000 word essay discussing the policy agenda on key skills

Using assessment criteria

There are many innovative methods used to assess learners, some of which have been introduced to reduce the burden of assessment on students as well as to reduce the marking requirements for busy staff (Rust, 2001). Whatever the assessment method employed, it is important that the learner is aware of what is expected. Many of the less used approaches to assessment need greater clarification than might at first be available. For example, an approach that includes an element of group presentation and peer assessment requires clear guidelines, including what to do if one group member does not engage fully in the process. Such clarity is necessary, for both the student and the lecturer managing the assessment, to ensure that equity is maintained.

Different types of assessment

When evaluating the appropriateness of different assessment methods it is useful to consider what it feels like to be a student engaged in the assessment activity. You will see below a number of assessment strategies explained in terms of how they impact on the student experience. In the interests of fairness and equity it is important that assessment is not only fit for purpose but also achievable within reasonable expectations of time, place and personal cost to those involved.

Group assessment

As part of the oral assessment approach, learners may be required to work with a group of peers studying on the same programme. Working in groups can be stimulating and fun. It may also be threatening and unrewarding. If you are not used to group work then you may feel that group assessments place you at a disadvantage.

The group presentation method has many advocates in that it helps to develop presentation skills, oral communication skills and teamworking. In teacher training programmes it mirrors many of the team activities required in the real work environment of teaching and course development. Often unappreciated by learners, it is an excellent tool to practise skills of diplomacy, motivation and collegiate working. However, there are problems associated with the approach.

Case study Nikki

As part of her teacher training programme Nikki was required to prepare a group micro-teaching session on the Incas of Peru. She chose close friends whom she thought would be reliable, to work with her. One of the group, however, did not attend the planning meetings, thus creating anxiety and extra work for the rest. The reluctant contributor took part eventually but the team felt that their group grade would have been higher had she participated throughout.

Although teachers/tutor/trainers may be prepared to support teams that, for one reason or another, are not working, learners find it difficult to work with reluctant participants. The group presentation, with a group mark awarded as part of the final award classification (summative assessment), can be very controversial, leading to some participants feeling bitter about the experience.

Case study Roy

As a mature learner, Roy, living on limited budget, travelled to college only on days when he had to attend lectures. He agreed to attend on a non-college day to prepare for a group. He arrived after his 15-mile trip to discover that two of the other students in the group, who lived on the campus, had forgotten about the meeting, one having arranged to go shopping for the day. Roy was still angry three days later when the whole class met for their timetabled session. He refused to work with the group again.

9

One institution, experiencing problems of the kind met by Roy and not wanting to lose the group assessment methodology, introduced a 'yellow and red card' system for groups to award to members following consultation with the lecturing staff. If the award of the yellow card resulted in increased contribution by the offending team member, then it was withdrawn. If the card had no impact then a red was awarded and the offending learner received a 10 per cent reduction in their assessment grade for the activity (Jenkins, 2000). This rather unusual practice provides an acceptable, non-threatening way for teams to record the non-contribution of members and avoids one of the main pitfalls of group assessments.

The problems associated with group assessment may lead you to avoid this method in your course planning. Table 9.4 highlights some of the possible advantages and disadvantages of the method. It is worthwhile considering strategies to overcome the possible problems associated with this method as the approach has much to recommend it.

Table 9.4 Advantages and disadvantages of group-based assessment

Advantages	Disadvantages
Encourages learning by doing Develops teamworking Supports skills in communication and negotiation Enables students to learn from one another Mirrors many work situations that require teamwork	The final grade is a group grade and this raises issues of equity concerning who has contributed and how Some students, unused to group work and/or presentations, may feel uncomfortable with the method

Peer- and self-assessment

Moves towards different assessment designs are not just the result of the current increases in learner numbers (DfES, 2002b); they have been introduced for sound educational reasons as well. Theorists are concerned to ensure that assessment is functional as a learning experience not just as a test of what can be remembered for a brief period of time (Race, 1999). The benefits of learning by doing are not to be underestimated, and being involved in assessing fellow students is a powerful way to implement this process. Educational research (Race, 1999) illustrates that learning improves when students are involved in what is referred to as peer assessment. This is another approach to assessment that requires careful management and clear guidelines if it is to be effective. As a practising lecturer, introducing students to degree-level study, I include during induction a group marking exercise of work completed in the previous year (with the permission of the students who produced it and all names removed). This exercise enables the participants to focus on how assessment is conducted in higher education institutions and is something that could be adopted on a variety of courses.

Some guiding questions are presented below to help lecturers manage peer assessment:

- How could this work be improved?
- What would you have done differently?
- Does the work meet the specified assessment criteria? (See the end of this chapter for a discussion of the importance of designing clear assessment criteria.)

The trainee teacher/tutor/trainer might also like to consider the role of self-assessment as a tool for learning. Self-assessment, in this text has been discussed under the guise of reflective practice in Chapter 5. There are ways in which self-assessment can be planned for in a variety of teaching contexts. Learners can be asked to comment on the strengths and weaknesses of a piece of work prior to submission, or asked to reflect on a front sheet attachment to their written assessment on what went well and not so well. It is worth asking students occasionally to grade their work against set criteria before submission. The prompts listed above can be employed here as well.

Traditional assessment methods

Extended essays and written exams are still used as a means of assessing understanding and, in the case of the unseen paper, mainly memory. Staff setting such tests of student comprehension need to be clear about what they want to test and why they have adopted this method of assessment. Careful framing of questions is crucial: the learner must not be confused by ambiguously or badly worded questions.

Computer-assisted assessment

It is worth mentioning here the use of optical mark readers (OMRs) which rapidly allocate grades to the work of students by scanning marks or crosses made on a piece of paper. It is a useful tool for providing quick analysis of student learning. It is often used for those teaching large groups and forms a tool used in programme evaluation if you want to elicit information about your learners' views on the quality of the teaching they have received. The tool is only as good as the questions it asks, and the data, although useful for course evaluation purposes, give you a picture but not the whole story. For assessment purposes OMRs can read student answers to short knowledge-testing activities and provide data very quickly. They can also show which questions were answered well and which not so well. This information is useful to the reflective teacher/practitioner, who can ask what and why certain components of the course have not been understood. The data become a tool for the teacher to ask if low student understanding has anything to do with the way they delivered the course.

Computer-designed tests completed online and marked and graded electronically can produce similar data to those provided by an OMR. The test itself can be supervised or not, formative or summative and can provide numerical test scores and/or detailed feedback to support learning. Currently, those training to be teachers in the compulsory schooling sector have to complete, online, a number of tests to confirm their skills in literacy, numeracy and ICT before they can be designated qualified teacher status. The feedback that participants receive following the tests is instantaneous and it is possible to re-register immediately to sit a retest if you fail to achieve the desired skill level in any of the tests. Those seeking to gain QTLS will be required to demonstrate ability in these skills in a similar way (DfES, 2004a: 24).

There is more to the use of computer-assisted assessment (CAA) than the assessment of key skills. CAA may be used for short-answer questions, crossword puzzles, image identification, case studies, labelling activities and in many more interesting ways. Example 9.3 is taken from a computerised module of learning used on a psychology course to test student understanding of data. Learners are required to answer a number of questions based on the material provided.

9

Example 9.3 Computer-assisted assessment task 1

Question No 4. **10 marks** **Test-type Practice**

A biologist was interested in the weights of male and female Lappin rabbits. She weighed a random sample of both and calculated the following sample statistics. Test a suitable hypothesis.

	Sample size	Sample mean	Sample variance
Male	7	7.4	1.02
Female	11	8.3	1.22

Calculate the pooled variance, the test statistic and the tabulated statistic at 5% and 1%.

Choose the option which best describes the conclusion:
○ There is no evidence to reject the null hypothesis. Accept the null hypothesis.
○ There is some evidence to reject the null hypothesis and accept the alternative.
○ There is strong evidence to reject the null hypothesis and accept the alternative.
○ None of these.
Next Question ○

Source: Wolverhampton University CAA project http://www.caa.wolverhampton.ac.uk/demo.

Another example, this one from the Oxford Brookes University website, is provided in Example 9.4.

Example 9.4 Computer-assisted assessment task 2

Question 5
A web design company is developing a website for a health foods shop, and has created a prototype site. One of the company's employees explores the prototype site carefully and systematically, looking specifically at responses to any actions that potential customers might perform. For example, in response to a customer clicking on a button to put an item into a shopping basket, there should then appear a clear indication to the customer that an item has been put into the shopping basket, and which item it is. Any responses that are missing, or inadequate, are noted and reported to the design team.

Please indicate whether the statements below are True, False or that you Don't Know.

	True	False	Don't Know
a) The evaluation by the employee was *formative*.	☐	☐	☐
b) The evaluation involved GOMS *analysis*.	☐	☐	☐
c) This situation describes an example of *heuristic evaluation*.	☐	☐	☐

Scoring for Question 5:
Correct answer = +2, Incorrect answer = -2, Don't Know = 0

Source: http://cms.brookes.ac.uk/staff/SharonCurtis/publications/hciq.pdf.

There are a number of advantages and disadvantages with the computer-facilitated approach to assessment. These are set out in Table 9.5.

Table 9.5 Advantages and disadvantages of computer-assisted assessment

Advantages	Disadvantages
Your progress can be monitored through frequent use You can be given detailed and specific feedback very quickly	There is no real check as to who is completing the test You have to be a confident user of ICT The tests may be superficial

Portfolio task 9.1

Discuss your experiences of CAA. What potential does it have in your subject area? What are the likely opportunities and difficulties with implementation?

Design an electronic assessment for a group of learners in your subject area. You can use whichever technologies you wish: video, computer, CD-rom, electronic whiteboard. Be as adventurous as you are able. Evaluate the outcome.

External testing

To gain QTLS you will be required to demonstrate your skills in literacy, numeracy and ICT by completing an external assessment. External testing is an essential component of many of the vocational qulaifications studied by students in the further education sector. Skills test in the areas of literacy, numeracy and ICT are part of the key skills award (a qualification introduced with Curriculum 2000, as an A level equivalent, accepted by some but not all universities in credit towards university access). To deal with the large number of students taking part in these tests there is a growing trend in the use of electronic assessment devices. External tests for vocational courses tend to use a multiple choice approach. The students you meet during your training and employ-ment will need help in how to succeed with this assessment method. Example 9.5 is taken from a key skills Number paper. Further exemplar test materials can be accessed at http://ferl.becta.org.uk or www.qca.org.uk.

9

Example 9.5 External assessment test for key skills in numeracy

Question 3

A store cafeteria is providing packed lunches for 54 employees. This will include 2 filled rolls each. The requests are for 50 ham, 20 cheese and 38 tuna rolls.

The table below shows how many rolls a given ingredient will fill.

Ingredients	No. of filled rolls	Amount of ingredient needed for rolls requested
1 kg butter	200	
1 kg tomatoes	25	
1 kg ham	20	
1kg cheese	30	
1 tin tuna	10	
1 lettuce	15	

Complete the end column of the table to show the ingredients needed to meet the requests. Give your results to the appropriate levels of accuracy.

Source: http://ferl.becta.org.uk

When first produced, the tests received a great deal of criticism from practising lecturers in the sector. Test questions are, however, quite difficult to write.

Portfolio task 9.2

Consider a number of ways in which you might use assessment in your subject area. Design two different assessment tools, try them out with a group of learners and evaluate the outcome. It would be interesting to include the learners' perceptions of each method as well, so design an evaluation tool to elicit their opinion. Reflect on their views and compare them with your own.

Keep records of the assessment results for your learners and use them in your next ILP interview to discuss the learners' perceptions of the assessment process.

 Helping students prepare for assessment

There are a number of key rules that apply to assessment. If you follow these then you will be some way towards helping your students to succeed.

The list below offers some guidelines; it is not exhaustive.

- Are you clear about what you want your learners to do?
- Will the majority of the learners be able to do the task set, i.e., is it reasonable?
- What will they have to do to succeed?
- By what criteria will you judge their success?
- Have you made the success criteria explicit, i.e., do the learners know what they have to do to succeed?
- Have you piloted the question/test to make sure it is clear?
- Do the learners know how, when, where and why they will be tested?
- Are the learners clear about the outcome if they do poorly in the assessment tasks?

Be prepared to rethink your assessment processes and to rewrite questions and tasks a number of times. Remember, the results of assessment are not just a reflection on your learners, they are a reflection on you as well.

Understanding assessment criteria

For mature learners (perhaps more so than for the younger learner), gaining a recognised qualification is a lifelong ambition. Such participants may fund their own study and work hard to fit study into a demanding home life. For them, a low grade can be very demoralising. The problem often lies in their failure to understand what is expected of them. This can apply to all learners, no matter what age or study level. Reading and understanding the basis upon which work is to be judged – the *assessment criteria* – is crucial to your success as a student.

Research carried out by Rust et al. (2003) showed that student achievement improved when time was spent explaining the assessment criteria to the group. The research used an assessment grid similar to that in Table 9.6 and to those often used by universities and colleges to award marks for student work. The contents of the grid will change from course to course and from one institution to another but the main themes and criteria will remain the same. Criterion-based assessment (as this is named) is very much part of the good practice followed in universities and colleges today.

The example in Table 9.6 is taken from the first stage of a degree programme leading to a Certificate in Classroom Support for Learning Support Assistants. The grid sets out, as recommended by the Quality Assurance Agency for further and higher education (www.qaa.ac.uk) the basis upon which decisions are made about the quality and grade of student work, 'institutions should publish, and implement consistently, clear criteria for the marking and grading of assessments'. The grid illustrates very clearly what has to be achieved by the learner.

9

Table 9.6 Assessment criteria: level 1

Grade	Knowledge and understanding	Synthesis evaluation	Reading research	Communication presentation
A 70% and above	Comprehensive knowledge and perceptive interpretation of the course content	Well-developed and balanced analysis encompassing a range of viewpoints	Thorough grounding in appropriate and wide-ranging information sources appropriate to the topic	Written fluently and effectively; good structure, grammatically correct, all sources referenced correctly
B+ 60-69%	Good knowledge and sound understanding of all pertinent aspects of relevant course content	**Clear evidence of analysis and critical evaluation. Theory and developing practice is linked and a comparison of alternative viewpoints is evident**	**Good use of a range of background information and reading**	Clear structure, work is well presented with few grammatical errors. **Most sources are referenced correctly**
B 50-59%	All major aspects of relevant course content are described and explained satisfactorily	Evidence of analysis of most material relevant to the topic together with an evaluative conclusion. Is aware of the link between theory and practice and alternative viewpoints are acknowledged	Adequate reading/ background information which is incorporated appropriately	Adequate structure and presentation, stilted writing style, some significant grammatical/stylistic errors. Some sources referenced correctly
C 40-49%	Some, but not all, major aspects of relevant course content are described but any explanations are incomplete	Minimal analysis and evaluative comment which is not always supported by the material presented	Evidence of some background information/reading	Weak structure and presentation, stilted writing style, some significant grammatical/stylistic errors. Approved referencing system not used
Fail 40%	Course content misunderstood/ misrepresented	Descriptive with little or no attempt at analysis or evaluation	No evidence that work is based on reading/ background information	Poor structure leading to incoherent work, evidence of major grammatical/stylistic errors. No list of references provided

Areas of the grid have been highlighted in bold type to emphasise the importance of certain criteria that are the focus of academic study. The grid clearly shows that accurate referencing and the use of theory to support your debate are key issues in this level of work. Careful reading of the highlighted parts will show you how important the reading of research is in the achievement of this qualification. So also is the use of theory, best used here to make an informed comment on what the theorists are suggesting. Failure to meet the criteria will always result in a lower grade. It is recommended you also notice how important the accurate use of referencing is in the allocation of a high grade. The criteria illustrated here are similar to those used on many teacher training courses. It would be easy to produce an assessment grid for a less academic course, which contains expectations about basic spelling, computation, sentence construction and key subject-specific knowledge. The exemplars below illustrate how understanding assessment criteria can help learners to succeed.

Case study Sonia

Sonia was concerned that she was not gaining any marks above a C in her assessed coursework. During a discussion with her tutor it became apparent that she did not understand how to use the referencing system. Although she was reading the work of many others theorists she was not mentioning their work for fear of using the reference system incorrectly. After spending some time integrating the work of theorists into her work, and using the appropriate referencing system, she improved her grades.

Task 9.5

Review the feedback you have received on a programme of study. Do the comments made relate to your achievement (or otherwise) of the learning outcomes for the course?

Giving feedback

There are ways in which feedback can and should be given to the learner. For the less confident student, fear of a poor mark and the resultant public humiliation can lead to poor behaviour and even withdrawal from the externally tested parts of the curriculum. Research has shown that some further education students would rather not participate in an activity at all than be seen to have failed (Browne, 2002b). Think for a moment about how you would feel receiving a disappointing result. Would you like this made public on a noticeboard or read out to your classmates? It is important to consider the dignity of your learners and to give them the opportunity to make their results public or otherwise.

Adjustments for learners with a disability

Since 2002, all educational institutions have had a responsibility to make 'reasonable adjustments' for learners who have a diagnosed learning difficulty or disability and, where appropriate, to make adjustments to the way they are assessed. Examples of amended assessment methods can be found on the Plymouth University website (http://www.plymouth.ac.uk). By way of illustration, one of the examples relates to Phil who has cerebral palsy and is finding it difficult to carry out the research for an extended piece of work. Instead of being required to submit an independent study of 4,000 words, Phil produced a multimedia CD rom as part of an interactive website design. Another case is that of George who has dyslexia. George received one-to-one support covering all aspects of literacy and extra time in his written examinations. An amendment to the set task, from a written assignment of 3,000 words to a viva voce (verbal or discussion-based assessment), enabled Farukh, who had eyesight problems, to gain her qualification.

9

Task 9.6

Brainstorm the range of possible alternative forms of assessment that might help students with a disability to succeed in a vocational subject. Consider how you could adjust an typical assessment activity to accommodate the needs of a disabled learner (Chapter 10 might be useful here). You may wish to use a mindmap for this task.

Using feedback to help learners to improve

With assessed coursework comes the additional advantage of detailed feedback to help you improve. As a lecturer you will realise that there is nothing more annoying than to spend hours marking work, providing detailed feedback on how to improve, only to find some months later that the student has not collected the work from the course administrator. In an article entitled 'The MacDonaldisation of higher education', Hayes and Wynyard (2002) argue that educational change has led to a production line mentality, resulting in students engaging in the product without benefiting from the aftercare service. As a teacher/tutor/trainer you will become frustrated when your attempts to help students do not appear to make any difference. It is worth considering the use of verbal group feedback prior to returning marked class work. This needs thoughtful planning and should take up only a short introductory part of the teaching session. Another strategy, which ensures that learners do read what you have written in your feedback, is to require learners to keep a developmental log where they record points raised. Yet another is to ask them, as part of the next piece of work you set, to comment on previous feedback and illustrate how they have responded. It is through this dialogue that a focus on continuous improvement can be fostered.

In all assessment the feedback given should be linked directly to the criteria by which the learning is being assessed (see Example 9.6). Many institutions use a standardised feedback sheet designed to provide the student with a comment that is directly linked to the assessment criteria.

Example 9.6 Linking feedback to the assessment criteria

Learning outcome	Assessment task	Feedback
Learners should be able to use a recognised research method to carry out a small-scale investigation and evaluate their findings in relation to the social aspects of childhood	Interview someone with a childhood different from your own. Discuss your findings in relation to the themes studied in this module	You have carried out an interesting interview with your elderly relative and explored the differences between her experiences and your own. Greater discussion in relation to the sociological themes of age, generation and culture would have given you a higher grade. Evidence of wider reading and research is also required

As can be seen from the example, the teacher/tutor/trainer has linked her assessment feedback to the declared learning outcomes for the course and made reference to the need for more reading and research.

Task 9.7

Look back to the assessment grid in Table 9.6 and decide the grade category awarded for this work. (See the end of this book for the answer and an explanation of how the grade was awarded.)

Assessing learning

Learners can be encouraged to assess their own progress in their learning journey. Individual learning plans are intended to encourage this process. Aids to self-assessment might include specially designed progress checks, regular performance reviews, and the use of 'buddy pairs' to practise text recall, compare notes and set questions for each other. There are a number of strategies that can be employed to encourage students to become effective learners, to help them reflect on tasks after completion and to look for ways to improve performance in the future.

Portfolio task 9.3

Select a group of learners with whom you have been working. Take one topic you are required to teach and produce a list of available resources (books, CD-roms, websites). Produce a topic guide for the learners, a reference list of the resources and some worksheets containing a student activity. Set tasks for your learners to complete. Having given time for individuals or groups to work through the tasks, produce answer sheets for the learners to check their progress. Introduce a tracking sheet to monitor individual progress and agree further points for action. Evaluate the outcome in terms of encouraging independence in your learners, the opportunity for learners to work at their own pace, and the time this approach created for you to focus on the assessment of all learners in your group. Present the materials and your evaluation in your portfolio.

9

Record keeping

Within the compulsory school sector it is a statutory requirement for teachers to keep accurate records of assessment decisions and to provide reports for parents on an annual basis. Those teaching 14–16-year-old pupils are required by law to keep such records. There are a number of other reasons, however, for keeping accurate records. Accurately kept records of each assessment task can tell a variety of stories. An assessment mark sheet can illustrate individual student strengths and weaknesses, help detect a decline in student commitment and provide material for personal reflection for the lecturer. Where the usually successful learner, or indeed a large group, receives a low mark, then the facilitator may need to think about how the topic was delivered or whether the assessment strategy was appropriate. Where one group of students succeeds in a task and another fails, the reflective practitioner will begin to consider what the strategy was that has enabled this group to succeed where other strategies have failed. Teaching/tutoring/training is not a science and theorists will never be able to create categorical rules about how to teach, but the lecturer who is prepared to reflect on their skill and use available data to inform that process, will be the one who receives the most personal satisfaction from their work.

Technology tip

Keeping a record of learner achievement on the organisational intranet or on a disk can save a great deal of time should any monitoring of individual learner progress be required. Some institutions will have data tracking facilities for you to record your learners' progress. These are very useful for course leaders and tutors, enabling them to tell at a glance what progress their learners are making in a range of areas. If you are required to produce ongoing reports on your learners it is advisable to keep an electronic copy of the reports so that you have not only a quick reference guide but you also have a template for updating the content without having to reproduce the basic information (name, class group, course and so on).

Key tips to take from this chapter

- Assessment tasks should be designed to measure what students have been asked to learn. Learning outcomes and assessment tasks need careful planning and alignment.
- Understanding the assessment criteria is crucial to success.
- Whatever the assessment method employed it is important that the student is aware of what is expected.
- Assessment strategies should be clearly explained and fairly employed. The student is entitled to be told what has gone well and what is not considered acceptable. Lecturers should provide detailed feedback, linked to clear objective criteria.
- Education institutions have a legal duty to anticipate the needs of students with a diagnosed learning difficulty or disability and, where appropriate, to make adjustments to the way assessments are organised.
- Assessment results provide interesting reading for students and lecturers. Data gathered from assessments can be used in a variety of ways.

Assessment grid mapped to the standards

This chapter introduces the knowledge requirements for the areas in scope set out at the start of this chapter. Completion of the set tasks will provide you with evidence that can be matched to the standards, as set out below, for gaining awards in the learning and skills sector.

Task	Summary activity	Level 3 award	Trainer award (level 4) leading to QTLS (level 5)	E-learning standards CPD awards
Task 9.1	Source of assessment evidence	EK 1.1 EP 1.1 DP 4.1 DP 4.2	EK 1.1 EP 1.1 DP 4.1 DP 4.2	
Task 9.2	Types of assessment	EK 1.2 EK 1.3 EP 1.2 EK 1.3	EK 1.2 EP 1.3 EP 1.2 EP 1.3	
Task 9.3	Assessment tasks	EK 1.2 EK 1.3	EK 1.2 EK 1.3	C 1 (potentially) C 2 (potentially)
Task 9.4	Evaluating assessment activities	EP 1.3	EP 1.3	
Task 9.5	Reviewing and responding to feedback	EK 1.3 EK 1.1	EK 1.3 EK 1.1	
Task 9.6	Providing alternative assessment strategies	AP 2vi EP 1.2 EP 3.2	AP 2 EP 1.2 EP 3.2	C*1 (potentially) C*3 (potentially)
Task 9.7	Grading learner work	Not essential	EP 5.1	
Portfolio task 9.1	Design an assessment using computer aids	Not essential	EP 2.3 EP 1.3	F 1 F 2 F 3 (potentially)
Portfolio task 9.2	Encourage learners to work independently and to assess their own progress and developmental needs	EK 5.1 EK 5.3 EK 3.1 EK 3.2	EK 5.1 EK 5.3 EK 3.1 EK 3.2 EP 1.2 EP 5.3 AP 5.1	E 1 (potentially) E 2 (potentially)
Portfolio task 9.3	Resources for assessing learners	Not essential	EP 3.1 EP 5.2 EK 5.1 EK 5.2	

9

Helping learners to achieve their full potential

Providing effective support to learners

Learning outcomes

By the end of this chapter you will:

- appreciate the importance of information, advice and guidance
- have explored the components of an effective induction programme
- have designed an effective tutorial programme
- have considered the role of initial assessment in your curriculum area
- have planned to meet individual needs
- have explored the use of individual learning plans for your learners
- have set targets to support learner retention, success and achievement.

Areas in scope in this chapter in relation to the standards for teachers, tutors and trainers working in the sector are AS 1, AS 2, AS 7, CS 2, CS 3 , CS 4, ES 3, ES 4, ES 5, ES 6, FS 1, FS 2, FS 3, FS 4.

A key feature of what it means to be professional in the learning and skills sector involves working with learners to provide them with every opportunity to succeed. This is a responsibility that starts at the first point of contact and extends beyond the time when the learner exits the course.

This chapter explores the nature of support to which all learners are entitled, discusses some specific requirements for those with additional needs, and explores the role of the teacher/tutor/trainer in enabling learners to achieve the most from their programme of study.

Information, advice and guidance

Government documents have increasingly reflected high levels of concern about the qualification levels of those leaving schools and colleges in the twenty-first century. Research shows that around half of all students who take their GCSEs get fewer than five at grade C or above. The number of students failing to achieve level 2 skills in numeracy, literacy and ICT (level 2 @ 19) is considered too high (DfES, 2005f). One of the strategies already discussed, aimed at increasing participation, is that of personalisation (see Chapter 8). In terms of policy, government ministers want to pursue three new strategic thrusts:

- Personal coaching and advocacy support for individuals, targeting those who need more support.
- Building the capacity of individual learners so that they are expert and effective independent learners.
- Creating 'collective learner voice' to shape provision and improve the quality of experience and success for all learners.

These aims require greater focus on the individual learner to ensure they are able to follow the pathways that best suit their needs, skills and abilities. They also require expert tutoring on the part of the lecturer appointed to oversee the individual learner's personal development needs. The availability and accessibility of information, advice and guidance (IAG) plays a crucial role in learner retention and achievement. It is proposed that IAG will be provided by trained and qualified support advisors. However, every teacher, tutor and trainer will need to be familiar with information about additional support specific to issues such as financial help, counselling advice, nursery provision and all other available services. It may not be your role to know all the answers but you should be able to direct your learners to appropriate sources of information in your workplace.

City College Manchester has a website dedicated to ESOL learners and their IAG needs (www.ccm.ac.uk/esol). The site contains the following materials that are accessible if you search the website:

- IAG resources for use by staff (in a variety of languages and formats – large print, etc.)
- Attendance monitoring form
- Attendance reminder form
- Attendance reminder letter
- Withdrawal letter
- Progress test form
- Progress test results tracker
- New enrolment information cards (in seventeen different languages)
- Student folder contents checklist
- Student programme checklist
- Summary CV form
- Placement information for ESOL learners
- Monitoring progress form.

The site also contains resources for induction and other useful materials.

10

Induction

Well-planned induction programmes are a key to successful and content students (Martinez, 1999). Time invested in planning a worthwhile experience now will save time and effort later. The sooner you get to know your tutees the better: so plan well for your first meeting. Below is a list of what learners expect to achieve, or what they have at the back of their minds, at the point they first become involved with a course:

- Name of the tutor
- Programme timetable and room number
- Work commitment in terms of time
- Likely costs
- The names and some personal details of those I will be learning with
- Arrangements for food and other comfort requirements
- Have I chosen the right course for me? Will it be interesting? What will it lead too? What career opportunities might it provide?
- Where is the library? How do I access the computers?
- Are there any rules I need to know about?
- Is this venture really going to be worthwhile or should I get a job instead?

Icebreakers

There are a number of tried and tested icebreaker activities to use with a new group of learners to help remove their anxieties. One such activity might be to ask them to write a list of questions to which they need answers today. These lists can then be shared in triads and fed back to form a whole-class question list. Other ideas involve individuals drawing six pictures which give personal information and sharing these with peers who are required to guess what they represent. Interviewing the person next to you and summarising the information to feed back to the group, is another. One slightly risky method requires you and the group to invent an unusual name for yourself based on the first initial of your name, so that Mat Brown becomes Muscle Body or Lucy Fletcher becomes Lovely Flower (individuals should chose their own names and only share them if they feel willing and are prepared to be known as such for ever more).

Task 10.1

Produce a list of effective icebreakers you have taken part in, have seen used with learners or have used yourself. Make notes about age appropriateness and preparation requirements. Design a table, as shown below, which supports preparation for a variety of Icebreakers.

Icebreaker	Resources	Age appropriateness
Share three pieces of information with two peers: two truths and a lie. Peers to guess which is the lie	Group of more than three learners	Adult only
Build a bridge from newspaper and elastic bands	Newspapers, elastic bands, real space, more than five learners	Adult only
Charades (perhaps for a media and film group)	Prompt names of a book, film or play	14 plus
'What's my line?' role play game	Possible occupation lists	14 plus

Some of the above will be more effective than others in helping learners to find out something about each other. This needs to be considered when planning the Induction, particularly in respect of how important it is for learners to work cooperatively at a very early stage in the progamme.

Tutorial schemes

As a trainee teacher you will be expected to take part in tutorial sessions. These sessions vary in time but can be up to 60 minutes long. Example 10.1 is a recommended scheme of work for a tutorial programme devised by a further education college.

Example 10.1 Scheme of work for student induction

Week	Element	Activities	Resources	Comments
Week 1	Student induction	To prepare the learners for their course by introducing them to their peers and the college by environment by: • instigating an Icebreaker • giving out course handbooks, timetables, etc. • visiting Student Services and Learning Resources (perhaps set a brief discovery quiz for learners to find out what is available) Ensure learners are enrolled on the course and have computer access Discuss the college code of conduct, bullying policy, etc.	Student lists Icebreaker Copy of timetables Course handbooks Map of campus Quiz Computer log in arranged Copy of policies	

Week	Element	Activities	Resources	Comments
Week 1	Student records	Complete the records as far a possible. Introduce the idea behind an ILP	Blank copy of ILP	
	Course structure and assessment	Issue course and student timetable (keep your copy in a file) Hand out assessment schedule Detail how performance will be judged Ensure key dates are noted and understood	Timetables Assessment schedule	
	Check entry qualifications	Qualifications checked on entry, record kept, development needs (resits) identified	Students to supply original qualification certificates	
	Plagiarism and cheating	Ensure students are aware of the institutional policy	Exemplars of what constitutes cheating and copy of policy	

In the weeks following, a number of other tasks will have to be completed such as:

- the election of course representatives to ensure you hear the student voice, either formally in agreed course committees or informally as required
- completion of individual learning plans (see later in this chapter)
- registration for examinations and with awarding bodies
- key skill registrations where appropriate
- study skills advice (time management, research techniques, notetaking, learning styles analysis)
- health and safety issues
- one-to-one feedback.

At some time it will be essential with young full-time learners to address citizenship issues such as:

- valuing diversity and respecting others
- drugs awareness and sex education
- work experience
- money management
- avoiding plagiarism and cheating.

There may well be other sessions that need planning or become necessary depending on group needs:

- planning visits or debriefing after visits
- pre-visit health and safety information and risk assessments
- debriefing after assignments, work experience, performances, exhibitions
- dealing with bereavement, conflict, responding to external events
- discussions around group behaviours as these emerge and change.

In addition to what has been good practice in terms of induction for learners, government policy in *Every Child Matters* (DfES, 2005e) and *Youth Matters: Next Steps* (DfES, 2006) has provided a focus on the expansion of issues that could be addressed in the induction curriculum. *Every Child Matters* identifies four themes:

- being healthy, staying safe
- enjoying and achieving
- making a positive contribution
- economic well-being.

Youth Matters describes the personalisation of services, with greater choice for young people. There will be funds allocated to support this in terms of a Youth Opportunity Fund and the Youth Capital Fund. It will be your role to ensure that your learners have access to the support that is available. It will be the responsibilty of local authorities to ensure that young people have access to a wide range of positive activities, and secure places to go and things to do. Your role will be to direct your learners to the appropriate sources of advice and guidance.

Task 10.2

Think back to a programme you engaged in once. Which of the elements listed above were most needed? Are there any other initial needs or questions? Design a scheme of work for an induction period specific to the needs of a groups of learners you may be working with. Find out what types of information, advice and guidance are available for learners who may need extra support.

10

Initial assessment

It is a requirement that all learners in full-time education, and those enrolled on National Employer Training Programmes (NETPs) and registered with an education provider, receive an initial assessment of their functional skills in the subjects of numeracy, literacy and ICT. A number of bespoke tools are available to aid the completion of the assessment. What is used will vary from organisation to organisation. The tool used should be able to identify the individual's operational level in the key areas and highlight whether they will need additional support to be able to continue with their programme of study (see Chapter 8 for a description of the levels).

The outcome of the assessment will need to be discussed with the individual and appropriate support will need to be provided. All learners have an entitlement to free additional support in the functional skill areas should the assessment show that they are operating below the standard needed for the course of study they are deemed able to follow. Sometimes additional support will be provided for whole-class groups; on other occasions it will be offered on a one-to-one basis. The assessments usually inform the decisions about which level of key skills an individual learner may work towards. Again, information about key skills and levels is available in Chapter 8. The information from the initial assessment, together with reports from previous institutions, academic results achieved, and the record made at the point the learner applied for the course and was interviewed all form part of the individual learning plan.

Use of individual learning plans

Individual learning plans are used by teachers, personal tutors and students to plan the students' programmes and to track their progress. In the college environment, and one would hope elsewhere in the sector, it is considered appropriate that all learners should be entitled to a negotiated and agreed programme of study. This should be planned with their personal tutor or teacher taking their individual needs into account. Progress in relation to the ILP needs to be reviewed regularly. These are the principles associated with personalised learning and they are at the heart of the IAG strategies designed to keep learners motivated and on course.

The standard 'model' ILP combines a number of functions: planning the student's programme, keeping a student record, and monitoring the student's progress. For most students, the ILP brings together various documents that are used at different stages of their programme. The ILP provides the tutor with a guide to what work needs to be covered with the student, and a structured record in which to log outcomes and actions. The scale of the ILP will vary according to the duration and nature of the programme, for example whether full-time, part-time over 180 hours, short part-time, or work-based.

The ILP model used in your college or institution will probably be available on the corporate intranet. The format may be varied according to the needs of the individual programme. However, the overall structure and the ground covered usually remain consistent.

ILPs normally cover:

Examples of ILPs for your learners can be downloaded from the companion website (Web 18)

- Student record (full-time/part-time)
- Key skills planning and tracking
- Initial assessment and study support planning
- Proformas for student self-assessment and one-to-one tutorial interviews
- Tutor log to record discussions and reviews against the set targets.

As a course tutor you will be required to keep up-to-date information on the learning needs of all your tutees. Part of this information should be a record of the initial diagnostic test results. During each ILP interview the progress of your tutees should be checked to make sure they are persevering with the achievement of the basic and key skills required to complete their qualification and progress to the next stage. Examples 10.2 and 10.3 are tutors' records of a group of learners who have literacy and numeracy needs. These learners are the group identified as level2@19, targeted in the 14–19 reform agenda (DfES, 2005c) as typical underachievers who need support to develop and progress in the core skills. The three columns headed 'initial assessment', 'diagnostic result' and 'free writing score' identify the three diagnostic tools used in the institution. (All names are fictitious.)

Example 10.2 Tutor record for a group with literacy needs

Name	First name	DoB	Student no.	Date	Subject	GCSE English	Initial assess-ment	Diagnostic result	Free writing score	Identified needs	Current status	Type of support
Allen	Ewan	15/10/89	007630	6/9/07	Literacy	F	L1	L1/76	11	Lit	OK	
Brown	Chris	22/06/90	007549	6/9/07	Literacy	D	L1	L1/62	12	Lit	Withdrawn	
Brown	Mat	18/04/90	007657	6/9/07	Literacy	E	L1	L1/87	13	Lit	Support	In class
Crisps	Simon	20/04/90	007541	6/9/07	Literacy	D	L1	L2/60	14	OK		
Fletcher	Lucy	3/12/89	007292	15/9/07	Literacy	D	L1	L1/65	12	Lit	Support	In class
Taylor	Emma	12/4/90	007293	6/9/07	Literacy	F	E3	E3/71	5	Dyslexia assessment 13/10/07	Additional support	1-to-1
Elan	Narjit	21/3/90	007294	6/9/07	Literacy	D	L1	L1/50	10	Needs dyslexia assessment	Support	In class
Moore	Mary	3/10/89	007300	6/9/07	Literacy	D	L1	L1/45	absent			
Radshaw	Carl	20/10/89	007298	6/9/07	Literacy					ESOL		

Source: Adapted from a form used in a college of further education.

Example 10.3 Tutor record for a group with numeracy needs

Name	First name	DoB	Student no.	Date	Subject	GCSE Maths	Initial assess-ment	Diagnostic result	Free writing score	Identified needs	Current status	Type of support
Allen	Ewan	15/10/89	007630	6/9/07	Numeracy	D	L1	L1/76	11		OK	
Brown	Chris	22/06/90	007549	6/9/07	Numeracy	D	L1	L1/62	12		Withdrawn	
Brown	Mat	18/04/90	007657	6/9/07	Numeracy	E	L1	L1/87	13	Hearing loss	Support	In class
Crisps	Simon	20/04/90	007541	6/9/07	Numeracy	F	E3	E3/72	10			
Fletcher	Lucy	3/12/89	007292	15/9/07	Numeracy	U	Absent	Absent	10			
Taylor	Emma	12/4/90	007293	6/9/07	Numeracy	U	E3	E3/20	10	Additional support		1-to-1
Elan	Narjit	21/3/90	007294	6/9/07	Numeracy	D	L1	L1/79	13		Support	In class
Moore	Mary	3/10/89	007300	6/9/07	Numeracy	E	L1	L1/87	13		Support	In class
Radshaw	Carl	20/10/89	007298	6/9/07	Numeracy					ESOL	Support	

Source: Adapted from a form used in a college of further education.

Task 10.3

Review Examples 10.2 and 10.3. What does this information tell you about this group of learners? If you were the tutor for this particular group, what actions would you instigate as a result of receiving this information. Some suggestions are offered at the end of the book.

Planning to meet individual needs

Once you are in possession of information about your learners it is your responsibility to use this information effectively to help learners stay on track. Whether a trainee teacher on placement or one already employed and developing your skills 'on the job', any experience you can get working directly with individual learners is worthwhile. Once you take on full responsibilities as a course tutor you will be required to keep a record of your learners' progress and to monitor this throughout their time with you. Regular meetings with learners need to be planned into any tutorial scheme of work.

At these meetings you will keep a record of the learners' progress and development, highlighting any areas or problems and acknowledging their successes. This is also point at which you set targets and motivate learners to reach the end of their training. Such targets will be recorded on an individual learning plan (ILP) similar to the one you may be completing as part of the your record of the tasks set in this book. The ILP should belong to the learner but, as a course tutor, you should keep an independent record.

Simple steps to success

The stages involved in supporting learners to succeed may be illustrated as steps. The idea in Figure 10.1 was developed by a group of trainees on an initial teacher training programme. Have they left anything out?

Statutory responsibility

There are a number of areas of activity involved in teaching in the learning and skill sector which bring with them statutory responsibilities. These were discussed in Chapter 8, when health and safety requirements were addressed, and in Chapter 9, when attention was drawn to the disability legislation. This latter is addressed again below.

The Disability Discrimination Act 1995 was amended in 2005 to place a duty on all public sector authorities to promote disability equality in all aspects of their work. This duty will have a significant impact on the way in which all public services, further education colleges, prisons, and adult and community education centres are run, and on improving the lives of disabled people.

Figure 10.1 **Stages in supporting learners to succeed**

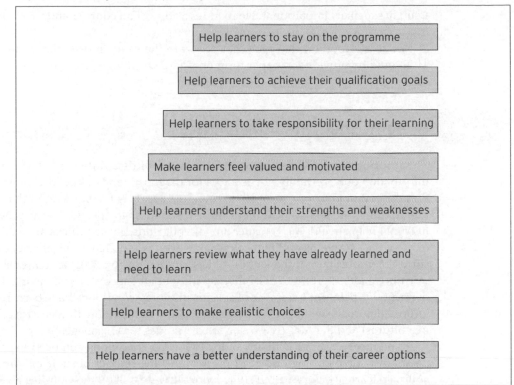

Learners with specific needs

In supporting all learners you have a legal responsibility to make 'reasonable adjustments' to counter the substantial disadvantage faced by disabled students for reasons relating to their disability (www.senda.gov.uk). The term 'reasonable adjustment' may be difficult to define, and below you will see a number of examples illustrating the use of the terminology:

Example 1

Ayesha has dyslexia. She needs her exam test to be printed on blue paper and extra time to complete any in class tests. Is this reasonable?

Yes, these requirements can be arranged easily. In the case of external examination papers, letters requesting special requirements need to be sent to the awarding body well in advance of the date of examination.

Example 2

Joe uses a walking stick and finds climbing stairs exhausting. He requires the venue for his course to be changed to one on the ground floor or near to a lift. Is this reasonable?

Yes, it is appropriate for a room change to be made to accommodate Joe's specific requirements.

10

Example 3

Liam has a visual impairment. He requires a copy of all course handouts to be produced in a larger font size. Is this reasonable?

Yes, it is important that Liam has access to the same information as other learners. This could be provided in paper form or as large print in electronic copy on a computer screen.

Specific identified disabilities

The information provided below on a number of disabilities is offered as summary information only, certainly not as a tool for diagnosis, and is intended only as guidance to help you in your role as teacher/tutor/trainer. It is recommended that you do not attempt any personal allocation of these disabilities to specific learners but seek professional help should you consider any of your undiagnosed tutees are exhibiting some or all of the symptoms outlined below. However, you do have a legal responsibility and, since the publication of the Disability Discrimination Act 2005, all reasonable attempts must be made to promote disability equality in all aspects of your work. The detailed descriptions below of a number of specific disabling conditions have been adapted from information made available by the Learning and Skills Council (www.lsc.gov.uk/learningcultures) and the AoC (www.aoc.co.uk – guides for FE colleges).

If you meet a learner with any of the following conditions you need to consider their needs in your planning and read more about the impact of their condition on their ability to learn, by carrying out some follow-up research on the websites given below.

Attention deficit/hyperactivity disorder

Attention deficit/hyperactivity disorder (AD/HD) is a neurobehavioural disorder that affects an estimated 3–7 per cent of the population. It can present itself in three forms:

- Inattentive: the learner is unable to focus or stay focused on a task or activity.
- Hyperactive or impulsive: the learner is highly active and often acts without thinking.
- Combined: the learner demonstrates inattentive, impulsive and very active behaviour.

Learners presenting with AD/HD will have difficulty paying close attention to details. They will appear not to be listening when spoken to directly and be easily distracted. The organisation and completion of tasks will be problematical, as will normal conversation. The sufferer will interrupt conversation, will fidget continuously and avoid tasks that require any mental effort.

Helping learners with AD/HD

Provide preferential seating, for example seat the learner near the front of the room and away from distractions if such a location helps them to maintain better focus. Stand near the learner when giving instructions and put the daily routine in writing where it is easy to see. Where possible, include opportunities for physical activity in the lesson plan.

In terms of teaching and learning:

- Allow tape recording of lectures
- Provide a written outline of material covered

- Use overhead and other visual media with oral instruction
- Incorporate technology, for example computers, calculators, videos
- Accept typed or word-processed assignments.

  In terms of assessment:

- Provide practice questions
- Give open-book tests
- Vary the format
- Read questions and allow the learner to respond to questions orally
- Encourage the use of technology, for example calculator, word-processor
- Provide extra time to complete tests
- Give parts of a test in more than one sitting
- Allow the opportunity to take tests in another room or at another time of day
- Give more short quizzes and fewer long tests
- Mark correct answers rather than mistakes.

  When grading work consider the following:

- Base grades on modified standards, for example ILP objectives, effort, amount of improvement, content, rather than spelling
- Specify the skills the learner has mastered rather than give a letter grade.

Remember, however, not to give false hope in terms of examination success if this not achievable, ensuring always that learners are enrolled on appropriate courses.

Useful websites

www.hi2u.org   For people with hidden impairments
www.adhd.com   Help and support for people and families coping with AD/HD
www.adders.org   Promoting awareness of AD/HD and providing information

Dyslexia

The word 'dyslexia' means 'difficulty with words', and the condition affects skills that are needed for learning one or more of reading, writing, spelling and numeracy. The underlying cause of dyslexia is largely unknown but it is thought to be due to a problem in processing auditory or visual information, or both. It is possibly genetic, but it is not related to intelligence.

Potential strengths:

- Creative, practical – art, design, drama, architecture, computing, sport or dance
- Innovative, imaginative and skilful with hands
- Care and empathy, often excellent communication skills
- Good visual spatial skills – can see the 'whole picture'
- Often highly intelligent – Einstein was dyslexic.

Symptoms and difficulties that might affect ability to study:

- A discrepancy between academic achievement and real-life performance in practical problem solving and verbal skills
- Finds notetaking difficult – frequently misreads or miscopies
- Difficulties expressing ideas on paper, planning work and producing essays in a logical, sequential order
- Omission or misuse of punctuation
- Word recall difficulties when speaking
- Poor short-term memory
- Difficulty with organising self, work or time
- Easily distracted and loses concentration
- Experiences left/right confusion
- Often loses place when reading; may demonstrate a lack of speed and misread words
- May have difficulty sorting and selecting materials, understanding and retaining what was read and decoding unfamiliar words. May mispronounce multi-syllabic words
- Experiences persistent, erratic or severe problems with spelling – may spell as the word sounds, omit, add or reverse letters, may misrepresent sounds.

Learners may find their dyslexia causes unforeseen problems, which are difficult to cope with. They may be anxious, tense or even angry, particularly if they had a negative experience at school. They may have lost their self-confidence, doubt their abilities and feel insecure.

Helping learners with dyslexia

- Be supportive, show understanding and give encouragement where appropriate
- Focus on achievement
- Do not regard dyslexic people as a problem
- Concentrate on their strengths and do not force them to do things against their will
- Be explicit in expectations
- Be clear in your own communications
- Never accuse a dyslexic learner of being careless or lazy, they usually work twice as hard to rewrite work many times before they hand it in. Also, having proofread their work several times, they still may not see their errors
- Find out the students' learning style – observe and listen to them, then try to implement what they tell you
- Use multi-sensory teaching methods and aids – present material visually (pictures), orally (spoken) and kinaesthetically (practically)
- Use plenty of diagrams, mindmaps or pictures but do not present too much information on one sheet
- Print text on pale coloured paper – experiment with colours

- Use a larger print size and vary typefaces
- Ensure writing is clear on the board and on worksheets – write key words on overhead transparencies and give a separate handout with explanations
- Make verbal instructions brief and clear
- Vary pace and activities, for example include discussions and presentations in small groups
- Set up experimental and hands-on activities which allow students to bring existing skills to the present task
- Give an overview of the topic and provide a framework by stating the aims of the class and expected outcome. Make explicit links from particular examples to the general overall idea
- Give out work in manageable amounts
- Break up tasks into small steps and allow time for reinforcement and 'over-learning' of information
- Give specific instructions for assignments. Explain titles and purpose explicitly. Check understanding
- Encourage alternative ways of recording work – tapes, diagrams, flowcharts, computers
- Allow assignment to be word-processed
- Help with checking text, if asked
- When marking learner's work, try to separate the marking of spelling, punctuation, written expression and vocabulary from the content so that the learner's knowledge and understanding are acknowledged and valued
- The learner may require extra time to complete their assignment especially if there is a significant amount of research and reading involved
- Build in lots of feedback to monitor understanding and encourage students to ask questions
- Encourage the learner to attend study support for an educational assessment, where appropriate.

Useful addresses

SKILL (National Bureau for Students with Disabilities)
www.skill.org.uk

British Dyslexia Association
98 London Road
Reading
Berkshire
RG1 5AY
Tel: 01189 668271
www.bda-dyslexia.org.uk

10

Dyslexia Institute
Park House
Wick Road
Egham
Surrey
TW20 0HH
Tel: 01784 222300
www.dyslexia-inst.org.uk

Task 10.4

In the light of the advice given above, consider how you would now design your lessons to address the needs of learners with either dyslexia or AD/HD. Design two new lessons plans, one to accommodate a learner with dyslexia, one to accommodate someone with AD/HD.

It is likely that your learners will exhibit a number of other disabilities, some more obvious than others. You will meet some with mobility problems, those with reduced sight and/or hearing that will impact on their ability to learn. The legislation on disability requires you to consider the needs of all learners.

For more information on sight impairment contact:

Royal National Institute of the Blind
105 Judd Street
London
WC1H 8NE
Tel: 020 7388 1266
www.rnib.org.uk

Action for Blind People
14–16 Verney Road
London
SE16 3DZ
Tel: 020 7635 4800
www.afbp.org

The Guide Dogs for the Blind Association
Burghfield Common
Reading
Berkshire
RG7 3YG
Tel: 0118 983 5555
www.guidedogs.org.uk

For those with hearing impairment contact:

Royal National Institute for the Deaf
19–23 Featherstone Street
London
EC1Y 8SL
Tel: 020 7296 8000
www.rnid.org.uk

British Deaf Association
1–3 Worship Street
London
EC2A 2AB
Tel: 020 7588 3520
www.britishdeafassociation.org.uk

Hearing Concern
7–11 Armstrong Road
London
W3 7LJ
Tel: 0845 0744600
www.hearingconcern.org.uk

Task 10.5

Using the websites identified above consider how you will adapt your teaching to address the needs of learners with sight and or hearing impairment. Complete the table to show what adaptations you will make.

Disability	Needs	Adaptations
Impaired sight		
Impaired hearing		

Now consider learners with mobility problems.

Disability	Needs	Adaptations
Mobility problems		

To help you complete this task you may wish to access the website of City College Manchester (www.ccm.ac.uk) which has a signed video clip explaining how additional support may be accessed for the deaf and/or hard of hearing.

Information on disabilities can be downloaded from the companion website (Web 19)

10

171

The autistic spectrum

What is autism?

Autism is a complex lifelong developmental disorder that affects the way a person communicates and relates to people and the world they inhabit. The provision of specialised education and structured support helps individuals to maximise skills and achieve their full potential. Whether you teach a learner with autism or not, you are likely to meet such learners in educational institutions such as further education colleges. In fact it is one of the strengths of the LSS that such learners are embraced and fully integrated into everyday activities and places (college restaurants, libraries)

First identified in 1943, autism is still a relatively unknown disability. Figures provided by the National Autistic Society (1997) show that the current prevalence of autistic spectrum disorders in the UK is estimated as 91 in 10,000. This figure includes people at the higher functioning end of the spectrum who may not need specialist services and support, for example people with Asperger syndrome, but who will benefit from early recognition and sympathetic understanding.

What is Asperger syndrome?

Asperger syndrome is a form of autism. However, people with Asperger syndrome usually have fewer problems with language and learning than those with autism. They are usually able to speak fluently, though their words can sometimes sound formal or stilted, and they can be, and often are, of average or above-average intelligence.

How to recognise autism and Asperger syndrome

Features of autism and Asperger syndrome can vary widely from one individual to another. There is no single feature that, if missing, indicates whether autism or Asperger syndrome is present (for example ability to make eye contact). It is the overall pattern that is relevant.

The degree to which people with autistic spectrum disorders are affected varies, but all experience difficulties to a greater or lesser extent with some of the following:

- Social interaction
- Difficulties with social relationships
- Poor social timing
- Lack of social empathy
- Rejection of normal body contact
- Lack of eye contact
- Inappropriate use of gaze
- Difficulty judging social distance/personal space – individuals may talk 'at' people instead of 'to' them.

Communication – language impairment across all modes of communication:

- Speech, intonation, gesture, facial expression and other body language (non-verbal communication)
- Literal interpretation – often unable to understand jokes, metaphors, sarcasm and irony.

- Imagination – the 'triad of impairments':
- Rigidity and inflexibility of thought process
- Resistance to change
- Special interests and love of routines

In addition, individuals may have poor physical and visual motor skills. Clumsiness is often seen as a characteristic of Asperger syndrome.

Symptoms and difficulties in relation to study

Learners with autism/Asperger syndrome may:

- Be unable to transfer, or experience difficulty in transferring, skills learned in one environment to another
- Have orientation problems and need support or guidance at break or in unstructured periods of time
- Find environments too stimulating
- Experience stress and anxiety which may be heightened by:
  - room or class size
  - proximity of other students
  - changes in routine
- Experience sensory overload from sound, light, smell, touch or taste
- Experience difficulties in sequencing, prioritising and meeting deadlines, staying on task and maintaining attention on other tasks.

Current research states that people on the autistic spectrum tend towards a visual learning style and may experience difficulties with abstract thinking and problem solving.

The pedantic style of speech and impressive vocabulary may give the false impression of understanding as these learners may have a tendency to learn by rote and not by reason.

Helping learners with autistic spectrum disorders

It is your responsibility to be aware of the issues surrounding the specific and individual needs of learners with autistic spectrum disorders and endeavour to:

- Modify teaching styles and resources
- Differentiate and use visual aids and objects of reference
- Check and adapt the learning environment to avoid sensory overload
- Provide clear guidelines for study time, homework, free time, equipment and materials
- Work in a calm, clear and structured manner
- Be aware of calm, safe places that are accessible within the college for time out if required
- Try to limit sensory stimuli that may distract or distress the learner
- Reinforce and check understanding

10

- Check and modify own language, avoiding using sarcasm, jokes and facial expressions/body language to communicate
- Be specific when giving feedback. Praise the activity; for example, instead of saying, 'that was good', say 'that was good listening'
- Encourage active listening skills
- Encourage and demonstrate appropriate social and communication skills
- Encourage awareness of self and others and check learner's understanding of the perspective/intention of others' actions and speech
- Advise learners of any changes as soon as possible
- Be aware of exam concessions.

Useful address

The National Autistic Society
393 City Road
London
EC1V 1NG
Tel: 020 7833 2299
Helpline: 0845 070 4004
Education advice line and tribunal support scheme: 0845 070 4002
www.nas.org.uk

Task 10.6

Learning checklist

Read the notes made by your learners at the end of one of your sessions

- Do they make sense? Have you explained things clearly enough?
- Check font size, line spacing and layout of any handouts you produce or PowerPoint presentations you use. Are they accessible to all learners?
- Have you used appropriate examples to illustrate your points? Are they appropriate to the learning group (for example, references to Guy Fawkes might be difficult for a group of ESOL learners)?
- Have you used a range of teaching strategies suitable to meet the needs of all types of learners?

Technology tip

Technology can be a great enabler for learners with specific difficulties. Explore as many ways as possible for supporting your learners using technological support. Specific examples are provided in the text.

Portfolio task 10.1

Consider a group of learners you work with. Identify the special needs that two learners in this group may have. Produce two anonymous case studies describing the learners, their needs and how you address their needs when working with the individuals concerned and the group in which they are located. Each case study should be detailed and run to about 500 words.

Using evaluation to inform practice

Most organisations will use formal systems of evaluation to ensure learner satisfaction. These may take the form of questionnaires, course evaluation proforma or requests for confidential feedback in the form of an issues log. The versatility and quality of the evaluation tool will determine how useful the feedback might be. It is important for your professional development that you review feedback from your learners and use this to improve and adapt your practice.

As well as organisationally devised evaluation, it is useful to carry out your own investigation to ascertain what was appreciated by your learners and what did not receive such a good response. You may wish to design a questionnaire, run a focus group or ask your learners to give you some informal feedback.

Portfolio task 10.2

Carry out a piece of small-scale action research by gathering data from a group of learners with whom you work. Critically evaluate the information and identify one area where you may need to adopt a different approach. Adjust your teaching/tutoring/training and evaluate learner response. Produce a report on the outcome of this activity. (200 words)

10

Setting targets

It will be part of your role as a teacher/tutor/trainer to set targets for all your learners. Target setting usually takes place during regular one-to-one discussions recorded in the ILP. Targets need to inspire and motivate. They need to be SMART: specific, measurable, achievable, realistic and time-bound (see Chapter 3). They need to take into account individual learners' abilities and disabilities as well as their social and cultural circumstances. It would not be SMART, for example, to set a Muslim student on a sports studies programme a target requiring dramatically increased physical exercise during Ramadan (a time when strict Muslims fast from sunrise to sunset).

Task 10.7

Design a SMART target for a learner who has not been attending additional literacy and numeracy support. Make sure the target is SMART. What do you want to happen, when and how often? How will you review the target and what evidence will you accept to show that the target has been achieved? This may involve making an appointment with the learner (once they have agreed) to meet staff who are trained to provide additional learning support services. Make sure you are clear about all the support services available to your learners. Finally, the learner has to agree to the target and commit to its achievement.

Reflect on the strategy you have used. Write a report on the issues involved in supporting learners with literacy and numeracy needs. To help you in this you will need to access the Talent website (www.talent.org) and read the article entitled 'Supporting numeracy and literacy in post-16 education'. Other supporting texts include Brumfit and Johnson (1979) and a range of research articles available from the Basic Skills Agency. You might also carry out internet searches on the two key phrases 'language and communication' and 'number acquisition'.

It is the role of the tutor (and anyone who works with the individual concerned) to be alert to signs of demotivation, partners in absence, lateness, tiredness and so on. It helps many learners to know you are interested in them. If you cannot help directly, use other support services such as Connexions, institutional advisors, study support and student finance departments. In your contacts with learners, help them to focus on success, try to remotivate and re-engage them. Involve other colleagues responsible for the learners' programmes. Some learners may be very capable but not stretched or stimulated enough in terms of the challenges that you are presenting them with. Target setting can be used to motivate and challenge students who have disengaged. There is particular concern in the LSS about learners in the 14–19 age range who may start on programmes of study but then fall away. Strategies to keep them motivated are crucial.

Retention and achievement strategies

Learners joining institutions straight from schools will bring with them a great deal of information (SATs results, school reports, copies of GCSE results) Such information should be used to gather a picture about the individual and inform the ILP record. The learning environment of a college (or a workplace learning placement) is very different from that of a school. Some learners adapt well to the freedoms created by reduced timetable contact hours, the responsibility of choice in attendance, course options and other additional commitments, and a more fluid timetabling structure. Some do not. Research by Martinez and Munday (1998) demonstrated the following factors as crucial in students' decisions to stay on course or to withdraw:

- the suitability of their programme of study
- the intrinsic interest of their course
- timetabling issues
- the overall quality of teaching

- the help and support received from teachers
- help in preparing to move on to a job or higher education.

It is highly likely that learners who drop out blame the institution rather than themselves. However, there are a number of strategies that you can adopt to reduce student loss:

- Offer advice that is learner-specfic and recruit learners on to programmes that are appropriate to their needs and abilities
- Pay particular attention to induction activities, to ensure all learners are welcomed and embraced
- Monitor and follow up poor attendance
- Work closely with colleagues who are delivering programmes for your students. If such colleagues do not attend team meetings, ask them to produce a written report or to complete 'cause for concern' documents should your tutees not be performing
- Help learners to build on their existing skills
- Plan activities and assessment so that learners experience success
- Use target setting to challenge and motivate
- Work with the support services: Connexions; careers and learning support departments; counsellors; financial advisors.

Portfolio task 10.3

Identify a learner who is showing cause for concern (if you are a student using this text you may need to ask your coach/mentor to help you). Review the paperwork available concerning this learner, talk to other staff delivering parts of their programme and set up a meeting with the individual concerned. During the meeting complete and update the ILP for the learner, setting targets that are SMART.

Produce a reflective account of the meeting. Review the learner's progress over time and comment on the success or otherwise of this strategy. After a period of one month, review the situation and meet again with the learner. Reflect on the advantages and disadvantages of this process. (500 words)

10

Diversity issues

There are statutory requirements that underpin the focus on diversity. These are enshrined in disability legislation (discussed earlier in this chapter) and legislation associated with race and gender equality. Legislation pertinent to age discrimination is also applicable. In one institution, a poster (reproduced in Figure 10.2) articulates the scale of equality and diversity issues using an acronym approach.

Figure 10.2 **Spelling out a focus on diversity issues**

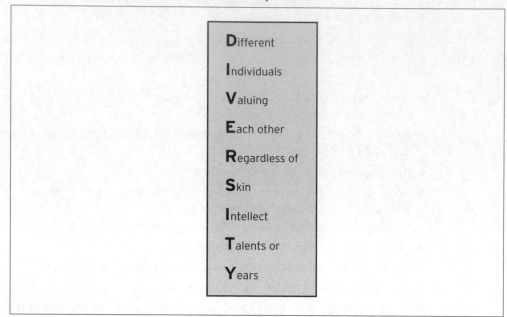

Diversity checklist

When planning episodes of teaching/tutoring/training it is important to ensure that your resources, methodological approaches and classroom climate embrace the needs of all learners. You may wish to perform a diversity check on all your resources and teaching materials.

The checklist below can be used to evaluate your teaching materials. It is adapted from material provided by the LSC (www.lsc.gov.uk).

- Is the handout/text culturally acceptable to all learners?
- Does the text encourage students to value minority cultures?
- Does the text in any way underestimate the intelligence/maturity/experience of your students?
- Does the text in any way reinforce gender, race, nationality or class stereotypes?
- Does the text in any way challenge and positively seek to counter stereotyping?
- Does the text help students to develop language skills for use in situations of discrimination or abuse?
- If the text is not appropriate for your learners, could it be used with others?
- Could you use the text with bilingual learners?

Task 10.8

Submit some of the materials you use in your teaching to the diversity checklist above. Take five pieces of resource and amend them to make them more inclusive. Create five new resources in your subject area that will support learners with particular learning needs. Describe these resources and show how you will use them with your learners.

Portfolio task 10.4

This task requires you to carry out some research. There are a number of steps involved:

1 Observe some ESOL classes.
2 Research issues associated with cultural difference.
3 Identify the teaching methods that are suitable for such learners.
4 Compile a number of teaching resources (in your subject) that would be suitable for such learners (minimum of five resources).
5 Reflect on your findings and the implications of these for your teaching.
6 Test a number of these resources with learners (and/or your mentor). Evaluate the results and make the necessary amendments to your work.

The following websites might prove useful:

http://www.lang.ltsn.ac.uk/resources/goodpractice.aspx?resourceid=421
http://www.ling.lancs.ac.uk/groups/slarg/links.htm

Key tips to take from this chapter

10

- Induction sessions require a process of design prior to implementation.
- You have a responsibility to become aware of the learning needs of different types of learners and to plan your lessons accordingly.
- There are statutory requirements placed upon you to take account of the needs of all learners, specifically those with special requirements.

Assessment grid mapped to the standards

This chapter introduces the knowledge requirements for the areas in scope set out at the start of the chapter. Completion of the set tasks will provide you with evidence that can be matched to the standards, as set out below, for gaining awards in the learning and skills sector.

Task	Summary activity	Level 3 award	Trainer award (level 4) leading to QTLS (level 5)	E-learning standards CPD awards
Task 10.1	Icebreaker activities	AK 1.1 AK 1.2 DK 1.1	AK 1.1 AK 1.2 DK 1.1	B 1 (potentially) B 2 (potentially)
Task 10.2	Induction scheme	AP 2 AP 3.1 AP 4.1 FK 1.1 FK 2.1	AP 2i AP 3.1 AP 4.1 BP 3.2 BP 3.3 BP 4.1 BP 5.1 FK 1.1 FK 1.2 FK 2.1	B 1 (potentially) B 2 (potentially)
Task 10.3	Assessment information	Potentially not essential, dependent on role	AK 2 DK 2.1 DK 2.2 BP 3.2 BP 3.3 BP 4.1 BP 4.3	A 1 (potentially) A 2 (potentially) A 3 (potentially)
10.4	Lesson planning for specific learning needs	BP 3.3 BP 4.1 CP 1.2 FK 1.1 FK 1.2 FK 2.1	BP 3.3 BP 4.1 CP 1.2 FK 1.1 FK 1.2 FK 2.1	D 1 (potentially) E 1 (potentially) E 2 (potentially)
Task 10.5	Sight and hearing difficulties	DP 1.2 BP 1.1	DP 1.2 BP 1.1	B 1 (potentially) B 2 (potentially)
Task 10.6	Learning checklist	EP 1.1	EP 1.1 DP 3.1	
Task 10.7	Target setting	May not be essential	FP 1.1 FP 1.2 FP 2.1 CP 1.1 CP 4.1	A 2 (potentially) A 3 (potentially)

Task	Summary activity	Level 3 award	Trainer award level 4 leading to QTLS (level 5)	E-learning standards CPD awards
Task 10.8	Diversity checklist	AP 1.1 AP 2.1 CP 3.2	AP 1.1 AP 2.1 CP 3.2 CP 3.3	B 1 (potentially) B 3 (potentially) D 3 (potentially) D 4 (potentially)
Portfolio task 10.1	Case studies of two learners	May not be essential	DK 2.1 DK 2.2	A 2 (potentially) A 3 (potentially)
Portfolio task 10.2	Learner evaluations	May not be essential	DP 3.1 DP 3.2 EP 4.1 EP 4.2 EP 5.4 EP 5.3 EP 6.1	F 2 (potentially)
Portfolio task 10.3	SMART targets	May not be essential	EP 4.1 EP 4.2 DP 3.1 DP 3.2	C 1 (potentially) C 2 (potentially) C 3 (potentially)
Portfolio task 10.4	Research project	May not be essential	AP 2 AP 4.2 AP 6.1 BP 4.1 DP 2.1	

10

11 Enhancing learner behaviour
Establishing and maintaining an effective learning environment

> **Learning outcomes**
>
> By the end of this chapter you will have:
>
> - identified elements of behaviour you want to enhance and those you wish to minimise
> - explored what is meant by the term 'classroom climate' and considered how best to establish one which is conducive to learning
> - identified some of the reasons for poor behaviour and applied strategies to address them
> - trialled the use of behavioural control techniques within the boundaries of acceptable policy and practice.

Areas in scope in this chapter in relation to the standards for teachers, tutors and trainers working in the sector are AS 1, AS 2, AS 4, BS 3, DS 1, DS 2, DS 3, FS 3.

It could be argued that this chapter should appear nearer the beginning of this text. It is likely, as a text for the beginner teacher, to be one of the most referenced. It is placed near the end of the book for a specific purpose, namely to remind the reader that:

- teaching/tutoring/training is a skill that has to be practised and developed
- it does not come naturally
- we learn most from making mistakes, reflecting on our errors and making adjustments to our practice
- it is your role to establish an environment that is conducive to learning.

The initial chapters of this book were structured to provide you with the thinking, theoretical and conceptual tools to make you an effective teacher. This chapter offers practical advice and further opportunities for personal reflection on the skills you have developed so far.

Enhancing, not managing

The use of the word 'management' in relation to behaviour has been avoided as a chapter heading since the word has connotations of coercion, control and dominance (Browne, 2005). In addition, it has always been the case in the lifelong learning sector that the relationship between students or course participants and their teachers/tutors/trainers is more about mutual respect and co-working than it is about management. Research into the impact of teaching 14–16-year-olds in colleges of further education (Harkin, 2006) has identified how conducive this approach can be to motivating the disenchanted learner. But it is not necessarily an easy approach. Classroom or workshop climates that adopt a more flexible and liberal style need established boundaries and clearly defined behavioural expectations.

Classroom climate

During your training and throughout your career you will observe a number of different approaches and examples of a classroom climate. There are no hard and fast rules, although the nature of the climate, the expectation and approaches will differ depending upon the needs of the group. Task 11.1 examines some of the dimensions of a learning environment and is designed to encourage exploration of the types of climate that need to be established with different groups of learners.

Task 11.1

This activity provides you with the opportunity to consider your natural teaching style in relation to the needs of a particular group of learners.

From the statements below, tick the five that most accurately describe your natural style of behaviour enhancement.

1. Enforce rules and routines ☐   2. Tell pupils what to do ☐
3. Assist decision making ☐   4. Clarify rules and routines ☐
5. Be obeyed ☐   6. Control the learners ☐
7. Demand obedience ☐   8. Manage learner behaviour ☐
9. Train people ☐   10. Teach appropriate behaviour ☐
11. Model appropriate behaviour ☐   12. Expect compliance ☐
13. Encourage self-discipline ☐   14. Encourage cooperation ☐
15. Prevent problems escalating ☐   16. Isolate problems ☐
17. Support learner effort ☐   18. Guide behaviour ☐
19. Reward appropriate behaviour ☐   20. Provide opportunities for good behaviour ☐

There are no right or wrong answers: there are situations and particular groups of learners where all of the above might be necessary. Think about a group of learners that you are teaching now or have taught in the past. The continuum below represents a range of possible learner needs. At one end of the continuum would lie those groups of learners who require very strict limits and clear boundaries for their behaviour (perhaps a group with severe learning difficulties and disabilities). At the other end lies the group of able learners who are attending because they are self-motivated and want to achieve maximum benefit from the experience. Decide where the group should be placed on this continuum and mark with an X.

Adult control   Independence

| 24 | 21 | 18 | 15 | 12 | 9 | 6 |

Return now the tick-box activity above and, using the scorechart below, add up your points

Question no.	1, 7, 9, 12	5, 6, 8, 16	2, 10, 15, 18	4, 13, 19, 20	3, 11 , 14, 17
Scores	5 points	4 points	3 points	2 points	1 point

When you have added up your total score, mark a tick where you fall on the continuum (i.e. inclined towards clear adult control (24) or towards promoting independent decision making (6)).

A behavioural strategy analysis form can be downloaded from the companion website (Web 20)

Task 11.2

Complete the above exercise for two different groups of learners. What have you discovered? Does your score match your perceived behavioural teaching style? What have you gained from completing this exercise?

Having completed the above task in respect of your approaches, the next task requires you to observe another practitioner. Where possible, you should aim to observe the group of participants that you work with thus giving you an opportunity to observe how the climate established by someone else works effectively or otherwise with the same group. If it is not possible to observe the same group of students then try to observe a group that matches as nearly as possible the groups you teach.

Task 11.3

Observe another teacher. Reflect on the climate established and strategies used, and compare with your approaches. Which worked better and why?

List five components of a positive classroom climate and five of a negative classroom climate, Consider how to establish a positive climate.

Portfolio task 11.1

Tasks 11.1 and 11.2 were designed to help you consider your underpinning philosophies in relation to classroom behaviour and to encourage you to think about the climate in which you wish to operate. Return now to the values in Chapter 2 and check whether your approach to creating a learning environment concurs with the professional values set out for those teaching in the sector. Consider issues of health and safety, and equality and diversity. Comment on what you have achieved from completing the exercises above. (500 words)

A reflective practitioner is one who thinks about the outcomes of their sessions and makes changes in the hope of fostering improvement. Teaching can be a lonely and demotivating job. Using reflective practice is a good way to maintain motivation as a teacher as it ensures you are always evaluating your skills and looking for ways to do things differently.

Creating a positive climate

The hard fact to face is that creating a positive climate is down to you. Positive classroom climates don't just appear at the first point of contact with groups; they have to be established, developed, adjusted and sometimes reworked altogether. Creating them is one of the hardest parts of the job since they involve people, developed communication skills, perception and the ability to cope with the unexpected. There are three important stages that have been focused on throughout this text:

- planning
- teaching
- evaluating (reflecting and learning from your experiences).

Detailed planning enables you to be proactive rather than reactive in establishing an enhanced environment for learning. Research conducted by the BBC into comedy programmes has identified that the writer has approximately 5 minutes in the first episode to convince the audience to stay tuned and watch the whole programme. Decisions that affect viewing figures, and ultimately the careers of the comedy writer who has invested months in writing the series, hang on those first few moments of a programme. There are similarities here with teaching: if you don't create an impression of competence, knowledge and ability to direct the learners towards their goal, they will switch off very quickly. The different ways they might demonstrate their frustrations are discussed later in this chapter.

If you have not planned for this session, do not know what the syllabus is, arrive late having lost your file, forget what you are teaching, do not plan enough material, and so on, then you are doomed. Unlike the comedy writer you have other opportunities to impress, meeting different groups of learners, new cohorts each year and in some cases a captive audience, attending to achieve the qualification they so desperately need. They may also have paid for the course you are delivering and will complain bitterly if they do not receive what they deem to be appropriate teaching.

Rights and responsibilities

The act of teaching or training involves a relationship of mutual rights and responsibilities. You may feel that, to be responsible, participants should arrive on time, provide some basic equipment (pens, paper) and listen attentively to your words. This, in turn, places the responsibility on you to be well prepared, interesting and to have something worthwhile to impart. It is worth formalising this as a contract. At the first point of meeting with a group, set down in writing what you are prepared to offer and what you expect in return from your learners. This can be tried with all groups, no matter what age. One successful diet programme uses this approach with adults who sign a contract to follow the programme for 100 days, attend all sessions, be punctual and to respect and keep confidential the information revealed by others in the group (www.lighterlife.co). In return the weight loss counsellor agrees to offer support and to answer all telephone messages and requests within 24 hours, guaranteeing that, if the participants follow the programme exactly, they will lose a stone in weight during the first month.

Task 11.4

Design a contract for a group of learners. Make it age appropriate. The statements need to be SMART: specific, measurable, achievable, realistic and time-bound. An example solution is provided at the end of the book.

Agreeing the ground rules on a contractual basis

The contract can be agreed with the group at the first session. It may be recorded electronically and shared with the group (in paper or electronic form) and revisited on a termly basis or as and when considered necessary.

Task 11.5

1 Think about a group of learners you know and consider the following:
- What are your expectations of the session?
- In what aspects of the session do you need to maintain order?
- Where can you be more flexible?
- What can you negotiate on and what do you need to establish?

2 Design a contract with a group of learners. Reflect on the experience. What have you learned? What did you achieve? What would you do differently?

3 Think again about classroom climate and complete the following table.

Learners' rights	Learners' responsibilities
Staff rights	Staff responsibilities

If you access the website for City College Manchester (www.ccm. ac.uk/ESOL) you will be able to download the contracts that have been written for their ESOL learners. Contracts are available in seventeen different languages. This is a clear reminder that the contract is with both you and the learner and has to be understood by all.

Task 11.6

Think of a group of learners you have met. How would you describe your experiences with this group? Was the climate conducive to learning? Do you think that the needs of all learners were met? Given the opportunity, what would you do differently? What expectations would you like to establish, what changes in behaviour might you like to instil? Complete the table below in relation to two other groups you have worked with.

Describe your experiences with this group. Was the climate conducive to learning?	
Were the needs of all learners met?	

11

What might you do differently given the opportunity to start afresh with this group?	
What expectations would you like to establish, what changes in behaviour might you like to instil?	

Having completed the exercise with two different groups, what have you learned about your practice, about your learners and about the environments in which you teach? Share your thinking with your mentor/coach and/or another colleague who knows these learners.

Classroom misbehaviour

Writing a contract and establishing behaviours is only one step towards creating positve classroom environments that are conducive to learning. There are certain types of behaviour that individuals may demonstrate that will be unacceptable and, indeed, impact on your ability to maintain an effective classroom environment.

It is likely that misbehaviour has a purpose in the mind of the perpetrator, unless of course the individual has some learning behavioural problems that might unwittingly impact on their behaviours (see Chapter 10). It is important to know your learners so that you can distinguish real challenges to your authority from behaviour over which the learner may have little control.

Five roots of misbehaviour are:

- attention
- power
- revenge
- display of inadequacy
- displacement activity to hide the individual's anxiety or ignorance.

There are various strategies that can be applied to deal with misbehaviour:

- Apply consequences: 'If you do this, then this will happen.'
- Demonstrate and draw attention to positives, not negatives: 'Thank you for that contribution, can we see the impact.'
- Encourage positive behaviour.
- Focus on rewarding the behaviours: devise and consistently apply a reward system.

It is also important that you understand yourself. There will be occasions when you feel less able to cope with challenging behaviour than others. It is important that you try to remain constant in your expectations and standards. You need to be confident at all times and able to respond calmly and competently to all sorts of challenges. This is not easy: confidence and skills develop only with time and practice.

Observe an experienced lecturer (your coach or mentor) working with a group you may find challenging. Discuss the session beforehand, plan together and then identify what strategies the experienced lecturer is using that are successful with this group. Record your reflections. (500 words)

Motivational dialogue

As part of the Success for All strategy, the Department for Education and Skills has sponsored the development of resources to help teachers, tutors and trainers. Some of these are referred to in Chapters 7 and 8. In addition, the continuing professional development materials, prepared by the DfES Skills for Life team and available in the Standards Unit Materials, contain some useful training activities on motivational dialogue. Designed for use with Entry to Employment (e2e) learners, the materials are transferable and could be used to support staff working with a learner or groups of learners who might display unwanted behaviour.

Motivational dialogue is described as being distinctive for the following three reasons:

- It is directive, in the sense that you direct the learner to examine and resolve their ambivalence to change, while at the same time focusing on the needs of the learner.

- It acknowledges that people will have mixed feelings about making changes, and that trust needs to be established over time before changes can be introduced.

- When changes are made, individuals progress through distinct stages, known as the wheel of change (Figure 11.1).

Figure 11.1 **The wheel of change**

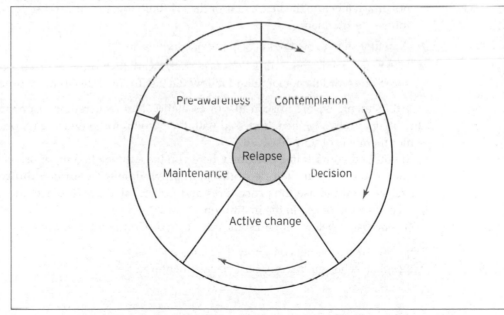

Source: adapted from *Entry to Employment Resources* (2003) Wheel of change diagram. Crown Copyright. Reproduced under the terms of the Click-Use Licence.

Portfolio task 11.3

Try out the approaches described in the wheel of change with two of your learners. Work with your learners to help them progress through the wheel of change. Keep notes of each meeting and discussion you have with the learner. Describe the process and comment on the outcome. (500 words)

Challenging behaviour

There will be times when you come across what might be defined as challenging behaviour. This behaviour may occur outside the classroom or workshop environment where you feel more in control. The operating culture of the environment in the LSS needs to be one of mutual respect, where learners and staff behave appropriately towards one another. Organisations will have established disciplinary procedures setting out the code of conduct which learners are required to follow. The following guidelines may provide you with support when confronting unacceptable behaviours:

- Explain calmly why you are asking the individuals to change their behaviour.
- Avoid sarcasm or belittling comments that demean the person.
- Avoid racist or homophobic language or comments.
- Remain calm and polite and do not lose your temper.
- Use assertive rather than aggressive body language.
- Try to establish facts in a calm manner and do not jump to conclusions (it may be necessary to defuse the situation if a crowd has gathered by asking the key provocateurs to accompany you elsewhere.
- Condemn the deed rather than doer ('That was an inappropriate way to behave'). Do not attach labels to the behaviour or the act (bullying, racism, and so forth, as this can infuse the situation).
- As a first step, invite the participant(s) to apologise.
- Where no serious misconduct has occurred, a verbal warning may suffice, but make sure you record the incident and follow the institutional disciplinary procedures.

All incidents, severe misconduct or escalation and recurrences of unacceptable conduct that has already been discussed with the perpetrator(s) must be reported and more senior members of staff involved.

If you find yourself in a position where you have threatened to report an incident to a higher authority, but then do nothing, you will damage your credibility and status. Never be afraid to use the procedures and policies that are in place: they are there to protect you and others in the institution.

The websites below contain some advice on disciplinary techniques and approaches:

http://www.teachernet.com/how–to/manage
http://theteachersguide.com/classmanagement.htm

Portfolio task 11.4

Consider how you promote a learning environment which stimulates the following four key values for those working the LSS:

- Reflective practice and scholarship
- Collegiality and collaboration
- The centrality of learning and learner autonomy
- Entitlement, equality and inclusiveness. (500 words)

You may wish to use the standards for teachers/tutors /trainers working in the sector to carry out this task (see www.ifl.org.uk.)

A link to the **QTLS** standards can be found on the companion website (Web 6)

Key tips to take from this chapter

- It is important to establish a climate that is conducive to learning. This is really down to you and, although difficult, can be achieved in most scenarios.
- There are strategies you can employ when working with individual learners to make them feel valued and to take more personal responsibility for their behaviour.

Assessment grid mapped to the standards

This chapter introduces the knowledge requirements for the areas in scope set out at the start of the chapter. Completion of the set tasks will provide you with evidence that can be matched to the standards, as set out below, for gaining awards in the learning and skills sector.

Task	Summary activity	Level 3 award	Trainer award (level 4) leading to level 5	E-learning standards CPD awards
Task 11.1	Evaluating your classroom climate preferences	Not essential but could be useful		
Task 11.2	Observation and evaluation of strategies	Not essential but could be useful	AP 5.1 CP 3.2 DP 2.1	
Task 11.3	Collaborating with colleagues	DP 3.2	DP 3.2 EP 2.4 EP 5.3 FP 4.2	B 1 (potentially) B 2 (potentially) B 3 (potentially)
Task 11.4	Establishing ground rules	DP 1.1 DP 1.2 DP 4.1	DP 1.1 DP 1.2 DP 4.1	
Task 11.5	Creating a positive climate	DP 1.1 DP 1.2 BP 2.2	DP 1.1 DP 1.2 BP 2.2	

11

Task	Summary activity	Level 3 award	Trainer award (level 4) leading to level 5	E-learning standards CPD awards
Task 11.6	Meeting different needs	DP 1.1 DP 1.2 DP 3.3	DP 1.1 DP 1.2 DP 3.3	B 1 (potentially) B 2 (potentially) B 3 (potentially)
Portfolio task 11.1	Climate assessment	Not essential but could be useful	AP 3.1 AP 3.3 AP 4.1 AP 4.2 DP 1.1 DP 1.2	
Portfolio task 11.2	Reflection on behavioural styles	Not essential but could be useful	DP 1.1	
Portfolio task 11.3	Class climate	Not essential but could be useful	CP 3.2 DP 1.1 DP 2.1	
Portfolio task 11.4	Completing a contract	Not essential but could be useful	AP 6.2 DP 2.2 EP 2.4 FP 2.1 FP 4.2	B 1 (potentially)

12 Continuing professional development

Developing by participating in formal and informal professional activities

> ### Learning outcomes
>
> By the end of this chapter you will begin to:
>
> - think about your professional needs
> - consider additional modules of study you may wish to engage in
> - address your personal skills development needs
> - consider your professional and career development pathway.

Areas in scope in this chapter in relation to the standards for teachers, trainers and tutors working in the sector are AS 6, BS 1, BS 3, FS 3.

If you are reading this chapter because you have just achieved QTLS, congratulations. This is a worthy achievement and one of which you can be proud. A requirement for remaining in good standing as a qualified teacher is to register with the Institute for Learning (IfL) and then, on an annual basis, to engage in further study. Those who gained PGCE/Cert. Ed. qualifications some years ago may wish to achieve qualified teacher status (QTLS). To achieve this you will be required to prepare a portfolio and engage in further study. How 'further study' will be defined, how much will be required and how it will be recorded are still to be decided. This chapter makes some suggestions of what, at the time of writing, the sector seems to be suggesting in relation to CPD requirements. It also proposes some ideas which it hopes the sector itself will address as the reforms gain momentum.

Your skills and development pathway

If you have been reviewing the standards for teachers in the LSS as mapped in this text, you will have a clear view of your personal skills and competences. If you are new to teaching, your competence in these standards is, in some respects, at the threshold or early stages of development. You will need to develop your skills further if you are to work as a lifelong learner. Your personal development needs are crucial and need to be assessed. This chapter guides you through those processes and helps you to consider your future training and development pathway.

First, however, given the complexity of the roles carried out by staff in the LSS, it would be useful to consider the types of teacher/tutor/trainer that might be employed. Four categories are suggested:

- The *full-time generalist* who teaches a range of subjects, is able to offer key skills (and/or basic skills) in ICT, number and communication and who may be employed full-time in one institution.

- The *portfolio generalist* who teaches a range of subjects, is able to offer key skills in ICT, number and communication and who may be employed by a variety of different organisations, with different types of students, in different settings, on various contractual arrangements (permanent, hourly paid, annually renewable).

- The *full-time specialist* who teaches only their subject in one institution who may not feel competent to teach key skills and/or basic skills in ICT, number and communication but is increasingly being required to do so.

- The *portfolio specialist* who teaches only their subject in a variety of institutions or settings who may not feel competent to teach key skills and/or basic skills in ICT, number and communication but is increasingly being required to do so.

Task 12.1

Consider the four broad categories of teacher/tutor/trainer described above. Which one best describes you? If you are currently studying for a qualification in the LSS and wish to gain status as a full-time lecturer then willingness to be a full-time generalist may increase your employment opportunities unless your specialism is in an area where there are severe staff shortages such as ICT, mathematics and science. Are you happy with your role? What might you need to do to change it? Consider where you would like to be in your career in two, five and ten years' time.

Case exemplars

At this point it will be useful to revisit some of the staff we met in Chapter 1 to see how their careers have progressed. Michelle, the trained nurse, who had completed stages 1 and 2 of the 'old qualification' now has a full-time post and is required to complete the full 'licensed to practise' award. She has put together a portfolio of evidence of her competence to be assessed for Accreditation of Prior Learning (APL) in terms of her existing qualifications and is now completing modules at her local university which will be accredited towards a PGCE with QTLS.

Armid, who is still working in the prison, is about to register for the same PGCE qualification as Michelle. He will study at his local college of further education on a programme delivered in partnership with his local university. Armid will study core modules at the university and an optional specialist strand in literacy which will support him in his work.

Farah, who completed her PGCE(FE) some years ago, is preparing a portfolio of evidence to demonstrate her skills, providing evidence also of having recently attended courses to keep up to date so that she can apply for QTLS.

Peter, who has qualified teacher status, would like to be awarded QTLS. He is exploring opportunities at his local university and hopes that his portfolio record of attending CPD events on a regular basis will be all that is required.

It is apparent from reading each of the case studies that *portfolio evidence of skills, achievement and regular attendance at CPD events* will be essential for all practitioners working in the sector.

Recording your development activities

Once having gained QTLS everyone is required to provide evidence of their participation in sessions of CPD in order to remain in good standing. It will be the role of the IfL to ensure that a comprehensive system is in place which can be used across the sector to record and monitor such activity. Accurate records will have to be kept, on an individual basis, recording activity undertaken as part of the requirement for teachers to remain in 'good standing' and retain their QTLS status.

The Every Step Counts project undertaken on behalf of IfL recommends a template for recording CPD (www.ifl.ac.uk/documents). In summary it contains the following sections:

- Current activities and responsibilities
- What am I good at?
- What do I need to develop?
- What are my personal development objectives?
- Why do I want to develop this area?
- What will I do?
- The criteria for my success
- Target dates for review and reflection.

This is followed by a section that addresses:

- Action completed so far
- What did I learn?
- How have I used/how will I use this learning?
- Any further actions?
- Opportunities.

A PCP framework template can be downloaded from the companion website (Web 21)

A similar design of template is available on the website for this text although it is strongly recommended that you use the official IfL recording mechanism.

The planning cycle

The members' page of the IfL website contains a CPD portal (www.ifl.ac.uk/cpd-portal) outlining five steps in the process of compiling and maintaining a CPD record. The stages are as follows:

12

1 Initial reflection
2 Where am I?
3 Compiling the personal development plan
4 Compiling the personal development record
5 Keeping track of professional activities.

The aims of the CPD process are to enable you to:

- highlight your professional competences and needs
- keep a personal record of your CPD activities, which can be used for compiling a CV or as an agenda for discussion within a system of appraisal
- plan your self-development and future career.

The planning cycle can be presented diagrammatically as shown in Figure 12.1.

Figure 12.1 The planning cycle

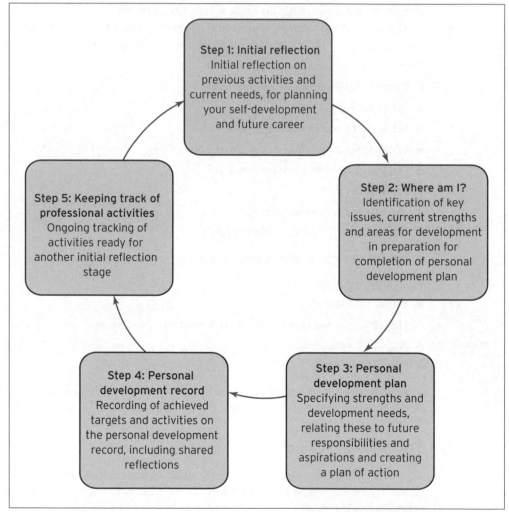

Source: This figure is reproduced with the permission of the Institute for Learning. At the time of publication initial teacher training is in a period of significant change with the implementation of *Equipping our Teachers for the Future*. Within its remit for advancing the teacher professionalisation agenda the Institute for Learning is developing a new model of professionalism which supersedes this figure. For the latest information on the professional development agenda please visit www.ifl.ac.uk

Training routes

The LSS will require those in training to follow a variety of paths to support the need for staff to be available to teach in a number of specialist areas. When undertaking CPD you may have a particular career route in mind. The following are some that you might consider (although many more are available). They fall into six categories:

- basic skills lecturer
- e-learning practitioner
- health and safety specialist
- mentor/coach supporting other teachers or those in training
- teacher trainer
- leadership roles.

Specific qualifications linked to these development routes have been or are being designed. The sections below describe the routes in more detail.

Basic skills lecturer

There are opportunities already available for those wishing to specialise in teaching numeracy, literacy and ESOL. These qualifications are offered at level 4 and require a set number of hours of face-to-face learning and a period of observed teaching practice. Some universities offer full PGCE pre-service qualifications with a specialist strand in basic skills teaching (Wolverhampton University is one such institution). Students completing this course on a full-time basis currently qualify to receive an annual training bursary of £9,000.

If you are interested in completing this qualification on a part-time basis then you need to contact your local college or higher education institution. Information is also available on the basic skills website (www.basicskills.org.uk).

E-learning practitioner

Qualifications in e-learning will be available to support the different roles likely to be required of those working in the sector. Some of these are specific to the teacher, others to different professional roles that require developed e-learning skills. The roles identified are those of:

- e-practitioner
- e-learning support
- e-learning development
- internal advisor
- e-leadership
- e-adviser
- e-strategist.

12

The CPD units are presented as follows:

- A core unit: e-learning fundamentals

followed by

- Pedagogy-based practitioner units
- Specialist e-learning developer units
- Leadership units

and complemented by

- Additional 'wraparound' units which support additional developmental needs dependent on the specialist route selected.

For more information about these units see www.lsn.org.uk or www.ifl.org.uk.

Health and safety specialist

There is likely to be an increasing demand for specialists in this area as the concept of the safe learner and changes in legislation become more apparent. The traditional route undertaken by health and safety practitioners is that provided by the Institute of Occupational Safety and Health. To find you more about the qualifications offered go to www.iosh.org.

Mentor/coach role

Once you have been teaching successfully for a number of years you will be ideally placed to act in the role of coach/mentor to newly qualified teachers (NQTs) and other lecturers who may benefit from some training to help them tackle the challenges in teaching today. If you are interested in this route you should consider undertaking training as a subject learning coach. The training leads to a qualification delivered as part of the National Change Programme in the LSS.

The subject learning coach programme is designed to cover six areas of learning. Following an induction which provides an overview, the modules focus on the following issues:

- Transforming the individual: focus on self
- Transforming teaching, training and learning: focus on subject pedagogy
- Coaching as a tool for transformation: focus on self and others
- Transforming the organisation: focus on self in the workplace
- Transforming the LSS: focus on self and the wider learner and skills context.

The model of coaching proposed is one of peer coaching (Joyce and Showers, 2002), the core concepts of which are set out in the government's national framework for mentoring and coaching (www.dfes.mentoringandcoaching) based on the work of the Centre for the Use of Research and Evidence in Education (CUREE). The peer or co-coaching model is described as one which sets aside existing relationships based on experience and hierarchy and provides permission for the expert, the novice, the slightly jaundiced and the demotivated practitioner to form relationships of mutual benefit and to identify their own learning needs, goals and aspirations.

Joyce and Showers' research shows that teachers, following initial training, gain more from their work if working in a coaching relationship, that is, if they share aspects of their teaching, plan together and pool their experiences, practise new skills and strategies more frequently and apply them more appropriately than do their counterparts who work alone. Peer coaching encourages the development of study teams where teachers and trainers plan lessons, share objectives, divide the labour, support one another's practice and study the impact together. The classroom observation person doing the teaching is the coach; the person observing is the coachee; and observations are carried out to support personal learning based on the view that examples and demonstrations are powerful teaching and training experiences. Peer coaching works on the premise that all members of the peer coaching team have something to contribute.

The issue of the title 'subject learning coaching' is interesting and feasibly problematical but none the less intentional. The combination of subject pedagogy and coaching in the title reflects a focus on two of the key enablers in the programme, namely the subject learning materials (discussed in Chapters 7 and 10) and the skills of coaching. Some might argue that the two skills are incompatible; the programme designers contend that skills of subject specialist and coaching facilitator are complementary, coming together in a powerful way to combine professional knowledge with skills of process to create one of the most challenging yet powerful forms of CPD (DfES, 2004a).

Teacher trainer

Those wanting to lead teacher training courses will themselves be required to demonstrate their competence on an ongoing basis. A qualification framework is being designed to support this requirement. It is likely that such training will be the responsibility of Centres for Excellence in Teacher Training.

Centres for Excellence Teacher Training

Centres for Excellence in Teacher Training (CETTs) will be the main home for the APL process towards QTLS and for the delivery and recording of CPD. It is in these institutions, formed in partnership with further education colleges, possibly clustered around a higher education institution, that you will complete your QTLS qualification and any other recognised and validated modules of CPD. CETTs will have to be recognised by the IfL, which will be the recognised body for recording CPD to ensure that an individual remains in good standing.

If you are interested in supporting others to become teachers you may wish to look at the Talent website (www.talent.ac.uk) which contains an interactive explanation of different types of teacher training models using a scaffolding approach to teaching practice with five scenarios explained:

- Model 1: Training groups in which twelve trainee teachers in two groups take turns to teach a group while their peers and trainer observe.
- Model 2: Buddy apprenticeships in which two trainees teach together.
- Model 3: Two trainees take turns to teach the whole group with the teacher trainer (or mentor) present.
- Model 4: One trainee is paired with a teaching practice mentor and they work together to plan and teach the class.

12

- Model 5: In this model the teacher is in paid employment while training to become fully qualified. The use of a mentor or teacher training advisor is important in this context as well as in all the others.

Leadership roles

The Centre for Excellence in Leadership (CEL) plays a key role in providing training opportunities for principals, managers and leaders of teachers (sometimes known as advanced practitioners). CEL will play a key role in providing CPD opportunities in the sector and plans to offer a masters-level qualification entitled Leading Professional Practice. This will have six modules, the content of which is yet to be decided but is likely to cover the following:

- Induction: how to remain in good standing
- Dual professionalism: subject knowledge and pedagogy
- Supporting other professionals: working with colleagues with QTLS
- Using action research to extend professionalism
- Developing a community of practice
- Developing and embedding reflective practice in whole organisations.

This qualification route is very much at the planning stage. More details will be made available on the website for this book once the qualification has been validated.

Developing a professional and career profile

A **PCP framework** template can be downloaded from the companion website (Web 21)

The portfolio of tasks you have completed for this text and your ILP can form the starting point of your professional and career profile (PCP). If you have just achieved QTLS you will need to review and update your ILP. It is suggested that you begin to collect your evidence for your PCP using an electronic medium (floppy disk or CD-rom) that can be readily accessed and updated. If you are not able to achieve this, then your first CPD need is to upgrade your IT skills.

The framework PCP that is available on the website for this text contains sections entitled:

- Starting points
- Assessment of skills against the standards
- Professional development activities
- Career opportunities
- Training and development needs
- Learning journal
- CV
- Career map.

As the requirements for CPD become clearer they will be posted on the website for this book, along with any additional information about CPD.

Keeping your CV up to date

Why maintain a CV?

A CV is a brief history of your career and professional experience. At the very least a CV is your personal record. Most of the time you use it to give prospective employers an insight into who you are and the means of matching your experience and potential with the requirements of the post they are offering.

What is in a CV?

Generally, a CV contains personal details, such as who you are, your contact details and IfL Teacher Reference Number; details of your education, qualifications and professional experience; and additional information such as significant professional development and how you have gained this. It usually includes information about your leisure interests and identifies your referees (people who will be willing to verify what you have stated and add their own views about your suitability for a particular job).

Why keep an electronic CV?

As you move through your career you will update and replace information. Having an electronic CV allows you to do this easily. Reviewing your CPD (PCP) log and learning journal are time-efficient ways to extract key information and remind yourself of your progress. You can also, if you wish, email your CV to a critical friend or referee and, of course, to a prospective employer.

Will all employers ask for a CV?

Employers vary in their expectations and needs in recruitment. Some may ask only for a CV, some may request only a letter of application, others may ask for both. In some instances, an employer may ask you to enter CV information on a specific form. In any of these circumstances, having your CV easily to hand will enable you to deliver the information quickly and efficiently.

Is there a standard model of CV?

In education, the model is usually the format offered in the template on the website for this book. However, there is nothing to prevent you from customising the information to suit the job you are applying for.

A CV **template** can be downloaded from the companion website (Web 22)

In common with other professions, initial qualification now represents the first stage in a continuum of learning throughout every teacher's career. By now you will have begun to think about your future development needs as a lifelong learner and career professional. Good luck on your journey.

12

> ### Technology tip
> Keep a record of all your training and CPD activity. Record internal staff development courses attended, attendance at network events, any research you are asked to undertake and papers you write. Keep an accurate copy on disk or on your home computer, and update the record regularly.

Portfolio task 12.1

Review the ILP you completed at the beginning of your training period. What have you achieved? What still needs to be done? What happens next?

Key tips to take from this chapter

- There will be considerable focus on continuing professional development for staff working in the sector.
- It will be your responsibility to maintain a record of all CPD you might engage in.
- This book has demonstrated the importance of record keeping and portfolio building for those training to teach in the lifelong learning and skills sector.

Assessment grid mapped to the standards

This chapter introduces the knowledge requirements for the areas in scope set out at the start of the chapter. Completion of the set tasks will provide you with evidence that can be matched to the standards, as set out below, for gaining awards in the learning and skills sector. The tasks will also support you in the next step in your learning journey and provide a framework for presenting evidence of CPD on an annual basis.

Task	Summary activity	Level 3 award	Trainer award (level 4) leading to level 5	E-learning standards CPD awards
Task 12.1	Personal evaluation	AK 6.1 AK 6.2 BK 4.1 BK 4.2 FK 3.1	AK 6.1 AK 6.2 BK 4.1 BK 4.2 FK 3.1	
Portfolio task 12.1	Target setting	AK 6.1 AP 6.1	AK 6.1 AP 6.1	G 1, G 2, G 3, G 4 (potentially if teacher/tutor/trainer is considering becoming an ILT champion)

Example answers to selected tasks

1.1

Head – full of ideas and knowledge about their subject

Brain – trying to think of different ways to make learning accessible and fun, while encouraging learner anatomy

Arms – full of paper, schemes of work, lesson plans, targets to meet, marking, paperwork, registers, records, individual learning plans

Heart – warm, understanding, open to giving learners a second chance to succeed

Fingers – quick to help those who want to learn and prepared to try with those who don't!

Body language – purposeful and confident

Approach – helpful, kind and suportive, aware of all learners and their needs, providing support to help them to succeed

Interests – enthusiastic about their subject, often having been employed in the work environment, now wanting to share their experiences and having direct knowledge of what it is like to work in their specific area of interest

Linguistic skills – keen to discuss how they can motivate the learner and share ideas with others

Eyes – observing everything, specifically focus on health and safety issues

Ears – able to listen to problems

Shoulders – capable of carrying large amounts of marking

Stomach – calm, prepared to accept challenges and act with integrity

Legs – able to change direction quickly if appropriate

Feet – on the ground but responsive to change when it has a clear rationale and is in the interest of the learner

Toes – willing to dip in and try out new ways of motivating and engaging their learners

2.7 The answer is 'all of them'. In fact there is no such thing as a typical skills sector student. The recipients of education and training in this sector can come from all walks of life, have a range of skills and qualifications and a breadth of experience and needs. In one classroom studying a new language can sit a medic, a plumber, a pensioner, a child, an academic and a student with learning difficulties. Such diversity in age and qualification may not exist in all the various learning environments that make up this sector. Full-time day classes, for example, could contain what, at first sight, appears to be a more coherent group of people brought together by pursuit of a common course of study such as an Applied Vocational Course (AVC) a National Qualification, a National Diploma, a foundation degree, GCSEs and A levels. Coherence in the population of those studying in this sector, however, can never be guaranteed. The LSS embraces all people in its concern to provide, through education, better opportunities for all throughout the whole of life.

5.4 The class could have been divided into groups, with some given a more specific research task. The setting of an in-depth research task would have appealed to the theorists in the group. In addition you could have asked the groups to nominate a leader (or leaders) with responsibility for timekeeping, monitoring progress and driving forward the task. This would have met the needs of activists in the group. Notice that the more structured responsibility you give to your learners, the more chance you have of meeting their individual needs

6.1

IT	ICT	ILT
Computer	Students producing assignments for a set essay	Accessing a pre-purchased or pre-prepared CD-roms to gain information for a teaching session
Electronic whiteboard	Teacher use the whiteboard to present pre-prepared Powerpoint presentations	Students become actively involved in selecting materials, accessed through a range of sources, and stored for further use
Website	Students access a number of pages available through the internet to select their options and/or courses	Students access a travel website as part of a research project on life in France
Access to the internet	Students/lecturers may use the internet as a route to access pre-prepared data/ information (e.g. Ofsted reports)	Lecturers and students might research an area of interest, perhaps a journal article or a magazine to prepare for an assignment
Access to the organisation's intranet	The intranet may hold timetable information, registers, copies of reporting forms required by lecturers	Students may wish to access available policy documents for a project on equality Issues

9.2

Type of Assessment	Explanation	Function
Diagnostic assessment Book reviews Initial tests Mock exams Computer usage tasks	The term 'diagnostic' refers to the identification of difficulties that might influence the learning process	To gauge different entry levels, rates of progress or potential weaknesses. The assessment is used to provide support where necessary
Formative assessment Course essays Class presentations Activities designed to help the learner but that may not result in a final grade classification	The term 'formative refers' to assessment which provides the student with an indication of their strengths and weaknesses but does not necessarily provide a grade which counts towards the final degree classification	To support the learning process by providing advice and feedback in order that the student might improve
Summative assessment Exams Coursework Course essays (where grades are accumulated and used in the final grading) Dissertations	The term 'summative' refers to any form of assessment which gives a precise account of achievement at the end of a set assessment period	To determine whether the student can progress from one stage in the academic calendar on to the next To determine the final degree classification

9.7 Although the student had carried out an interesting piece of research and identified a wide range of information about her grandmother's childhood, the use of theory in the work was very limited, as was the evidence of any reading and research. The grade given was within the C (40–49%) category, at the higher end (i.e. 48%) because there was evidence of some description and explanation and a little analysis but minimal reference to background reading.

10.3 There are a number of actions that you, as tutor, would be required to do. The first one would be to contact the student who has withdrawn (Chris) to discuss with him the reasons for his withdrawal and, if appropriate, encourage him to re-engage with the course. You may wish to meet with him and suggest an alternative course or offer him careers advice.

Second, Lucy needs to be encouraged to sit her numeracy tests. Her profile suggests that she may be avoiding facing facts in terms of her skill level in this area. Third, all staff who come into contact with this group need to be alerted to the fact that Mat Brown has a hearing loss and Narjit Elan may have dyslexic support needs and must be encouraged to attend the learning support department to ensure her levels of functioning are assessed.

Carl is identified on the form as an ESOL learner, but there is no other information available. You need to talk to Carl on a one-to-one basis and arrange for him to receive an assessment and additional support. This is urgent. The fact that there is no information available about him shows a major weakness in the organisation's IAG systems. Action needs to be taken quickly to correct this.

You will need to liaise with staff in the learning support department to ensure that they have up-to-date timetable and rooming information so that, where support needs to be provided, the appropriate staff can be swiftly allocated.

During meetings with all your learners you need to monitor their progress and set them individual targets, to be recorded in the ILP, to monitor progress in basic skills. The City College Manchester website (www.ccm.ac.uk) contains exemplars of some resources you may wish to use.

Anything else?

11.4 Contract with Foundation Health and Social Care Students

Students agree to:

- attend all sessions unless unavoidably detained
- arrive punctually, ready to start the session on time
- complete all set tasks
- listen attentively
- respect the views of fellow learners
- hand in homework at the due date
- ask for help with they do not understand.

Lecturer agrees to:

- attend all session unless unavoidably detained
- arrive punctually, ready to start the session on time
- prepare interesting lessons which address the needs of the learners
- mark submitted work and return it to students within one week of the due date
- respect the views of the students
- provide help when it is needed
- deliver well-prepared sessions matched to the agreed syllabus
- a promise that if students work you will do your best to help them succeed.

Glossary

Academic Focusing on the acquisition of facts, information and abstract theoretical, rather than practical, knowledge.

Action learning set A small group of peers (ideally four or five people) who come together on a regular basis to critique and challenge actions on a supportive way.

Action research A form of small-scale, workplace-based research in which teachers, trainers and other professionals investigate their practice with the aim of developing it.

Active learning Learning that involves learners in practising important skills and in applying new knowledge in such a way that their understanding is improved.

Advanced Extension Awards (AEA) An examination available in seventeen areas for advanced level candidates who are particularly gifted and expected to attain a grade A. The AEA is graded as merit or distinction.

Analysis The breaking down of complex situations and arguments into many related points in order to examine the relationship between these parts.

Application Application, in academic language, refers to the ability to use knowledge and understanding in different situations.

Area of learning A subject or topic within a specified field of knowledge.

Assessment for learning Judgements used to support teaching and learning, monitor learners' progress and illuminate their strengths and weaknesses. Also known as formative assessment/judgement.

Brainstorming Putting together a small group of learners to produce a large number of creative ideas in a short time for subsequent evaluation. Also known as 'word storming', this activity can take place on an individual basis.

Buzz group A small groups of learners who spend a few minutes discussing an idea or thought-provoking question among themselves.

Change agent Any member of staff who is engaged in enabling and facilitating change in practice within their organisation.

Common knowledge, skills and attributes (CKSA) The knowledge, skills and attributes that all young people need for learning, employment and adult life. For example, personal awareness, problem solving, moral and ethical awareness. CKSA forms part of the **core**.

Communities of practice Groups of individuals sharing common beliefs and values who group together to share and develop practice.

Complementary learning Learning related to the focus of a learner's **main learning**, such as Latin for a learner with a modern foreign languages focus. It may contribute towards achievement of the **threshold** or be additional to it.

Component The building blocks for the proposed diploma system. A discrete subject or **area of learning** with its own assessment arrangements, achievement in which gives credit towards the award of a **diploma**. Components will build on existing qualifications, such as GCSEs and A levels and other existing qualifications.

Comprehension or understanding in academic terms requires not just the mere recall of information, but the insight into the ways in which the information may have been derived or how it relates to other information available on the topic.

Continuing professional development (CPD) Sometimes referred to as staff development. Any activity that helps teachers/tutors/trainers maintain, improve or broaden their knowledge, understanding and skills, and become effective in their role.

Cooperative learning A strategy in which small groups, each with students with different abilities, use various learning activities to improve their understanding of a subject. Each member of a group is responsible not only for learning what is taught but also for helping fellow learners learn, thus creating an atmosphere of achievement.

Critical analysis The ability to break down complex situations and arguments and to objectively assess the implications for one's practice.

Critical incident An episode of teaching, a single session or one event during a session that is subjected by the teacher to close analysis by means of reflection in order to develop their practice.

Critique To critically examine something, such as a session plan, to give feedback, to recognise strengths and suggest strategies for improvement.

Core (learning) Skills, knowledge and experiences common to and required for the achievement of all **diplomas: functional literacy and communication; functional mathematics; functional ICT; extended project; CKSA; personal review, planning and guidance**; and an entitlement to **wider activities**.

Credit Value ascribed to a **component** based on a measure of notional learning time. Nothing smaller than a component can provide credit towards a **diploma**.

Deep learning A term used to describe learning that is committed to the permanent memory as opposed to **surface learning** which is retained for as long as is needed and then discarded.

Diagnostic assessment Assessment which gives in-depth information about an individual's strengths and weaknesses in relation to literacy, language and numeracy, enabling tutors to design a **programme** of work specifically to meet the needs of the learner.

Differentiation Identifying and addressing the different needs, interests and abilities of all learners to give them the best possible chance of achieving their learning goals.

Diploma Proposed qualification recognising achievement in a **programme** that meets **threshold** requirements for **core** and **main learning**.

E-learning The generic term for learning facilitated and supported through the use of information and communications technology. It may involve the use of, for example, computers, interactive whiteboards, digital cameras, the internet, the institutional intranet, virtual learning environments and electronic communication tools such as email, bulletin boards, chat facilities and video conferencing.

End-user Ultimate beneficiaries of the 14–19 education and training system, especially higher education and employers.

Extended project A significant autonomous piece of work completed by each learner as part of their **core learning**. Completing the extended project would require learners to develop and demonstrate a range of skills such as planning, research and problem solving. The final outcome would be dependent on the nature of the project selected by the learner. It might be a written report, but could also be a piece of artwork, a construction or a performance.

Extension activities Additional activities provided for learners who have completed basic learning tasks. The activities should be more complex and challenging than the ones that have gone before, thus supporting the development of talented learners.

Evaluation The skill of making judgements based on a clear assessment of the available evidence; also, specifically, the process whereby learners, teachers/tutors/trainers or an organisation evaluate perceptions of a learning experience, a study programme or a particular course or activity. Evaluation is usually part of a formative process aimed at improving standards. It may be carried out by questionnaire or by interviews.

Formative assessment/judgement *See* **Assessment for learning**.

Functional ICT The ICT skills that young people need to function as informed citizens and effective learners and in the workplace. A **component** of the **core**.

Functional literacy and communication The literacy and communication skills that young people need to function as informed citizens and effective learners and in the workplace. A **component** of the **core**.

Functional mathematics The mathematical skills young people need to function as informed citizens and effective learners and in the workplace. A **component** of the **core**.

GCE General Certificate of Education or A levels – an advanced level general qualification.

GNVQ General National Vocational Qualifications – intermediate and foundation level qualifications covering broad vocational sectors, such as health and social care. They are in the process of being withdrawn.

In-course assessment Work set and marked by teachers over the duration of the course that contributes to the award of a grade in a subject or **area of learning**.

Individual review A formative **assessment** that encourages learners, either on an individual basis or as part of a group, to evaluate their progress in a given task or programme and to plan and set targets for the next stage of development.

Individualisation Recognising and responding to individual needs.

Initial assessment The process of recognising individual learners' needs, aptitudes, preferences and prior learning in order to plan and provide an appropriate learning programme to meet those needs.

Kinaesthetic Practical or tactile approach to learning using the sense of touch.

Knowledge The information and experience that a learner has acquired or learned and is able to recall or use in a given situation or activity.

Learning cycle A process, identified by Kolb whereby the experience of trying something new is followed by reflection and evaluation. The process is cyclical and can be iterative and is thought to be central to the way individuals learn and develop.

Learning outcomes Statements indicating what a learner should know or be able to do at the end of a given period.

Learning preferences The way a learner likes to be engaged in the process of learning, whether it be through the use of computers, self-study, or through visual, kinaesthetic or practical activities.

Learning styles inventory A diagnostic instrument used to help individuals assess their preferred approach to learning.

Level Demand or difficulty of a qualification, **programme** or **component**.

Lines (of learning) Related subjects or **areas of learning**. **Programmes** and **diplomas** will be based on one of a number of lines.

Main learning Learning chosen by the learner which constitutes the bulk of each **diploma**. It should ensure achievement and progression within individual subjects and **areas of learning**.

Mindmap A diagram which summarises information or ideas, with linkages drawn between ideas and themes.

Moderation A process of checking a sample of assessed work for the consistency of marking and to arrive at a grade for work. Moderation is carried out by examiners other than those involved in the original marking.

Objectives Precise and measurable statements describing what the teacher/tutor/trainer intends that learners should achieve in a specified period.

Pathway A progression route through the **diploma** framework.

Pedagogy The theory of learning. Tried and tested ideas about how best to organise episodes of learning, i.e. theoretical and procedural knowledge about teaching.

Peer assessment Using learners to check each other's work, applying clear criteria to make judgements to support the learning of others and themselves.

Personal review, planning and guidance Support for the young person to understand themselves as a learner and how the different parts of their **programme** relate to one another, and to identify their learning and career goals and how to achieve them.

Programme Overarching term for a combination of **components** followed by a learner or group of learners. Programmes may differ in content, **volume**, **level** and length, but share the characteristic of bringing components together into a whole. Achievement in a programme should be recognised by the award of a **diploma**, provided that **threshold** requirements are met. A programme may be bigger than a diploma, and additional achievement beyond the required threshold should be recorded on a **transcript**.

RARPA Recognising and recording progress and achievement in non-accredited learning. This is an approach to measure learners' success in non-accredited learning. There is some debate about extending this approach to measure improvements made in adult education environments.

Reflection The process whereby a learner (teacher/tutor/trainer) takes time to consider a given learning experience with a view to making changes in order to continuously improve their approach to learning or their practice.

Resource-based learning An approach to learning which often involves a specific area or designated learning environment where individuals use a range of resources (computers, books, journals) to carry out set tasks.

Resources Discovery Network (RDN) A free national gateway to internet resources for the learning, teaching and research community.

Screening A process that indicates, following an initial assessment, the likelihood that a learner has support needs over and above those normally required to complete a programme of study.

Self-assessment The type of assessment undertaken by the learner (the teacher/tutor/trainer) to evaluate their performance, strengths and weaknesses.

Self-awareness Implies an understanding of the individual's strengths and weaknesses, the ability to identify learning goals and areas for improvement.

SMART Objectives that are specific, measurable, achievable, realistic (or relevant) and time-bound.

Strategic learning An approach to learning which sees knowledge as a means to an end (such as passing an examination). In such cases the learner selects the knowledge they need to retain and consciously commits it to their short-term memory purely for the purposes for which it is initially intended.

Study skills The skills needed by learners in order to successfully participate in or complete a programme of study. They may include notetaking, researching information, time management, essay writing.

Subject pedagogy Accepted good practice, underpinned by theory, in designing teaching/training episodes associated with a specific area of the curriculum.

Summative assessment The final evaluation point, used at the end of a unit, module or programme, to assess a learner's attainment of that unit of learning.

Surface learning Learning which is retained in the consciousness on a short-term basis, for practical application, to be discarded once it has been utilised.

Synthesis The ability to bring a number of issues together and describe links and associations that make this link possible. Linking theory to support the findings of your own research requires the skill of synthesis.

Teacher(-led) assessment *See* **In-course assessment**.

Threshold The minimum **level** and **volume** of achievement in **core** and **main learning** required for the award of a diploma.

Transcript Document providing details of the **components** that constitute a learner's **programme** and achievement in them. This includes non-assessed activities such as **CKSA** and **wider activities**, and achievement beyond the **threshold** required for award of a **diploma**.

Triads Groups of three learners working together.

Understanding The learner shows the capacity to use the current knowledge, concepts and skills to solve a problem or task or to answer specific questions concerning that topic.

Unit Block of teaching and learning within a **component**. Units may be separately assessed but do not on their own provide **credit** towards a **diploma**.

Vocational learning Learning which develops the knowledge, skills and attributes directly relevant to the workplace in general or a job in particular. It is usually practical or applied, rather than abstract or theoretical.

Volume A measure of the amount of work required.

Wider activities Tasks set for learners to complete to demonstrate additional and/or more developed skill.

Work-based learning Learning which takes place predominantly on the job rather than in structured learning settings.

References

Alexander, R. et al. (1992) *Advanced Study in HE: The Role of Professional Development*. Guildford: Teacher Education Study Group.

Argyris, C. (1991) Teaching smart people how to learn. *Harvard Business Review*, May/June pp. 99–109.

Armitage, A., Bryant, R. Dunnill, R. Hayes, D. Hudson, A. Kent, J. Lawes, S. Renwick, M. (2002) *Teaching and Training in Post-Compulsory Education*. Buckingham: OUP.

Balderstone, D. and Lambert, D. (2000) *Learning to Teach Geography in Secondary Schools*. London: Routledge Falmer.

Ball, S. J. (1994) *Education Reform: A Critical and Post-Structural Approach*. Buckingham. Open University Press.

Bloom, B.S. (ed.) (1956) *Taxonomy of Educational Objectives: The Classification of Educational Goals: Handbook 1, Cognitive Domain*. New York: Longmans.

British Educational Research Association (1992) *Journal of British Education Research*, vol. 12, no. 1.

Brown, S. and McDowell, E. (1998) *Assessing Students: cheating and plagiarism*, Red Guide no. 10, series 11. University of Northumbria at Newcastle.

Browne, E. (2002a) The management of change towards greater reliance on ICT, *Journal of Post-Compulsory Education*, November.

Browne, E. (2002b) Listening to the voice of the student, *Support for Learning*, vol. 17, no. 2.

Browne, E. (2003) Conversations in cyberspace. *Open Learning*, vol. 18, no. 3.

Browne, E. (2005) Structural and pedagogic change in educational institutions, *Journal of Further and Higher Education*, vol. 29, nos 1/2.

Brumfit, C.J. and Johnson, K. (1979) *The Communicative Approach to Language Teaching*. Oxford: Oxford University Press.

Bruner, J. (1990) *Acts of Meaning*. Cambridge Mass: Harvard University Press.

Buzan, T and Buzan, B. (2000) *The Mindmap Book*. London: BBC/World Publishing.

Coffield, F., Moseley, D., Hall, E. and Ecclestone, K. (2004) *Should We be Using Learning Styles?* What Research has to say to Practice. London: LSRC.

Cohen, L. Manion, L. Morrison, K. (2001) *Research Methods in Education*, 5th edn. London: Routledge Falmer.

Cohen, L., Manion, L. and Morrison, K. (2004) *A Guide to Teaching Practice*. London: Routledge Falmer.

Demos (2006) Personalising post-16: summary of fieldwork findings. Unpublished report, Demos, London.

DfES (1995) *The Learning Age*. London: Department for Education and Skills.

DfES (1999) *A Fresh Start: Improving Literacy and Numeracy* (Moser Report). London: Department for Education and Skills.

DfES (2002a) *Success for All: Reforming Further Education and Training*, discussion document. London: Department for Education and Skills.

DfES (2002b) *Success for All: Reforming Further Education and Training. Our Vision for the Future*. London: Department for Education and Skills.

DfES (2004a) *Equipping our Teachers for the Future: Reforming Initial Teacher Training for the Learning and Skills Sector* (Tomlinson Review). London: Department for Education and Skills.

DfES (2004b) *Mathematics Resource Materials*. London: Department for Education and Skills (Standards Unit).

DfES (2005a) *Equipping our Teachers for the Future: One Year On (Success for All ITT2)*. London: Department for Education and Skills.

DfES, (2005b) *Harnessing Technology: Transforming Learning and Children's Services*. London: Department for Education and Skills.

DfES (2005c) *14–19 Education and Skills*. London: Department for Education and Skills.

DfES (2005d) *Skills: Getting on in Business, Getting on at Work*. London: Department for Education and Skills.

DfES (2005e) *Every Child Matter: Change for Children*. London: Department for Education and Skills.

DfES (2005f) *Realising the Potential: A Review of the Future of Further Education Colleges* (Foster Review). London: Department for Education and Skills.

DfES (2006) *Youth Matters: Next Steps*. London: Department for Education and Skills.

DoE NI (1999) *The Teacher Education Partnership Handbook*. Belfast: Department of Education for Northern Ireland.

Ellis, V. (2000) *Learning and Teaching in Secondary Schools: Meeting the Professional Standards*. London: Learning Matters.

Flavell, J. (1977) *Cognitive Development*. London: Prentice Hall.

Freire, P. (1972) *Pedagogy of the Oppressed*, Harmondsworth: Penguin.

Gagne, R. (1977) *The Conditions of Learning*. New York: Holt, Rinehart & Winston.

Gagne, R. (1985) *The Conditions of Learning*, 4th edn. New York: Holt, Rinehart & Winston.

Gibbs, G. (1988) *Learning by Doing: A Guide to Teaching and Learning*. London: Longman.

Ginnis, P. (2002) *The Teacher's Toolkit*. Carmarthen: Crown House Publishing.

Giroux, R. (1994) Teachers, Public Life and Curriculum Reform, *Peabody Journal of Education*, pp. 35–46.

Grabe, M. and Grabe, C. (2001) *Integrating Technology for Meaningful Learning*. Boston, Mass: Houghton Mifflin.

Hargreaves, A. (2003) *Teaching in a Knowledge Society: Education in an Age of Insecurity*. Maidenhead: Oxford University Press.

Harkin, J. (2006) *Behaving Like Adults: Meeting the Needs of Younger Learners in Further Education*. London: Learning and Skills Development Agency.

Harkin, J., Turner, G. and Dawn, T. (2001) *Teaching Young Adults: A Handbook for Teacher Education*. London: Routledge Falmer.

Hayes, D. and Wynyard, R. (2002) *The MacDonaldisation of Education*. Westport, Conn.: Bergin & Garvey.

Hill, C. (2003) *Teaching Using Information and Learning Technology in Further Education*. Exeter: Learning Matters.

HMSO (2004) *Social Trends*. London: HMSO.

HMSO (2005) *Reducing Re-offending through Skills and Employment*. London: HMSO.

Hokanson, B and Hooper, S. (2000) Computers as cognitive media: defining the potential of computers in education. *Computers in Human Behaviour*, vol. 16, pp. 537–53.

Jenkins, A. (2000) *Assessment Practices*. Learning, Teaching and Support Network Series no. 1. York: LTSN.

Joyce, B. and Showers, B. (2002) *Student Achievement through Staff Development*. Virginia Association for Supervision and Curriculum Development.

Kelly, A. V. (1999) *The Curriculum. Theory and Practice*, 4th edn. London: Paul Chapman.

Lave, J. (1988) *Cognition in Practice: Mind, Mathematics and Culture in Everyday Life*. Cambridge: Cambridge University Press.

Leask, M. (1999) What do teachers do?, in S. Chapel, M. Leask and T. Turner (eds) *Learning to Teach in Secondary School*. London: Routledge.

LEACAN (2005) *Curriculum Reform for the 21st Century*. Sheffield: Local Education Authority Curriculum Advisers Network.

LLUK (2005) *Skills for Learning Professionals*, available at www.lluk.org.uk.

LSDA (2002) *Key Skills in Modern Apprenticeships*. London: Learning and Skills Development Agency.

Martinez, P. (1999) *9000 Voices: Student Perspectives and Drop Out in FE*. London: FEDA.

Martinez, P. (2000) *Improving Student Retention and Achievement*. London: Learning and Skills Development Agency.

Martinez, P. and Munday, F. (1998) *9000 Voices: Student Persistence and Drop-out in Further Education*. London: Further Education Development Agency.

McGettrick, B. (2004) Keynote Address to the University Council for the Education of Teachers Conference, November 2004.

McGettrick, B. (2005) *Towards a Framework of Professional Teaching Standards*. Bristol: Higher Education Academy.

Meggison, D. and Clutterbuck, D. (2005) Establishing and Managing the Coaching Relationship, ch. 1, in *Techniques for Coaching and Mentoring*. Oxford: Elsevier

Miller, G., Galanter, E. and Pribham, K.H. (1960) *Plans and the Structure of Behaviour*. New York: Holt, Rinehart & Winston.

Minton, D. (1991) *Teaching Skills in Further and Adult Education*. Basingstoke: McMillan.

Morrison, K.R.B. (2002) *School Leadership and Complexity Theory*. London: Routledege Falmer.

National Autistic Society (1997) *Autism Update*. London: NAS.

Nisbet, J. and Schucksmith, J. (1986) *Learning Strategies*. London: Routledge.

Ofsted (2003) *The Initial Training of Further Education Teachers*, HMI 1762. London: The Stationery Office.

Ofsted (2005) *Outcome of Consultation on the Ofsted Framework for the Inspection of the Initial Training of Further Education Teachers*, HMI 2554. London: Oftsted.

Race, P. (1999) *Never Mind the Teaching Feel the Learning*. Birmingham: Staff and Education Development Association.

Reece, I. And Walker, S. (1999) *Teaching, Training and Learning*. Tyne and Wear: Athenaeum Press.

Rogers, C. (1951) *Client-Centred Therapy*. London: Constable.

Rust, C. (2001) *A Briefing on the Assessment of Large Groups*, Learning Teaching and Support Network Generic Assessment Series no. 12. York: LTSN.

Rust, C. Price, M. and O'Donovan, B. (2003) Improving students' learning by developing their understanding of assessment criteria, *Assessment and Evaluation in Higher Education*, vol. 28, no. 2.

Schneiderman D. (1994) *Readings in Information Visualisation*. New York: Morgan Kaufman.

Sousa, D. A. (2001) *How the Brain Learns*, 2nd edn. Thousand Oaks, Calif.: Corwin Press.

Teacher Training Agency (2003) *Newly Qualified Teacher Survey: Evaluation of Training*. London: TTA.

Wenger, A. (1998) *Communities of Practice: Learning, Meaning and Identity*. Cambridge: Cambridge University Press.

Young, M. (2005) *100 Ideas for Managing Behaviour*. London: Continuum.

Index

3